US economic history since 1945

For my parents and Kieran

US economic history since 1945

Michael French

Manchester University Press
Manchester and New York

distributed exclusively in the USA by St. Martin's Press

Published by Manchester University Press
Oxford Road, Manchester M13 9NR, UK
and Room 400, 175 Fifth Avenue, New York, NY 10010, USA

Distributed exclusively in the USA
by St. Martin's Press, Inc., 175 Fifth Avenue, New York,
NY 10010, USA

British Library Cataloguing-in-Publication Data
A catalogue record for this book is available from the British Library

Library of Congress Cataloguing-in-Publication Data

French, Michael.
    US economic history since 1945 / Michael French.
        p.   cm.
    Includes bibliographical references (p.).
    ISBN 0-7190-4185-6 – ISBN 0-7190-4951-2 (pbk.)
    1. United States – Economic conditions – 1945–   I. Title.
HC106.5.F727   1997
330.973'091–dc21   96–46267

ISBN 0 7190 4185 6 *hardback*
        0 7190 4951 2 *paperback*

First published 1997

01 00 99 98 97   10 9 8 7 6 5 4 3 2 1

Printed in Great Britain
by Biddles Ltd, Guildford and King's Lynn

Contents

Tables

Acknowledgements

In the course of writing this book, I have received advice and assistance from many sources. The original idea really came from Anne Crowther in appraisal mode, for which I am grateful. The relationship between teaching and research can involve varying degrees of 'trial and error' so I owe much to the students in my USA classes for accommodating both elements, especially the class of '96, who kept their own sense of proportion. The University of Glasgow provided a period of study leave and support for travel which helped immensely. The project would have been impossible without the resources and support of the Glasgow University Library, and particularly its Inter-Library Loan service and staff who were unfailingly efficient and helpful. Their help enabled me to benefit from and enjoy the writings of many other people. More directly, the thoughtful comments of Neil Rollings and Ray Stokes on drafts of the chapter on the international economy were appreciated and straightened out several tangles. Dan Nelson performed a similar service on the section about labour. The comments of the publisher's anonymous readers on a earlier draft were thorough, sceptical and a great help, for which I thank them. The remaining errors and gaps are, of course, all my responsibility. The late Francis Brooke's interest and encouragement in commissioning the book was a vital factor, and the loss of his talents was a great sadness.

Roma, Nick and Kieran put up with the whole business and helped to keep it in perspective. The book is dedicated to my parents for their support and to Kieran for everything.

M.F.

Introduction

The America of 1945 had been affected profoundly by the experiences of the Depression of the 1930s and the volatile years of World War II.[1] From this starting-point the United States has been transformed over the past fifty years. The pessimism about a relapse into the economic stagnation of the 1930s proved ill-judged; rather, there was an extraordinary consumer boom during the 1950s and 1960s. The contraction of agriculture altered rural and small-town society and a vigorous civil rights movement challenged racial inequalities. American technology, business practices and productivity were examined and copied avidly by overseas firms and nations seeking the sources of economic growth. The United States exerted a profound influence as the exemplar of a consumer society. Post-war US society, culture and language have been displayed more than any other nation through the outpourings of images through films, television and the printed media. Moreover its international role, particularly through the Cold War rivalry with the Soviet Union, had profound effects on the rest of the world whether through diplomacy, military involvement, its multinational corporations or the transfer of US technologies overseas. The notion that when 'America sneezes the rest of the world catches a cold' captured another dimension of this relationship. The different facets of America hinge on the state of its economic life and the swings in economic performance and self-confidence make the half-century since 1945 an important and fascinating period. As the prosperity appeared to be firmly entrenched, the economy faltered during the recessions and inflation of the 1970s and early 1980s. In the new climate there was more scope for domestic conflicts and disagreements and other economies, notably that of Japan, possessed competitive advantages in important industrial sectors.

This book charts the main economic changes in the United States since 1945. In any historical study demarcation lines involve an uneasy compromises between placing an era in its long-run context or examining a short span more thoroughly. The period from 1945 to the early 1990s has often been treated as the tail-end to a longer book surveying two or three hundred years of American economic development. This establishes the grand schema, but at the expense of detail. Alternatively there have been excellent accounts of particular decades, such as Harold G. Vatter's *The US Economy in the 1950s* or Allen Matusow's assessment of the 1960s.[2] Both angles of vision are illuminating, but this book aims to cover a longer span in some depth. With less of the historian's advantage of hindsight than usual, the search for economic and social structures and explanations for processes of change is difficult. Such problems are compounded by the country's size and variety and the persistence of diverse attitudes and cultures in all corners of rural and urban America. Some form of selection is required and the focus on economic changes reflects an underlying belief in their importance in shaping social development. Inevitably, though, economic, political and social factors are intertwined, especially given the role of government since 1945. The chapters generally try to give a sense of the background to the period and then to analyse the changing character of a major aspect or sector of the American economy.

Notes

1 For a survey see Peter Fearon, *War, Prosperity and Depression: The US Economy, 1917–45* (Oxford, 1987).
2 Harold G. Vatter, *The US Economy in the 1950s: An Economic History* (Chicago, 1963); Allen Matusow, *The Unravelling of America: A History of Liberalism in the 1960s* (New York, 1984).

1

The US population since 1945

This first chapter examines trends in population as a convenient and useful way of summarising the changing character of American society. Among the distinctive features of post-war America were the 'baby boom' of the 1950s and 1960s and the expansion of the suburbs. The dimensions and sources of the 'baby boom', a phase of high birth-rates, are discussed, along with shifts in the nature of families and households, issues which have been the subject of much social and political comment. The second half of the chapter focuses on population movements in the form of the revival and changing composition of immigration and the internal migrations across regions and into the suburbs.

The number of people resident in the United States increased from 140 million at the end of World War II to 249 million in 1990 (Table 1.1). There were two distinct phases in the growth of population. Between 1945 and 1964 the rate of increase accelerated with the arrival of the 'baby-boom' generation, which abruptly reversed earlier trends and confounded predictions of population stagnation. There was then a pronounced slow-down over the next three decades which in certain respects returned to pre-war demographic patterns. The post-war period was distinctive in US demographic history, too, in that there were a greater number of women than men in the population for the first time. It was an ageing population: average life-expectancy at birth rose from 64 years to 72 years for men and from 68 years to 79 years for women between 1945 and 1990. Racial differences in life-expectancy remained, but narrowed. White men could expect

Table 1.1 *US population, 1950–94*

Year	Total (000s)	Increase by decade (%)	
1950	152,271		
1960	180,671	1950–60	18.6
1970	205,052	1960–70	13.5
1980	227,726	1970–80	11.1
1990	249,911	1980–90	9.7
1994	260,651		

Source: Economic Report of the President, 1995 (Washington, DC, 1995), p. 311, table B-32.

to live to 73 by 1990 compared to 64 in 1945, while for black men life, expectancy rose from 56 to 67. In the case of white women there was an increase from 70 in 1945 to 79 in 1990, and the greatest rise occurred for black women from 60 to 75.[1] Female longevity was evident in the ratio of men to women in the over-65 age group, which declined from 90 to 67 between 1950 and 1990.

Population trends were a product of changes in fertility, death-rates and net immigration. Average mortality rates declined, with the main reductions occurring during the 1940s, 1950s and 1970s. From 1940 to the mid-1950s better and more widely available medical services, including new drugs, had an impact and there were fewer deaths from previously major contagious diseases, such as influenza and tuberculosis. Improvements in medical care and nutrition were further contributory factors in dramatic falls in the rates of infant and maternal mortality. After a period of stability, mortality rates declined further during the 1970s with a reduction in deaths from heart disease due to changes in life-styles and diets. Overall lower mortality rates offset part of the tendency for an ageing population to raise death-rates. While all groups displayed similar trends, racial differences persisted, including higher mortality rates for black Americans and Hispanics.

The driving force of demographic change was the rate of natural increase, that is the excess of births over deaths, which principally reflected trends in fertility rates. A declining rate of population growth, beginning in the late nineteenth century, was accentuated during the 1930s as people responded to the economic crisis by delaying marriage and having smaller families. Low fertility might have been expected to continue since the postwar years saw a decline of rural America, which had traditionally high fertility. Instead, when the Depression passed, America embarked on a 'baby boom' which produced over 90 million children between 1941 and 1964 and encompassed all regions and races. The fertility rate was around 25 per thousand each year between 1952 and 1957 compared to 20.4 per thousand in 1945; among women aged between 15 and 44 the fertility rate leapt from around 70 per thousand in the 1930s to a peak of 123 per thousand in 1957.[2] Higher fertility resulted from a combination of changes. Men and women married younger and were more likely to marry: the proportion of women aged between 18 and 24 who were married increased from 42 per cent in 1940 to 60 per cent in 1957.[3] Couples had children more quickly after marriage and the average number of children per family increased. These trends were general, though fertility rates were higher in the Mountain and some southern states and among the Black and Hispanic populations.

To some degree the 'baby boom' brought demographic indicators back on track after the exceptional drop during the 1930s.[4] Underlying the fertility changes, however, were economic and social influences. In social terms family life was regarded as a source of security by a generation who had experienced the uncertainties of the Depression and the war, though this interpretation fits parents in the early stages of the 'baby boom' better than those in the later years who very young or not even born in the 1930s. The return of general prosperity and the greater availability of housing made family life more affordable. Easterlin's relative-income hypothesis focused more narrowly on the earnings and expectations of young couples. He identified a rise in the income of young men relative to their parents' income which, coupled with modest expectations after the hardships of the 1930s, encouraged young married women to leave paid work and start a family.[5] Easterlin's analysis did not address the social factors which channelled the returns from renewed growth and higher incomes into specific gender roles in employment and child care. There was, for instance, an outpouring of popular literature advocating motherhood and domesticity during the late 1940s and 1950s.[6] Elaine Tyler May argued that the Cold War and the threat of atomic warfare prompted a further search for security via the family and children. The extent of the Cold War influence is questionable since fertility attained levels which were similar to earlier peacetime rates rather than completely novel, and then fertility declined from the late 1950s without there being any particular diminution of Cold War tensions.

After 1957 fertility declined, particularly among married women, though the fall was less steep for the black and Hispanic populations because their average ages were lower. Age at first marriage rose modestly between 1957 and 1975 and far more markedly during the 1980s: by 1990 average age at first marriage was 23.9 for women and 26.1 for men. Finally the number of births per woman averaged 3.7 in the 1950s, but was only 1.9 in 1988. There was an upturn in fertility rates in the late 1980s consistent with an element of 'delayed fertility' from the 1970s, as the last cohort of the 'baby-boom' generation reached their thirties. The decline in fertility after 1964 might be explained in terms of the introduction of new methods of birth control, with contraceptive pills available from 1960, plus increased government support for family-planning services. Yet fertility rates had already peaked and the swings in fertility over the previous three decades implied a considerable degree of control over fertility with earlier contraceptive methods.

Easterlin's interpretation pointed to a deterioration in young men's relative incomes as the source of lower fertility. The entry of the first of the 'baby-boom' generation into the job market increased the supply of young workers, depressing their earnings. In response, Easterlin argued, young married women took paid work and raised family incomes rather than children, and this tendency was reinforced by a fall in real family incomes in the 1970s. Female employment can, however, be seen as a direct response to rising real wages for women and the decline in the proportion of nuclear families implied that more complex variables were operating. Married women's employment had risen during the 1950s at the peak of the nuclear family's popularity and appeared to sustain family incomes, which suggested that women's willingness to emphasise motherhood in the 1950s passed, as a new generation of younger, more educated women saw more scope for employment and greater autonomy, a development which contributed to, and reinforced, the new feminist movement in the 1960s. The generation who reached maturity in the 1960s had been raised in post-war affluence and perhaps reacted against, or felt less reason to seek security in, large families. Even so the persistence of gender divisions in work and domestic roles implied that changed economic roles for women should not be equated with changes in family relationships.

Families and households

In a recent article Steven Ruggles suggested that household and family composition was remarkably stable between 1880 and 1960, in spite of the profound changes associated with the expansion of urban, industrial society.[7] Among blacks and whites married-couple households were the largest element, though around 20 per cent of households took the form of extended families. The generation of young adults in the 1940s and 1950s placed particular emphasis on marriage, and were more likely to remain married, than either their parents' generation had done or than their own children were to do.[8] In 1950 60 per cent of families fitted the nuclear-family ideal of a working man and female home-maker, a situation reinforced by the suburban trend towards individual family homes. The divorce rate, which had risen steadily during the 1930s, leapt between 1945 and 1947 as wartime marriages fractured, but over the next decade, though high in international terms, it declined.

The post-war assertion of family life was followed by major changes. Ruggles identified a rise in the proportion of individuals living alone before 1940, but this accelerated strikingly after 1960 at the expense of the proportions of married couples and extended households. The proportion of men and women who were married declined: by 1990 only 56 per cent of households consisted of a married couple compared to 74 per cent in 1960 and around 78 per cent in 1950.[9] Among white Americans divorce and separation became more common, while for black Americans the main influence was a decline in the proportion of those who ever married. Single-parent families constituted 12 per cent of all households in 1950 and 21 per cent in 1989.[10] The majority of single-parent families were headed by women. The incidence of widowhood diminished and divorce and separation increased, but, whatever the circumstances, female-headed families remained disproportionately likely to be poor. Fertility rates declined among married women, but increased for unmarried white women and were stable for unmarried black women, so that the proportion of children living in single-parent families more than doubled from 12 per cent to 27 per cent between 1970 and 1992. By 1992 there were 6.9 million white single-parent families, which represented one-quarter of all white families with children under eighteen. The 3.2 million black single-parent families constituted 62 per cent of black families with children under eighteen.[11]

Changes in family structure defy neat explanations. There were influences associated with the population's age structure. Average family size and average household size declined as the 'baby-boom' generation established their own homes, and more elderly people, especially women, lived alone, a product of rising real incomes for many older people, longevity, and new expectations about remaining independent. Economic pressures probably weakened the nuclear family. The slower growth of real family incomes after 1973 exerted greater strain on family budgets than had been the case at any other point in the post-war years. The greatest decline in marriage rates and rise in divorces occurred during the 1970s, when unemployment and declining real incomes reduced the income potential and, thus, the marriage prospects of working-class men.[12] Higher female earnings offered women greater prospects of economic independence, but it remained a precarious margin and divorce resulted in steep declines in women's incomes, but was associated with a rise in men's incomes.[13] A particular gap in the literature concerns the attitudes of men to marriage and divorce, especially given the smaller number of men than women after 1945.

Whatever the economic influences, social attitudes changed. For men and women the rising divorce rate suggested a renewed unwillingness to accept unsatisfying marriages compared to their parents' generation, though the frequency of second marriages implied higher expectations rather than complete rejection of the institution.[14] Divorce became more socially acceptable, reducing the force of moral sanctions against it, and this received legal recognition with the introduction of 'no-fault' divorce laws in the 1970s, though these followed rather than triggered the upsurge in divorces.[15] The growing number of single-parent families was a result of divorce and separation, but conservatives have blamed the welfare system on the grounds that it provided incentives for single parents.[16] Such accounts do not fit neatly with the timing of changes in family life. In the case of unmarried black women, a target of much political rhetoric, fertility rates were falling from 1960 rather than rising in line with benefits. More broadly, the real value of welfare benefits declined during the 1970s, but the shift to female-headed families accelerated.

Differences in family and household composition between black and white Americans have generated a vast literature. The incidence of female-headed and extended family households was higher among African-Americans than for whites or Hispanics. Debate has centred on whether these features were a product of economic and social factors or of cultural influences. Recent work has indicated that female-headed households and extended families were more common among black Americans from the late nineteenth century, but each element increased in line with national trends after 1960.[17] Other data confirmed the rise, but implied higher initial rates than Steven Ruggles's study. In 1950 17.6 per cent of black families were female-headed compared to 8.5 per cent of white families.[18] By 1970 9 per cent of white families and 28 per cent of black families were headed by a woman and twenty years later the proportions were 13 per cent and 44 per cent respectively. In the 1960s Moynihan argued that slavery was the source of instabilities in black family life and portrayed the contrast to white family composition in pathological terms.[19] Although Moynihan also acknowledged the impact of unemployment, his emphasis on family structure provoked controversy. In response, Gutman's work indicated that the nuclear family predominated among rural and urban blacks before and after emancipation, thereby undermining the idea of continuities with slavery.[20] Gutman concluded that urban migrations produced a modest increase in the incidence of extended families as a means of coping with low incomes. Studies of post-war developments have emphasised stable aspects of black family life and its resilience and adaptability as well as links to different African family forms.[21] Wilson, however, argued that post-war economic and social changes which undermined the institution of marriage affected African-Americans disproportionately.[22] It remains a contentious and uncertain debate. The higher rates of single-parent and extended family arrangements among blacks since the turn of the century, and the greater frequency of extended families among African-Americans at all levels of income in 1980, implied the existence of long-term influences.[23] Yet the post-1960 rise suggested new influences shared with whites, but which affected blacks more acutely. The 'baby-boomers' relative income losses as they competed for jobs applied with greater force among African-Americans, whose population was younger than the average and faced particular discrimination. High rates of unemployment, imprisonment and mortality for young black men further reduced the supply of 'marriageable' men or disrupted domestic life. For instance, in 1990 the death rate from homicides per thousand was 69 for black men compared to 9 for white men.[24]

Immigration since 1945

Immigration accounted for around 10 per cent of population growth during the 'baby-boom' years before 1965, but thereafter its contribution rose, providing 28 per cent of the rise in population between 1980 and 1988.[25] Since its origins the United States had been characterised by high rates of immigration and emigration, principally from Europe. The number of immigrants and the rate of immigration in relation to the US population peaked in the first decade of the twentieth century. The disruptive influence of World War I was followed by the tightening of immigration

Table 1.2 *Immigration to the US by decade, 1931–90*

Decade	Total (000s)	Rate per 1,000 of US population
1931–40	528	0.4
1941–50	1,035	0.7
1951–60	2,515	1.5
1961–70	3,322	1.7
1971–80	4,493	2.1
1981–90	7,338	3.1

Source: US Bureau of the Census, *Statistical Abstract of the United States: 1993*, p. 10, table 5.

restrictions on the basis of national origins, particularly against people from southern and eastern Europe and Asia. There was less incentive for immigration, given high unemployment during the 1930s, and a federal repatriation scheme promoted the return of half a million Mexican workers.[26] As a result the proportion of the population who were foreign-born was only 8 per cent in 1945, below its pre-war level.[27] From the low point of the 1930s, immigration increased in absolute numbers and in relation to the US population. Between 1945 and 1990 18.6 million immigrants came to the United States plus an unknown number of illegal arrivals. After an initial recovery from the unusually low pre-war levels, the rate of immigration accelerated in the 1970s and 1980s. In 1990 the number of immigrants reached the high levels of the late nineteenth century. There was a corresponding rise in the proportion of foreign-born residents in the United States to 7.6 per cent in 1990, though this remained low compared to pre-1920 levels or other industrial economies.[28]

The 'push' of population growth, economic pressures and social instabilities encouraged migration from less developed economies, and the United States exerted a persistent 'pull' through high incomes and demand for labour plus the images of the American life-style, which were increasingly widely available through film and television. Levels of migration for particular nationalities were determined by immigration and naturalisation policies. As the United States extended its international political role, there were potential diplomatic advantages to liberalising immigration laws, but reform came slowly. The 1952 McCarran–Walter Act maintained the system of national quotas biased towards northwestern European countries which had been introduced in 1924. The McCarran–Walter Act confirmed the removal of earlier prohibitions on Asian immigration by assigning tiny quotas to the region. No quotas were applied to Western Hemisphere countries. Europeans still accounted for 60 per cent of all arrivals in the 1940s and 53 per cent in the 1950s; thereafter their importance diminished, as did the scale of Canadian immigration. This break with nineteenth-century immigration was a product of reduced incentives to leave as Western European economies prospered, and of new barriers to

Table 1.3 *Immigration to the US by area of origin, 1941–90 (000s)*

	1941–50	1951–60	1961–70	1971–80	1981–90
Total	1,035	2,515	3,322	4,493	7,338
Region					
Europe	622	1,328	1,239	801	706
Asia	32	147	445	1,634	2,817
Canada	172	378	287	115	119
Mexico	61	300	443	637	1,653
Caribbean	50	123	520	760	893
South America	22	92	228	284	456
Africa	7	14	39	92	192

Notes: The area figures do not equal the total due to rounding and the omission of some migration from other areas.
Sources: US Bureau of the Census, *Statistical Abstract of the United States: 1993*, p. 11, table 8; US Bureau of the Census, *Statistical Abstract of the United States: 1966* (87th edn, Washington, DC, 1966), p. 94, table 125.

leaving the Eastern bloc. Mexican immigration increased throughout the post-war period, especially during the 1950s and 1980s. Migration from Puerto Rico expanded substantially though, as American citizens, the entry of Puerto Ricans reflected job prospects and cheaper air travel rather than changes in immigration policy.[29] The share of immigrants from South America increased significantly to 1970 while the numbers from Africa rose steadily from a low base.

The major reform was the Hart–Celler Act in 1965 which aimed to remove discrimination by applying equal quotas and placed an overall limit, though no individual national quotas, on immigration from Western Hemisphere countries for the first time. Once individuals became naturalised, preferential access for close relatives allowed the usual sequence of family migrations to accelerate, giving added momentum to immigration flows from 'new' countries. Under the new measures, existing flows of seasonal and temporary migration from neighbouring countries now required visas, and the effect was most evident in the efforts devoted to controlling illegal immigration from Mexico. The 1965 Act was expected to facilitate migration from southern and eastern Europe, but its primary result was to allow far greater diversity in the origins of immigrants. The principle of equal treatment released a previously suppressed supply of Asian immigration.[30] Asia supplied only 3 per cent of migrants in the 1940s, but provided 13 per cent two decades later and 38 per cent by the 1980s. Changes occurred in the composition of refugees to the United States, which altered from Europeans in the 1950s to Cubans and people from Indo-China by the 1970s, as US political involvements widened and the war in Southeast Asia was lost. Within this general category there were pronounced national variations (Table 1.4).

Table 1.4 *Immigration to the US by country of origin, 1941–90 (000s)*

Country of origin	1941–50	1951–60	1961–70	1971–80	1981–90
China/Taiwan	17	10	97	203	389
Japan	2	46	39	48	43
Korea	7	n.a.	36	272	338
Vietnam			5	180	401
India	2	2	31	177	262

Sources: US Bureau of the Census, *Historical Statistics of the United States*, Part 1, p. 107, series C89–119; 1960–90: US Bureau of the Census, *Statistical Abstract of the United States: 1993*, p. 11, table 8.

As in the past, immigrants were on average younger and, therefore, tended to have higher fertility. Immigrants were more likely to be in the workforce than the native-born population and many immigrants were temporary, returning home after accumulating savings or coming and going regularly as in the case of migrant farm workers; even those who moved permanently often repatriated funds to relatives. Since 1945, however, a higher proportion of immigrants have possessed professional and technical qualifications as US immigration policy has encouraged such people, and the supply has increased, given the spread of education and technical employment overseas. More women than men entered from the 1930s and the 1965 Act strengthened the movement of families.

The conventional pattern of chain migration, a series of arrivals from one area who join family or friends in a new location, produced clusters of immigrant populations, particularly in entry ports and areas close to the home country.[31] Overwhelmingly, immigrants became urban residents, with New York, Los Angeles, Chicago and Miami as the most popular destinations. Mexicans were centred in California and Texas initially, but moved more widely across the country. Puerto Ricans and Dominicans largely lived in New York City, Cubans favoured Florida and Filipinos were concentrated in Hawaii and later, California. Such clustering provided networks of support in adjusting to urban America, ranging from accommodation, credit or access to employment to familiar cultural institutions.[32] The ethnic enclaves provided a basis for entrepreneurial activities in retailing, construction, restaurants, services and small-scale manufacturing as well as supporting professionals serving the community. The timing of immigration affected employment prospects, as did the migrant's skills and the degree of discrimination. Mexican and Puerto Rican workers found semi-skilled industrial jobs, but were more heavily concentrated in light industries and service employment. For the 'new' immigrants who arrived in urban America after 1969, there were fewer opportunities in the contracting older industries. Rather, employment tended to be in low-wage, labour-intensive industries, such as garment-making, where employment fluctuated. The expanding service sector offered better prospects of work by the 1970s and 1980s, but was divided into higher-paid professional work and less lucrative and stable activities. Those migrants who arrived with qualifications concentrated on certain professions: Asian Indians, Koreans and Filipinos had a considerable presence in medicine.[33] Self-employment and entrepreneurship offered another avenue. Retailing, with low entry costs and suited to reliance on family labour, provided another option: Koreans were prominent in retailing and even wholesaling in Los Angeles and New York.[34] In a similar fashion, Cubans in Miami entered the construction business. The 'new' immigrants of the 1970s and 1980s emphasised qualifications, with Asian immigrants in particular benefiting from educational performance. At the same time there were divisions between middle-class and professional people who moved into medical and other careers and those immigrants who worked in the clothing trades of Los Angeles or New York.

Regional demographic change

Although the frequency of movement declined slightly after 1960, Americans became even more mobile in the post-war period.[35] Certain states, such as Florida, Alaska, Hawaii and Nevada, were characterised by exceptional rates of population turnover, with arrivals and departures both high. The majority of moves were from rural to urban areas or from central cities out to suburbs within a particular state. Individuals often made several moves within one area or shifted back and forth between regions. The general directions of migration had been established before 1945 with a tendency for people to leave a broad swathe of central, rural states in the Plains and South plus migration from New England. The main destinations were California, Florida and Texas, though Michigan and midwestern industrial areas also gained population between 1910 and 1950.[36] After 1950 California, Florida and Texas still led the way. The West experienced high rates of in-migration from within and outside the United States, plus a high birth-rate.[37] Apart from the 1960s, the western population increased at double or more than double the national average. The Pacific states gained population consistently and California's population increased from 7 million in 1940 to 27 million by 1988.[38] Colorado, Nevada and Arizona experienced the greatest population gains among the Mountain states, but the Plains states generally lost people.

The South was characterised by high birthrates and out-migration between 1940 and 1970, though there were contrasting sub-regional patterns of migration.[39] The East–South Central states' population share diminished through out-migration from 1940 to 1970, but the West–South Central and South Atlantic regions attracted in-migration, primarily to Texas, Florida and Virginia. This pattern altered when southern emigration slowed in the 1970s and then the region attracted 4.8 million people,

Table 1.5 *US population by region, 1940–90 (%)*

Region	1940	1950	1960	1970	1980	1990
Northeast	27.2	26.1	24.9	24.1	21.7	20.4
Midwest	30.4	29.4	28.8	27.8	26.0	24.0
South	31.5	31.2	30.7	30.9	33.3	34.4
West	10.9	13.3	15.6	17.1	19.1	21.1

Note: Totals may not add up to 100 due to rounding.
Sources: 1940–50: US Bureau of the Census, *Historical Statistics of the United States*, Part 1, p. 22, series A172; 1960–90: US Bureau of the Census, *Statistical Abstract of the United States: 1993*, p. 26, table 28.

equivalent to 47 per cent of its population increase during the 1980s. Florida still gained migrants in the 1980s, but Texas was a less popular destination in the mid-1980s as the energy boom faded.

Just as southern economic development reversed previous trends, so movement away from the older industrial states of the Northeast and Midwest rose from the 1960s and accelerated rapidly during the 1970s and 1980s as heavy industry contracted. In the Northeast migration was concentrated in the Middle Atlantic states whose share of total population declined from 19 per cent to 15 per cent between 1960 and 1990. During the 1980s there was a net outflow of over 2 million from the Northeast with 1.5 million heading to the South Atlantic. Similarly the Midwestern trend primarily reflected the East–North Central states' experiences as previously below average rates of migration moved into line with the national average; their share of US population fell from 20 per cent in 1960 to 17 per cent in 1990. In the 1980s the Midwest experienced a net loss of 2.5 million people with over one million going to the South Atlantic states, chiefly Florida.

There were different racial patterns of migration. White Americans left the Plains states and parts of the Northeast and Midwest for the Pacific states, Florida and Arizona. White Southerners favoured Florida, Texas and Virginia, moved from border states such as Kentucky into Ohio or headed to the Far West.[40] A key element in demographic change in the twentieth century has been the migration of African-Americans from the South. The pace of this movement slowed during the 1930s compared to the 1910s and 1920s, but thereafter northern demand for labour and mechanisation in cotton-growing produced unprecedented levels of migration. In addition to economic incentives the exodus from the South offered an escape from the system of segregation. The majority of African-Americans still lived in the South in 1970, but the proportion had fallen to 52 per cent compared to 75 per cent in 1940; the states with the largest black populations were New York, Illinois and California.

There were distinct streams of migrants, following rail and bus routes and earlier pioneers. From the Southeast blacks tended to go to the major cities of the eastern seaboard such as New York, Philadelphia and Boston.

Table 1.6 **Black out-migration from the American South, 1920–70**

Decade	Net out-migration	% of mid-decade population
1920–30	877	−9.6
1930–40	398	−4.1
1940–50	1,468	−14.1
1950–60	1,473	−13.7
1960–70	1,380	−11.9

Source: Farley and Allen, *The Color Line and the Quality of Life in America.*

A central route channelled people to Chicago, Detroit, Cleveland and other midwestern cities. Finally there was a westward movement from Texas, Louisiana and Arkansas to the Pacific coast, notably Los Angeles, previously the recipient of white midwestern migration. The great migration was checked in the 1970s when fewer blacks left the South and there was a net return flow as economic growth faltered in the northern cities. African-Americans were transformed from a predominantly rural population to one which had an above-average concentration in urban areas.

Native Americans were in a very distinctive situation in 1940, with some tribes centred on reservations and subject to the policies of the Federal Bureau of Indian Affairs, a more active and liberal agency under the New Deal. Other Native Americans were widely dispersed. Mexican-Americans were concentrated in the Southwest with a high proportion of migratory farm labourers, though in-migration had been discouraged during the Depression. Both Native Americans and Mexican-Americans participated in the mass migrations during World War II, entering industrial work on a large scale for the first time, but often losing these jobs with the return of peace. From 1945 Native Americans continued to head for the cities, with a high proportion finding federal employment. The reservations fared poorly in the 1950s and 1960s, but experienced a revival in the 1970s and 1980s based on greater assertiveness over tribal rights, claims for larger royalties on minerals and in some cases by developing bingo and other gaming activities. The Mexican population was augmented by renewed immigration from 1942 which retained an agricultural strand, but the balance shifted towards urban destinations. Mexican-Americans continued to cluster in California and Texas. The arrival of other Hispanic migrants produced more complex ethnic patterns and by the 1960s there was a more assertive and less integration-minded Chicano movement which criticised discrimination.

Urban growth

The US population became more and more urban, especially during the first two post-war decades (Table 1.7). It continued a trend under way since

Table 1.7 *Distribution of the US population between rural and urban, 1950–90 (%)*

Year	Rural	Urban
1950	36	64
1960	30	70
1970	26	74
1980	26	74
1990	24	75

Note: the Census defines 'urban' as any place with a population of 2,500 or more.
Source: US Bureau of the Census, *Statistical Abstract of the United States: 1993*, p. 14, tables 12, 13.

the 1870s as people moved to the cities in order to obtain higher earnings, more opportunities and access to cultural and social amenities. The flow ebbed during the depressed 1930s, but resumed in the wartime boom. Pre-1950 migration was dominated by older metropolitan centres such as New York and Chicago, but thereafter the large cities of the North and Midwest tended to lose population. There was sustained expansion in the Sunbelt states of the South, where levels of urbanisation were initially low, and in the already predominantly urban West. The major cities were the destinations of generations of rural Americans and immigrants, and these processes continued in the post-1940 migration of African-Americans and the post-1965 wave of new immigration. By the 1950s and 1960s smaller cities were growing faster than the major centres.

Suburban growth

Cities had long displayed 'centrifugal' tendencies. The nineteenth-century pattern of a central core of offices, shops and industrial and commercial premises had altered as housing spread more widely and factories relocated, but the process slowed during the Depression. It gained renewed momentum after 1945. After 1945 sprawling cities developed with multiple local centres rather than a single core. This pattern was particularly evident in southern and western states with the vast regional conurbations such as Atlanta, Dallas–Fort Worth and Houston. Cities, particularly in the Southwest, tended to expand outwards creating relatively scattered, low-density settlements.[41] While older cities such as New York or Boston retained distinct neighbourhoods and close proximity between rich and poor areas, the trend has been a fragmentation of cities into more suburban and less centrally-focused places. It is by no means certain, however, that these new arrangements constituted a complete loss of identity or sense of place for urban residents. Improvements in transport, particularly car travel, and communications, notably telephones and television, allowed easier access across the larger cities and enabled people to maintain links to family and friends well beyond their local area. There is no reason to suppose that people, largely born and bred in towns and cities, were unable to comprehend structures or make use of available facilities and services. Moreover while older neighbourhood patterns altered, localities often displayed similarities in terms of the income levels, age structures or ethnicity of their residents which contributed to a sense of place.

By annexing surrounding land, central cities restricted the growth of politically separate suburbs which otherwise had the potential to attract people and jobs and, thus, tax revenues away from urban centres while still drawing on some services. Annexation maintained metropolitan resources in contrast to financial crises in northern cities as suburban growth drained higher-income populations and taxes out of city-centre jurisdictions.[42] Annexation was most common in the Southwest: Houston increased its area threefold from 1920 to 1950 and by a further 50 per cent between 1963 and 1978.[43]

The post-war housing boom was concentrated in lower-density developments on the fringes of cities.[44] Some 17 million people moved into suburbs during the 1950s and there was associated construction of new schools and other facilities. The transfer of stores from city centres to new shopping malls reduced the social significance of city-centre areas, and this process was given added impetus as offices, warehouses and industrial and commercial units, often in business parks, were constructed outside the urban core. There were incentives for such developments in the form of cheaper land and rents, the attractions of less congested sites and purpose-built facilities. At the same time the effects of ribbon development merged previously separate cities into larger metropolitan areas. Although the timing and extent of the process varied considerably, these centrifugal tendencies created a long-term crisis for older inner-city districts. Outflows of people and employment reduced tax revenues, especially where cities were unable to annex new suburbs. Older southern cities with assertive suburban neighbours were constrained. New Orleans was circumscribed by suburbs and politically influential rural parishes; Atlanta encountered opposition to annexations and suburban resistance forced Miami into agreements over service provision with surrounding suburbs. These problems were far more acute in the northern industrial cities in the 1950s and 1970s, but throughout the post-war period local elites attempted to counter this fundamental economic threat. Federal assistance was supplied through the 1949 Federal Housing Act and was substantially expanded during the 1960s in response to further decline and riots. Many older industrial cities underwent major rebuilding and improvement schemes, such as the rehabilitation of Pittsburgh. Equally there remained cases of severe dereliction, such as the Bronx and East St Louis, and serious financial crises, most famously in New York City in 1975.

The social consequences of post-war urban changes were many and varied. Despite recent revivals, many inner-city districts became 'hollow centers' as residents and offices were relocated into the suburbs, so that even commuting occurred more within the suburbs.[45] Images of the city were more and more associated with crime and violence and the urban decay of old industrial districts. To a considerable extent a divide between inner-city poverty and suburban wealth developed. Urban renewal schemes proved more effective at clearing slums than building replacement accommodation, and private capital flowed primarily to construct new offices in the central business district or convention centres which were frequently isolated in bleak landscapes.[46] During the 1950s the only counter to suburban flight was redevelopment in some middle-class conservation areas. By the 1970s suburban areas encountered congestion and social problems previously associated with inner cities, as well as steep rises in land and house values. These conditions triggered two different responses. On the one hand, there was a continuation of the scattering process and longer-distance commuting as people moved out to smaller towns and rural areas which had lost population three decades earlier. On the other hand, developers turned their attention to upgrading inner-city and older commercial districts to attract younger, higher-income residents. With the influx of Asian migrants from the mid-1960s, Chinatowns were revitalised and new enclaves were established in inner-city areas. In New York, Los Angeles and Chicago existing ethnic communities were augmented by immigration, particularly from Mexico and Central America.

Suburban migration in the 1950s and 1960s was predominantly a movement of white Americans as older ethnic inner-city neighbourhoods fragmented. By contrast, central districts were increasingly populated by African-Americans and the 'new' immigrants. During the 1940s and 1950s the boundaries of black neighbourhoods pressed out, creating new ghettos, under the pressure of rapid population growth in northern cities. In some southern cities, black districts were less centrally located initially and they spread out in segments as populations increased.[47] However, these changes in residential patterns operated within constraints. Public policies preserved segregation and new roads provided physical borders to black neighbourhoods, often as deliberate policy.[48] Urban renewal schemes and highway construction fragmented older black districts and, since private construction lagged behind demolition, overcrowding increased. The private sector's adoption of federal valuation criteria which prohibited or limited loans on properties in black or mixed-race areas further restricted black housing prospects.[49] Harassment of African-Americans who moved to predominantly white neighbourhoods was a further deterrent.[50] While the Supreme Court struck down restrictive housing covenants in the 1940s, suburban authorities deployed zoning to bar cheaper homes and resisted the introduction of public housing projects, thereby strengthening racial exclusion. Suburbanite residents' associations had the potential to constrain later developments, including industrial projects, less expensive homes or public housing.

Notes

1 US Bureau of the Census, *Historical Statistics of the United States, Colonial Times to 1970, Bicentennial Edition*, Part 1 (Washington, DC, 1975), p. 54, series B107–15; US Bureau of the Census, *Statistical Abstract of the United States: 1993* (113th edn, Washington, DC, 1993), p. 85, series 115.
2 US Bureau of the Census, *Historical Statistics of the United States*, Part 1, p. 49, series 8.
3 William H. Chafe, *The Unfinished Journey: America Since World War II* (2nd edn, Oxford, 1991), p. 123.
4 Andrew J. Cherlin, *Marriage Divorce Remarriage* (Cambridge, MA, 1981).
5 Richard A. Easterlin, *Birth and Fortune: The Impact of Numbers on Personal Welfare* (New York, 1980).
6 Elaine Tyler May, *Homeward Bound: American Families in the Cold War Era* (New York, 1988).
7 Steven Ruggles, 'The Origins of African-American Family Structure', *American Sociological Review*, 59, 1994, pp. 136–51.
8 Cherlin, *Marriage, Divorce, Remarriage*; May, *Homeward Bound* and Elaine Tyler May, 'Cold War-Warm Hearth: Politics and the Family in Postwar America' in Steve Fraser and Gary Gerstle (eds), *The Rise and Fall of the New Deal Order, 1930–1980* (Princeton, NJ, 1989), pp. 153–84.
9 The divorce rate increased from 17 per thousand in 1965–67 to 37 per thousand by 1987–89: US Bureau of the Census, Current Population Reports, P23–180, *Marriage, Divorce and Remarriage in the 1990s* (Washington, DC, 1989), p. 2, table A. David T. Ellwood and Jonathan Crane, 'Family Change Among Black Americans: What Do We Know?', *Journal of Economic Perspectives*, 4(4), 1990, pp. 65–84.
10 James R. Wetzel, 'American Families: 75 years of change', *Monthly Labor Review*, 113(3), 1990, pp. 4–13.
11 Steve W. Rawlings, *Household and Family Characteristics: March 1992*, US Bureau of the Census, Current Population Reports, P20–467 (Washington, DC, 1993), p. xiv.
12 William Julius Wilson, *The Truly Disadvantaged: The Inner City, the Underclass, and Public Policy* (Chicago, 1987).
13 On the impact of divorce on female living standards see Katherine S. Newman, *Falling From Grace: The Experience of Downward Mobility in the American Middle-Class* (New York, 1988), chapter 7.
14 May, *Homeward Bound*.
15 Leonore J. Weitzman, *The Divorce Revolution: The Unexpected Social and Economic Consequences for Women and Children in America* (New York, 1985).
16 Charles Murray, *Losing Ground: American Social Policy, 1950–1980* (New York, 1984).
17 Ruggles, 'The Origins of African-American Family Structure'; S. Philip Morgan *et al.*, 'Racial Differences in Household and Family Structure at the Turn of the Century', *American Journal of Sociology*, 98(2), 1993, pp. 799–828.
18 US Bureau of the Census, Current Population Reports, P-23, 26, *Recent*

Trends in the Social and Economic Condition of Negroes in the United States (Washington, DC, 1968); see also Frank Levy, *Dollars and Dreams: The Changing American Income Distribution* (New York, 1987), p. 35, table 3.3.

19 Daniel P. Moynihan, *The Negro Family: The Case For National Action* (Washington, DC, 1967).

20 Herbert G. Gutman, *The Black Family in Slavery and Freedom, 1750–1925* (Oxford, 1976).

21 Reynolds Farley, 'Family Types and Family Headship: A Comparison of Trends Among Blacks and Whites', *Journal of Human Resources*, 6, 1971, pp. 275–96; Lee Rainwater and William L. Yancey, *The Moynihan Report and the Politics of Controversy* (Cambridge, 1967); John H. Scanzoni, *The Black Family in Modern Society* (Boston, MA, 1971).

22 Wilson, *The Truly Disadvantaged.*

23 Reynolds Farley and Walter R. Allen, *The Color Line and the Quality of Life in America* (New York, 1987), pp. 165–87.

24 US Bureau of the Census, *Statistical Abstract of the United States: 1993,* p. 98, no. 134.

25 Richard A. Easterlin, 'American Population since 1940' in Martin Feldstein (ed.), *The American Economy in Transition* (Chicago, 1980), p. 313, table 4.A.1; US Department of Commerce, Bureau of the Census, Current Population Reports, series P-25, No. 1023, *US Population Estimates and Components of Change: 1970 to 1987* (Washington, DC, 1988).

26 Roger Daniels, *Coming To America: A History of Immigration and Ethnicity in American Life* (New York, 1990), p. 307.

27 James T. Patterson, *Grand Expectations: The United States, 1945–1975* (Oxford, 1996), p. 17.

28 Julian L. Simon, *The Economic Consequences of Immigration* (Oxford, 1989), p. 29.

29 Daniels, *Coming To America,* pp. 320–1.

30 David M. Reimers, *Still the Golden Door: The Third World Comes to America* (New York, 1985), chapters 3–4.

31 Ewa Morawska, 'The Sociology and Historiography of Immigration' in Virginia Yans-McLaughlin (ed.), *Immigration Reconsidered: History, Sociology and Politics* (Oxford, 1990), pp. 194–5.

32 Alejandro Portes and Ruben G. Rumbaut, *Immigrant America: A Portrait* (Berkeley, CA, 1990), pp. 44–6.

33 *Ibid.,* pp. 68–9.

34 On enclaves see Reimers, *Still the Golden Door*, pp. 112–13 and Morawska, 'The Sociology and Historiography of Immigration', pp. 202–3; Pyong Gap Min, 'From White-Collar Occupations to Small Business: Korean Immigrants' Occupational Adjustment', *Sociological Quarterly*, 25, 1984, pp. 333–52.

35 Larry Long, *Migration and Residential Mobility in the United States* (New York, 1988).

36 Harvey S. Perloff, *Regions, Resources, and Economic Growth* (Baltimore, MD, 1960).

37 Walter Nugent, 'The People of the West since 1890' in Gerald D. Nash and Richard W. Etulain (eds), *The Twentieth Century West: Historical Interpretations* (Albuquerque, NM, 1989), p. 37.

38 Michael B. Teitz and Philip Shapira, 'Growth and Turbulence in the Californian Economy' in Lloyd Rodwin and Hidehiko Sazanami (eds) *Deindustrialisation and Regional Economic Transformation: The Experience of the United States* (Boston, MA, 1989), p. 84.

39 Bernard L. Weinstein and Robert E. Firestine, *Regional Growth and Decline in the United States: The Rise of the Sunbelt and the Decline of the Northeast* (New York, 1978), pp. 3–11.

40 Jack Temple Kirby, *Rural Worlds Lost: The American South, 1920–1960* (Baton Rouge, LA, 1987), pp. 319–33.

41 Carl Abbott, *The New Urban America: Growth and Politics in Sunbelt Cities* (Chapel Hill, NC, 1981), p. 51.

42 Arnold Fleischmann, 'Sunbelt Boosterism: the Politics of Postwar Growth and Annexation in San Antonio' in David C. Perry and Alfred J. Watkins (eds), *The Rise of the Sunbelt Cities*, Urban Affairs Annual Reviews, 14, 1977, pp. 151–68.

43 David R. Goldfield, *Cotton Fields and Skyscrapers: Southern City and Region, 1607–1980* (Baton Rouge, LA, 1982), pp. 152–3.

44 For the idea of centrifugal forces see Jon C. Teaford, *The Twentieth Century American City* (2nd edn, Baltimore, MD, 1993), p. 152.

45 Sharon Zukin, 'The Hollow Center: U.S. Cities in the Global Era' in Alan Wolfe (ed.), *America at Century's End* (Berkeley, CA, 1991), pp. 245–61.

46 Herbert J. Gans, *The Urban Villagers: Group and Class in the Life of Italian-Americans* (New York, 1962).

47 Robin Flowerdew, 'Spatial Patterns of Residential Segregation in a Southern City', *Journal of American Studies*, 13(1), 1979, pp. 93–107.

48 David W. Bartlett, 'Housing the Underclass' in Michael B. Katz (ed.) *The Underclass Debate: Views from History*, (Princeton, NJ, 1993), pp. 118–60; Raymond A. Mohl, 'Making the Second Ghetto in Metropolitan Miami, 1940–1960', *Journal of Urban History*, 21(3), 1995, pp. 395–427.

49 Bartlett, 'Housing the Underclass'; Kenneth T. Jackson, *Crabgrass Frontier: The Suburbanization of the United States* (New York, 1985), chapters 11 and 13; Blaine A. Brownell and David R. Goldfield (eds), *The City in Southern History: The Growth of Urban Civilisation in the South* (London, 1977), p. 168.

50 Mike Davis, *City of Quartz: Excavating the Future in Los Angeles* (London, 1990), pp. 161–5.

2

US government since 1945

The scale and extent of government, especially federal, involvement in the economy provides the central theme of this chapter. After a summary of the dimensions of its growth, various explanations are considered which draw both on earlier precedents and developments as well as on new features of the post-war years. A more detailed examination is made of defence and welfare, which have been particularly important aspects of federal intervention and, thus, provide a good test of its origins. In the final part the reasons for a greater questioning of the federal government's role after 1970 are discussed.

Aspects of government influence are examined in later thematic chapters, but this chapter discusses the broad trends. From the nation's origins there have been contending visions of the proper purposes of government. Certain regulatory and policing functions were accepted, but the Constitution restricted federal powers and suspicion of central power limited extensions of federal authority. Consequently the political system developed a fragmented character. The main state and local responsibilities were education, transport, health and safety, finance and business licensing. The primary federal roles were defence, tariffs and land policies. Yet an expansion in the role of government, particularly the federal authorities, was a major element in US economic and social history after 1945, though in terms of its share of national income the US government remained comparatively modest compared to other industrialised countries.[1]

As a purchaser of goods and services, national and local government was most dominant during World War II and its purchasing diminished sharply in the late 1940s. However, there was then a rise in the early 1950s followed by more gradual growth.[2] As an employer the government's role also declined with the end of war mobilisation, but then rose consistently to the mid-1970s with the great bulk of the increase occurring in state and local government employment. Table 2.1 shows the growth in government expenditure. Expenditure captured only part of the story, since local and national governments exercised influence through their economic management and regulatory policies. In these spheres, too, governments played a larger role after 1945, but it was a contested and uneven process in which each step was

Table 2.1 *US government expenditure as a percentage of Gross Domestic Product, 1940–90*

Year	State and local	Federal	Total
1940	10.0	9.9	20.9
1950	6.9	16.0	22.9
1960	8.6	18.2	26.8
1970	11.7	19.9	31.6
1980	10.3	22.3	32.6
1990	10.8	22.9	33.7

Sources: US Bureau of the Census, *Statistical Abstract of the United States: 1993* (113th edn, Washington, DC, 1993), p. 331, table 513; *Economic Report of the President, 1982* (Washington, DC, 1982), p. 320 and *Economic Report of the President, 1994* (Washington, DC, 1994), pp. 359, 364.

subject to the US Supreme Court's shifting interpretations of constitutional propriety.

The balance between national and local governments varied across the post-war years. Generally federal direction over state and local government increased through an expansion in the number of federal 'grants-in-aid' given to state governments, plus more stringent and conditional criteria for the implementation of policies. However the Eisenhower administration's preference for local rather than federal activity contributed to the expansion of state expenditure between 1945 and 1960. The Johnson administration provided more central funding and direction of policy in the mid-1960s, but a decade later national government's self-confidence wavered and successive administrations tried to moderate spending to counter inflation and deficits. Federal 'grant-in-aid' peaked as a proportion of state spending and national income in 1978. Stagnant real incomes generated voter resistance to taxation and, along with a corporate critique of regulation, undermined support for federal intervention. Although by no means uniform, there was a shift back towards the state and local level plus reorganisations which increased their administrative and revenue-raising capabilities.

Earlier growth of government

There were many philosophies and proposals regarding the proper role of government, especially at the federal level, and the balance of opinion varied in relation to specific issues like welfare, business or public health. Post-1945 developments had their roots in the second half of the nineteenth century. Population growth and urbanisation increased the demand for existing government services, though cities and states varied in their willingness to respond. The rise of giant corporations challenged prevailing notions of competitive markets and Republican democracy and some, including smaller businesses, advocated regulation as a countervailing force. This was consistent with a political system which operated via the lobbying of different interest groups and the fragmented nature of government encouraged a similarly diffuse cast of lobbyists. During the Progressive era between 1900 and 1917 states, such as Wisconsin, responded to reform movements by extending welfare provision and widened their use of police powers to regulate urban conditions. The reform impulse included older elites anxious to check the economic and social consequences of urbanisation and industrialisation.[3] It also encompassed middle-class and professional people who embraced these changes, but considered that neutral experts could provide more efficient government. There were radical and socialist voices too. Even where the different tendencies favoured regulation or government intervention, there was often caution. This was partly based on the experience of existing institutions. Middle-class Progressive reformers were motivated by their rejection of the existing political machines and radicals and labour unions knew of the repressive force of government. The powerful advocates of states' rights questioned any federal action. Even positive views of federal government spanned prescriptions for decentralising economic and political power to those in favour of maintaining existing structures, but using specific regulations to ensure a greater flow of information and accountability.[4] The result was a patchwork extension of federal influence, based on the use of commissions with some independence from legislatures and on regulation rather than direct intervention.

The classic picture of reform movements initiating government action against vested interests identified an important element, but the targets of reform were resilient and had every incentive to try to shape the course of any regulation.[5] The commission form of government, which reformers favoured as a source of dispassionate expertise apart from popular pressures, could be influenced since the subjects of regulation possessed information relevant to any intervention. This form of 'capture' by the regulated was one possible outcome. In other cases business or other interest groups initiated government intervention in pursuit of their own competitive advantage and to reduce potential risks. Government possessed the power to modify market conditions, award subsidies or monopolies and provide legal protection for specific activities as well as maintaining the general framework of property rights and other laws. The balance of contending reformers and vested interests differed according to the issue at stake which led to variations in the forms and timing of intervention. Statist theories identified an element of autonomy for government officials who pursued their own agendas, such as bureaucratic empire-building, or priorities which did not mesh consistently with those of pressure groups. The scope for state autonomy increased if interest groups were divided or where the implementation of a measure left room for official discretion. Thus government possessed its own dynamic in the form of political and bureaucratic aspirations which shaped the formulation and implementation of laws and the development of government departments. One overarching interpretation identified professionalisation and the expansion of government and business as constituents of a general development of large-scale organisations.[6] The various influences led to discrete extensions of government's influence through interest-group lobbying or the bureaucratic endeavours of administrators.

In contrast to the gradualist impulses, dramatic changes in government policies occurred in response to crises which discredited existing measures, indicated forms of market failure or raised unforeseen problems. When the immediate difficulty had passed the extent of government influence tended to remain greater.[7] In 1929 government spending only constituted 2.5 per cent of national income and state and local government activities far exceeded those of the federal government. The economic crisis of the 1930s prompted fundamental change. President Hoover's vision of private voluntary action and limited government proved flawed, popular attitudes shifted to a greater acceptance of government intervention and local and state authorities, who were less able to raise revenues, became more reliant on federal resources. The scope of federal policy-making widened as established private-sector, local and voluntary institutions were unable to respond effectively to the Depression. As before, there were many visions of the way forward: wartime planning, versions of Hoover's corporatism, structural reforms and increased intervention. President Roosevelt's pragmatic advocacy of 'bold persistent experimentation' provided the opportunity for greater activity, but also frequent changes of direction. The pace and extent of federal intervention proceeded most rapidly in areas of established responsibility such as agriculture or those, like banking, which were regarded as critical for recovery. Elsewhere an expanded federal role was assumed cautiously by an administration wary of the financial and constitutional implications of extending its remit. Given its small size, there were organisational advantages for the federal government in providing financial support for programmes administered through local agencies rather than undertaking all duties centrally. Even in 1940 the federal share of all government spending was only 42 per cent and its civilian workforce of 1.1 million contrasted with 3.3 million employees at state and local levels.

The *ad-hoc* process of expansion in response to crisis accelerated during World War II when federal expenditure increased from $9.6 billion in 1940 to $95.2 billion in 1945; over the same period the federal deficit rose from $2.7 billion to $45 billion.[8] The growth in the established federal responsibility for defence and the assumption of new tasks resulted in a rapid growth in staff and, even more strikingly than during the Depression, in the financial resources of central government through the switch to 'pay-as-you-go' income tax and higher corporate taxes. However public works programmes ended. The New Deal and the war produced, therefore, a substantial, though uneven, expansion in the scale and scope of federal responsibilities and regulation and a legacy of precedents and pragmatic decisions extending government influence, though no coherent philosophy justifying state intervention.

Post-war influences on government

After the war conservatives in and out of Congress had some success in rolling back federal influence, particularly over planning and labour legislation.[9] Such efforts circumscribed government activity, but existing programmes retained their own dynamic through interest groups, lobbying and the momentum of the Administration itself. A considerable legacy of programmes remained from the New Deal, notably agricultural price supports, the Social Security system and public housing, which provided the foundation for a good deal of post-war government activity. There were also federal regulatory agencies of varying vintages such as the Interstate Commerce Commission, the Federal Communications Commission and the Federal Trade Commission. These organisations sought to expand their remit and new technologies provided scope for further regulation, as with the licensing of television stations and the broadening of controls on advertising to include the new medium. The Supreme Court judged whether such extensions of federal jurisdiction were acceptable.

A facilitating factor in the expansion of government was access to resources. The main revenue sources varied between the different levels of government with property tax being the main source of local government income, for instance. The tax system had been broadened and made more progressive during the war so there was a larger base of potential revenue. Post-war economic growth and inflation created a tendency for revenues to rise automatically as an individual's income moved into a higher tax bracket. Income tax accounted for a rising proportion of general government revenues, though the contribution of income tax was stable if social insurance payroll taxes are counted as a form of taxation, since their contribution increased very rapidly. Sales taxes contributed rather more to state government revenues over the post-war period.

Certain new features of the post-war years stimulated growth in accustomed government functions and supplied incentives for further accretions. Post-war demographic trends contributed to the rise in government expenditure and demands for increased services, especially at state and local levels. Rural depopulation transferred people to cities and states with higher levels of spending and suburban growth added to demand for road-building. The impact of the 'baby boom' produced a sustained demand for expenditure on education as school rolls increased by 13 million in the

1950s.[10] This was a contentious area where advocates of federal aid to education, notably teachers' organisations, were stymied by opposition from business and churches. As a result the expansion of schooling was a key element in the rapid growth of state and local expenditure. There was federal support for further education through the GI Bill of Rights which assisted some 7.8 million war veterans between 1945 and 1952.[11] In the case of education, voters demanded better facilities for their children and the 'baby boom' raised total numbers, but state governments also accepted education as a contribution to economic growth. The provision of federal aid to schools occurred in a piecemeal fashion linked to defence and welfare policies. The local elites who dominated post-war planning also supported the construction of roads and hospitals and in these spheres they were willing to accept federal contributions. Unlike education, business favoured highway construction and indeed, there was an influential lobby of car and road interests and little opposition. The major growth areas in federal activity occurred in defence and welfare.

Defence

In the case of military expenditure, the long-established federal duty to provide defence gained unprecedented peacetime momentum from the Cold War, and it was an area which met with broad public and legislative approval. Although declining from its wartime peak, defence spending remained well above pre-war levels at $22 million, or 8.5 per cent of the national income, in 1949. Defence budgets averaged between 6 per cent and 8 per cent of the national income in the 1960s and 1970s and rose steeply after 1976, so by the mid-1980s the real value of defence spending exceeded its Korean War or Vietnam War peaks.[12] Defence was a significant element in the overall expansion of the federal government's role, though its share of total federal spending diminished from over 60 per cent during the 1950s to between 40 and 50 per cent in the 1960s and 20 to 30 per cent in the 1970s and 1980s. Generally the largest items of defence spending were bases and personnel, but procurement budgets came to the fore during spending peaks and there was funding for research and development.

There was institutional support for the rise in defence expenditure. President Eisenhower's famous warning about the potential dangers of a 'military–industrial complex' in 1961 was a surprising note from a man whose own career so substantially combined military and political roles, but Eisenhower's conservative philosophy was based on a general suspicion of 'big government'. A broad definition of the 'military–industrial–complex' included employees, businesses, local politicians and universities or other agencies undertaking military research. A narrower definition, drawn from political science, focused on national politicians, officials and the executives of leading defence contractors who were connected by a flow of personnel between the different posts and by a shared perception of policy issues and appropriate responses.[13] Elements of the institutional framework of the 'military–industrial–complex' existed before 1939 due to steady increases in the scale of mobilisation and the complexities of military technology from the late nineteenth century.[14] There were links between business and national and local government too, for instance, in munitions and aviation.[15] However, the contraction of defence spending and the parlous state of major defence industries between the wars, plus the chaotic state of preparedness efforts in the late 1930s, indicated the weakness and fragmentation of the pre-war 'military–industrial–complex'. By 1945 the situation was radically different. The political and strategic concerns of the Cold War, reinforced by involvement in Korea and later Vietnam, ensured the retention of high levels of peacetime expenditure, and there was the expansion of a national security bureaucracy, a process given expression in the 1947 National Security Act.[16] The defence sector possessed unusual autonomy through its claims for priority and special expertise, as well as the secrecy which surrounded its activities.[17] National and local political leadership advocated high levels of military spending, marking it as an exception to the conservative critique of federal activism during the late 1940s and early 1950s. Indeed the assertion of links to defence was used to legitimate other forms of federal expenditure such as interstate highway construction and new education policies in the 1950s. Defence concerns provided a lever for increased federal support for education in general, after the Russian launch of Sputnik triggered a panic over the quality of American schooling, especially in science. The National Defense Education Act expanded federal aid to education and the creation of the National Aeronautics and Space Administration (NASA) was used to oversee a civilian space programme.

Defence policies were a major influence on employment and constituted *de facto* industrial and regional policies. Business–government links were strongest in the aircraft and electronics industries where military orders were fundamental to sales and the development of new technologies.[18] The armed forces' relationships with contractors broadened the constituencies interested in defence expenditure, and the desire of policy-makers to preserve manufacturing capacity related to defence was particularly evident in the case of the aircraft industry.[19] Since prime contracts for new products were generally on a 'cost-plus' basis, – total cost plus a percentage as profit – there was little incentive for producers to minimise costs, and this supplied a dynamic in favour of rising defence spending. Scientific developments added new dimensions of expense and the federal government displaced industry as the main financier of scientific research, including the nuclear energy and space programmes.[20] There was a rough division of labour: universities undertook basic research and corporations engaged more in applied research. In both cases the high cost of particular programmes

produced a concentration of research funding and had a profound influence on the types of scientific research undertaken and the character of disciplines such as physics and engineering.[21] There was a decline in the
pre-eminence of defence expenditure in federal research and development
spending during the 1970s when government support for medical-related
science increased.

US welfare policy since 1945

Defence was firmly established as a federal duty well before 1945, but
welfare policy had been a responsibility of local government and the
federal role was fairly new. Traditional ideologies of self-help and local provision of welfare had undergone a stiff examination during the 1930s when
the scale of need overwhelmed local sources of charitable support and
company welfare schemes, small in number and scope even in 1929, offered
little protection in the context of high unemployment and reduced profits.
Roosevelt's New Deal met the crisis with emergency measures of direct
relief and public works programmes. Despite ideological objections, federal
and state governments paid direct relief as the most prompt and economical means of supporting unemployed people and federal funds substituted
for lower state and local spending from 1932. Although the general crisis
moderated the force of the view that poverty was a reflection of individual
moral failings, such attitudes retained a hold and compared to the scale of
need, total expenditure and individual payments remained low. The
philosophy that direct cash payments ought not to be given to the undeserving or idle led to public works projects from the Public Works
Administration and short-lived Civil Works Administration to diverse
schemes under the Works Progress Administration. New Deal policies constituted a major growth in the federal direction and funding of welfare and
in the mid-1930s Roosevelt's position was strong enough to undertake
longer-term reforms through the Social Security Act of 1935. It was a land-
mark in committing government to a system of permanent provision for
the elderly, dependent children and unemployed. Nonetheless state and
local government agencies, charities and private philanthropy retained
important roles in the implementation of policy so there were marked variations in the criteria for eligibility and the value of benefits.

The return to full employment in World War II brought down the relief
rolls: the principal public works programme, the Works Progress
Administration, was wound up by Congress in 1943. The high level of
savings, the medical profession's success in defeating proposals for federal
health insurance and greater competition among the insurance companies
contributed to rapid growth in private medical insurance, pensions and
other benefits. Leading unions, stymied in their search for national
measures, successfully pursued job-related welfare benefits and increased

their influence over the administration of such schemes. The revived welfare capitalism primarily supported middle-class workers, though miners and car workers achieved gains for sections of the blue-collar workforce. State activities fared unevenly in the late 1940s. The Social Security Act's impact remained limited since only 21 per cent of the elderly received benefits under the Act in 1950, while double that number were in receipt of the old-age assistance payments.[22] The Social Security system remained in place and was extended to cover a greater proportion of the workforce. Its growth was partly inevitable as the system matured and indeed, the expansion held down the cost to individuals. The prospect for new schemes diminished after the National Resources Planning Board's proposals in 1943 to extend welfare provision made no headway. The primary extension to national support occurred through the GI Bill of Rights which provided assistance for unemployed or low-income veterans and through the expanded and more effective Veterans' Administration (VA).[23] VA activities encompassed pensions, hospitals, medical care and education, as well as benefit payments and loans to veterans and their dependants, and it accounted for 29 per cent of total government expenditure on welfare by 1950. Although its importance within overall provision declined subsequently, the VA's role remained significant, given the working-class origins of the majority of recruits.

Compared to defence spending, federal and state welfare provision attracted rather limited political support from 1945 to 1960. Unions and consumer groups advocated greater state provision and Berkowitz and McQuaid detected a strand of neoconservativism among employers, embodied by Marion Folsom, the first head of the Department of Health, Education and Welfare, in favour of federal finance for locally administered programmes. Such leadership, though thin on the ground, was significant in preserving the basic framework of New Deal provision. However, a conservative Congress and the election of the similarly inclined President Eisenhower in 1952 restrained the expansion of social programmes during the 1950s. As a result the expansion of federal welfare provision primarily proceeded in an incremental fashion via bureaucratic channels. Social Security administrators persuaded Congress of the merits of the contributory principle as a form of insurance which was preferable to public assistance. Federal aid also expanded through the diverse activities of the VA. If some currents of federal welfare flowed, others remained blocked. Although federal funding increased for hospital construction, national health insurance was defeated by the American Medical Association's expensive campaign against 'socialised medicine'. Moreover the return of economic prosperity allowed a revival of the earlier elements of corporate and private provision such as pensions and medical benefits.[24] Private charities and philanthropy revived in the more prosperous post-war years and were encouraged by tax exemptions for donations and charitable activities.

If the 1950s displayed growth through a mixture of government and private-sector welfare provision, the next fifteen years saw a particularly dramatic expansion in the scale and scope of federal welfare activities. Total welfare expenditure rose from 10.5 per cent of Gross National Product in 1960 to 15.2 per cent in 1970 with increased spending on social insurance programmes, like pensions and public assistance schemes. The sources and impact of this expansion have been the subject of considerable debate. In one formulation the policies signalled a new phase in a longer-run political cycle in which the reform impulse waxed in the 1910s, 1930s and again in the 1960s.[25] Certainly there were elements of continuity in that many policies implemented or extended programmes which had originated or been debated over the previous half-century. Moreover research in the 1950s provided the basis for later legislation. For instance, charitable foundations supported enquiries into issues such as juvenile delinquency and urban renewal in the 1950s, and the new notion of a culture of poverty transmitted from one generation to the next fostered the idea that intervention was required to break the cycle. Yet public opinion polls indicated little increase in popular support for greater intervention. The obvious change was the election of Democratic administrations from 1961 which were more receptive to the debates about social problems. After Kennedy's assassination, President Johnson strengthened the commitment to welfare measures because such policies offered a link to Kennedy, but one which gave Johnson scope to establish his own legacy. The volume of legislation following Johnson's 1964 election victory reflected his determination to capitalise on his position of authority to pass legislation which liberals had long favoured.[26] The wave of welfare legislation reflected a sense of optimism that economic growth would permit social problems to be solved at modest expense.

The new activism was symbolised by President Johnson's declaration of a 'unconditional War on Poverty' in 1964. In its strictest definition, the War on Poverty was represented by the Office of Economic Opportunity (OEO), but broader federal interest in welfare was evident in a raft of legislation under the Great Society banner. Johnson's powerful position after the 1964 election facilitated the passage of two pieces of health legislation, Medicaid and Medicare. Both had a long pedigree as liberal proposals, but had been blocked by opposition from the medical profession and Congress. Medicaid, administered locally, provided federal and state funds to people receiving benefits; Medicare was federally financed and assisted the elderly.[27] Both measures were significant extensions of federal welfare support, though it should be emphasised that the provision of services lay with existing medical services. Overall social insurance programmes and, more strikingly, public assistance schemes, whose eventual demise was frequently predicted, expanded. Greater assertiveness among welfare recipients provided a new impetus for extensions of coverage and relaxation of eligibility requirements.

Davies emphasised the feeling of liberal optimism in the early 1960s: the belief that a combination of prosperity and professional expertise offered the prospect of achieving equality of opportunity.[28] More narrowly, welfare policies can be examined in relation to economic policy and the role of economists in government. On assuming office, the Kennedy administration implemented fiscal policies to accelerate growth and this broad objective evolved in two directions. On the one hand, acceptance of Keynesian ideas led to reductions in corporate and individual taxes in 1964 with the aim of stimulating investment. In this context welfare measures were a means to pacify potential political criticism of the aid to business as Walter Heller, chairman of the Council of Economic Advisers, recognised. On the other hand, economists in government regarded certain welfare programmes as having the potential to improve the quality of human capital and thereby increase productivity and American competitiveness.[29] If fiscal policies generated growth, welfare could encompass education and training as ways of increasing the poor's prospects of employment, along with regional development schemes. The Manpower Development and Training Act of 1962, for instance, embodied such thinking, as did the 1964 Economic Opportunity Act.[30] The economists' assumptions that training would ensure better access to the labour market for the poor allowed increased welfare expenditure to be presented as a short-term measure which would lead to longer-term reductions in the relief rolls. Even the Head Start programme of children's education was consistent with this approach. In this sense reform could be conceived as cautious or limited in financial terms and this was one of the messages which Johnson used in an effort to counter conservative critics in Congress. Certainly the rhetorical flourish of a 'War on Poverty' contrasted with the comparatively modest budget given to the principal agency, the OEO, but even so the policies were a major departure in terms of the federal administration's commitment.

If economists held sway in the initial stages, many federal agencies joined the new thrust of social policy, especially in formulating and implementing the myriad schemes in Johnson's Great Society. Social policy advisers shared the economists' faith in the capacity of professional expertise to solve social problems. However a more novel strand was apparent in the OEO's Community Action Programme's aim of increased participation and self-help by the poor through sponsorship of local community organisations, which was directed to stimulating 'pressure from below'.[31] Other departments endeavoured to keep pace with the welfare parade. Public housing programmes were increased and the Department of Agriculture balanced farm and welfare interests in the Food Stamp Act in 1964.[32] The existing bureaucratic impetus behind the expansion of Social Security persisted: pension provisions were liberalised and the proportion of the elderly receiving Social Security benefits rose from 65 per cent in 1960 to 87 per cent in 1970.[33] Aid to Families with Dependent Children (AFDC) was extended to families with an unemployed father in 1962 and the proportion of those eligible who applied increased from 33 per cent to 71 per cent during the 1960s.[34]

Other interpretations have argued that new policies were a response to more effective lobbying by poorer people. Matusow, Aaron and Piven and Cloward all pointed to black migration to northern cities and the greater assertiveness embodied in the civil rights movement as sources of popular demands for reform.[35] For the Democratic Party there was the political prospect of consolidating their northern urban base by meeting African-American demands and averting the threat of greater unrest.[36] This would fit with the general notion of an increased awareness of, and demands for, rights as a driving force in post-war political change. The impact of 'pressure from below' in the early 1960s has been questioned, however. Sundquist asserted that 'the poor had no lobby' and the most immediate policy responses to the civil rights movement were the Voting Rights and Civil Rights Acts.[37] Both Kennedy and Johnson deliberately downplayed associations between new welfare measures and black urban poverty; both Presidents made well-publicised trips to areas of predominantly white rural poverty in Appalachia.

Despite the scale of Democratic political power in 1964, the legislation bore the marks of earlier defeats in that the measures contained elements of compromise and concession to conservative ideals. The broad strategy supplied additional federal funding via categorical grants, but preserved local administration with resulting variations in coverage and conditions. Where federal influence threatened established relationships, reforms encountered problems.[38] This was evident in the pruning of Community Action Programme activities following complaints from city and state politicians about the channelling of federal funds direct to community groups critical of local services. In the area of health reform, federal funding increased, but Medicare and Medicaid preserved considerable autonomy for hospitals, doctors and local administrators; as a result federal authorities possessed little capacity to control costs. The distinction between forms of public assistance to the poor and the social insurance schemes directed to higher-income groups also persisted, with the latter drawing on a wider, more vocal constituency which ensured more favoured political status.[39]

Since the precise impact of the programmes was hard to determine, both liberals and neoconservatives questioned the efficacy of the Great Society, though they drew very different conclusions. For some liberals urban protest signalled the need for additional expenditure and radical voices criticised the Great Society's failure to undertake more fundamental reform.[40] Johnson's involvement in welfare policy diminished under the competing demands of Vietnam and, although urban unrest triggered new initiatives, there was less sense of direction by 1968. The Nixon administration accelerated the OEO's decline, and emphasised local administration rather than central direction.[41] The absence of consensus was evident in the stalemate over Nixon's Family Assistance Plan which held out the prospect of guaranteed family income levels, attracting a mix of support from academic conservatives and suspicion from liberals.

Government in retreat?

The 1970s and 1980s produced conflicting trends in the role of government, but a broad swing away from national towards local activities. The Nixon administration curtailed elements of Johnson's programme, pruned public housing budgets, and emphasised local administration.[42] Even so, there was a continuation of the post-1964 trend towards increased expenditure as programmes maintained their own momentum. Bureaucratic forces remained influential in expanding programmes, liberal reformers maintained some momentum for more redistributive policies and the earlier programmes had stimulated more assertiveness among beneficiaries, often in the form of legal challenges over the implementation of policies. The Nixon administration countenanced increases in the traditionally well-regarded contributory schemes. Particularly striking was a sharp increase in the real value of benefits: the real value of Social Security benefits rose by 23 per cent between 1969 and 1972.[43] An automatic cost-of-living adjustment was added to Social Security payments in 1972 and accentuated the already rising real value of benefits. Rising unemployment increased the numbers eligible for welfare. Medicare and Medicaid costs were driven up by rising participant numbers, but even more by the above-average inflation of medical costs, the product of institutional arrangements which gave patients and doctors every reason to maximise expenditure.[44] The new strength of consumer, environmental and other interest groups provided further impetus to the post-1964 sequence of Congressional-inspired regulation with the passage of environmental, health and safety legislation.[45] These lobby groups were driven by a suspicion of business and by the belief that strict compliance rules were required in order to avoid delay or inaction on the part of government regulators. Such perceptions reflected a belief that federal agencies were susceptible to 'capture' by corporate interests and political events, notably the Vietnam War and Watergate, and signalled a weakening of liberal faith in government in favour of reliance on enforcement via the courts.

Earlier crises of war and the Depression had provided scope for extending the role of government. The 1970s and early 1980s were characterised by serious economic problems with a series of recessions and much higher rates of inflation, but these added to a critique of existing institutions, particularly the federal government. Johnson had promised that greater intervention would solve economic and social problems, but the measures had aroused higher expectations from some people who demanded further action. Liberal concern about 'capture' prompted restrictions on the autonomy of officials and in the process undermined the bureaucratic impulses which had contributed to the earlier expansion of government programmes. The result was a proliferation of groups demanding particular rights or aid. This assertiveness, which frequently involved racial tensions, and the persistence of social problems in turn triggered resentments among other people and a conservative swing in attitudes towards national government. The return of a Republican administration headed by President Nixon was one result, but the shift in attitudes was more far-reaching. As economic growth slowed and real incomes declined after 1972, acceptance of redistributive social policies and faith in government as a source of economic growth diminished. This process received particular momentum from a new corporate critique of regulation and government intervention which utilised techniques of lobbying and interest-group politics developed by pressure groups. External criticisms and the crisis of stagflation undermined bureaucratic self-confidence and alternative economic policies, such as monetarism, were associated with an emphasis on freer markets and a reduced government role. Since liberals and grass-roots campaigners criticised federal programmes as unduly bureaucratic, Johnson's Great Society approach lacked a unified body of support and there was little effective defence either in terms of ideology or political effort to the anti-statist aspects of the conservative attack on government and regulation.[46]

Even with the changed attitudes to government, some of the earlier sources of expansion retained their strength and the 1970s yielded mixed results. The pressures were evident in the case of Social Security, where the rising real value of benefits and rising levels of unemployment set in train a rapid decline in the system's solvency from 1972. As the system matured, higher contributions were necessary to sustain benefits and there was a squeeze on those workers actually contributing. Although taxes were raised, the growth of middle-class opposition to taxation threatened the mechanisms and political consensus that had underpinned earlier extensions to the Social Security system and the coherence of the bureaucrats' philosophy for expanding Social Security faltered. The economic crises of the 1970s drove up the costs of welfare, leading to a questioning of existing policies.

The resurgent conservatism was confirmed by the election of Ronald Reagan in 1980. The Reagan administration mounted a powerful critique of particular forms of government intervention, but its principal legacy was to alter the distribution of government expenditure rather than its overall level. Total federal employment rose because staff cuts in certain areas were offset by growth elsewhere, notably defence under the Carter and Reagan administrations. In this case national political leaders, the armed services and military contractors proclaimed earlier reductions in expenditure as a symptom of weakness. Social Security expenditure increased further, though taxes were also raised. Federal budget reductions fell most heavily on comparatively small programmes such as energy, regional and urban development, housing, transport and environmental policies.[47] The attack on welfare retained a traditional character since the primary focus was on schemes which primarily benefited the poor: public works schemes and entitlements to public assistance, food stamps and other programmes. The greater emphasis on local administration added to the variations in coverage, payments and conditions. In contrast to the deregulation of industry and the 'war on welfare', certain areas of government activity expanded via well-organised lobbying and the creation of a crisis atmosphere. The Reagan administration encountered resistance to budget reductions and pressures from crises, notably in the agricultural and savings and loan spheres, to extend federal commitments. The end of the Cold War cast doubt on the continuation of very high levels of defence spending, but international instabilities and well-entrenched resistance from the military plus the employment implications of any cutbacks limited savings. The return of a Democratic administration under President Clinton in 1992 reintroduced a more activist tone in some respects, but few practical changes. The creation of a national health-care system was a priority, but the final proposals were complex and failed to gain Congressional support. Indeed the 1994 Congressional elections resulted in Republican gains followed by a renewed emphasis on reducing welfare provision; even here the overall implications were for more government in some spheres, paticularly law and order.

Summary

Overall, post-war America was characterised by a far, larger government sector whose development was the contested result of numerous influences. Before 1945 there were many contrasting visions of the roles of federal and state government, both in general terms and in relation to specific issues, and these ideas were subject to constitutional and judicial checks. The post-war swings in thinking about government were, therefore, in line with tradition. In part there was a political cycle in which changes in national political leadership favoured or discouraged particular forms of spending or government policies. The most fundamental challenge to the role of government, especially federal regulation, occurred during the economic crisis of the 1970s and early 1980s. At the same time there were sustained demographic and political pressures for expenditure on roads, education and other local responsibilities, and at local and national level bureaucratic and institutional forces promoted the expansion of spending in specific areas. Such forces were evident in the persistence of New Deal programmes, such as

Social Security and farm policies, regulatory agencies and the retention of high levels of military expenditure. In these areas there was a symbiotic relationship between private interests and parts of government which blurred rhetorical contrasts between state and private activities. The specific forms of intervention in different spheres were the product of often highly-specialised lobbying by competing interest groups mediated, not necessarily neutrally, by officials. Even the dramatic shift to deregulation in the late 1970s involved a choice of reduced and different forms of regulation rather than an abandonment of all state influence.

Notes

1 Grahame Thompson, 'From the Long Boom to Recession and Stagnation? The Post-war American Economy' in Grahame Thompson (ed.), *Markets* (Milton Keynes, 1994), esp. pp. 106–111.

2 Robert Higgs, *Crisis and Leviathan: Critical Episodes in the Growth of American Government* (Oxford, 1987), pp. 20–7.

3 Richard Hofstadter, *The Age of Reform: From Bryan to FDR* (New York, 1955).

4 Ellis W. Hawley, *The New Deal and the Problem of Monopoly: A Study in Economic Ambivalence* (Princeton, NJ, 1966).

5 Gabriel Kolko, *Triumph of Conservatism: A Reinterpretation of American History, 1900–1916* (New York, 1973).

6 Louis Galambos, 'Technology, Political Economy and Professionalisation: Central Themes of the Organisational Synthesis', *Business History Review*, 57(4), 1983, pp. 471–93.

7 Higgs, *Crisis and Leviathan*.

8 Peter Fearon, *War, Prosperity and Depression: The US Economy, 1917–1945* (Oxford, 1987), p. 283, table 16.4.

9 Howell John Harris, *The Right To Manage: Industrial Relations Policies of American Business in the 1940s* (Madison, WI, 1982); Elizabeth A. Fones-Wolf, *Selling Free Enterprise: The Business Assault on Labor and Liberalism, 1945–60* (Chicago, 1994).

10 Lance Davis *et al.*, *American Economic Growth: An Economist's History of the United States* (New York, 1972) pp. 656–62; Ronald Lora, 'Education: Schools as Crucible in Cold War America' in Robert H. Bremner and Gary W. Reichard (eds), *Reshaping America: Society and Institutions, 1945–1960* (Columbus, OH, 1982), p. 232.

11 Diane Ravitch, *The Troubled Crusade: American Education, 1945–1980* (New York, 1983), pp. 12–15.

12 D. K. Henry and R. P. Oliver, 'The Defense Build-Up, 1977–1985: Effects on Production and Employment', *Monthly Labor Review*, 110(8), 1987, pp. 3–11.

13 C. Wright Mills, *The Power Elite* (Oxford, 1956).

14 Paul A. C. Koistinen, *The Military-Industrial Complex: A Historical Perspective* (New York, 1980)

15 Roger W. Lotchin, *Fortress California, 1910–1960: From Warfare to Welfare* (New York, 1992).

16 Charles E. Neu, 'The Rise of the National Security Bureaucracy' in Louis Galambos (ed.), *The New American State: Bureaucracies and Policies since World War II* (Baltimore, MD, 1987), pp. 85–108; R. D. Cuff, 'An Organisational Perspective on the Military-Industrial-Complex', *Business*

History Review, 52, 1978, pp. 250–67.

17 Robert Higgs, 'The Cold War Economy: Opportunity Cost, Ideology and the Politics of Crisis', *Explorations in Economic History*, 31(3), 1994, pp. 283–312.

18 Gregory Hooks, 'The Rise of the Pentagon and US State Building: The Defense Program as Industrial Policy', *American Journal of Sociology*, 96(2), 1990, pp. 358–404.

19 Donald J. Mrozek, 'The Truman Administration and the Enlistment of the Aviation Industry in Post-war Defense', *Business History Review*, 48(1), 1974, pp. 73–94.

20 Kenneth M. Jones, 'The Government-Science Complex' in Bremner and Reichard (eds), *Reshaping America*, p. 315.

21 Stuart W. Leslie, *The Cold War and American Science: The Military-Industrial-Academic Complex at MIT and Stanford* (New York, 1993); David A. Wilson (ed.), 'Universities and the Military', *The Annals of the American Academy of Political and Social Science*, 502, 1989, pp. 9–154.

22 Carolyn L. Weaver, 'Social Security Bureaucracy in Triumph and in Crisis' in Galambos (ed.), *The New American State*, pp. 66–7.

23 Paul Starr, *The Social Transformation of American Medicine* (New York, 1982), p. 348.

24 Edward Berkowitz and Kim McQuaid, *Creating the Welfare State: The Political Economy of Twentieth Century Reform* (2nd edn, New York, 1988), chapter 8.

25 James L. Sundquist, *Politics and Policy: The Eisenhower, Kennedy and Johnson Years* (Washington, DC, 1968).

26 Doris Kearns, *Lyndon Johnson and the American Dream* (New York, 1976), chapter 8; William H. Chafe, *The Unfinished Journey: America since World War II* (2nd edn, Oxford, 1991), chapter 8.

27 Martha Derthick, *Policymaking for Social Security* (Washington, DC, 1979), chapter 16.

28 Gareth Davies, 'War on Dependency: Liberal Individualism and the Economic Opportunity Act of 1964', *Journal of American Studies*, 26(2), 1992, pp. 205–31.

29 Carl M. Brauer, 'Kennedy, Johnson and the War on Poverty', *Journal of American History*, 69, 1982, pp. 98–119; Ira Katzenelson, 'Was the Great Society a Lost Opportunity?' in Steve Fraser and Gary Gerstle (eds), *The Rise and Fall of the New Deal Order, 1930–1980* (Princeton, NJ, 1989), pp. 185–211.

30 Mark I. Gelfand, 'Elevating or Ignoring the Underclass' in Robert H. Bremner, Gary W. Reichard and Richard J. Hopkins (eds), *American Choices: Social Dilemmas and Public Policy since 1960* (Columbus, OH, 1986), pp. 5–10.

31 Nicholas Lemann, *The Promised Land: The Great Black Migration and How it Changed America* (London, 1991).

32 Norwood Allen Kerr, 'Drafted into the War on Poverty: USDA Food and Nutrition Programmes, 1961–1969', *Agricultural History*, 64(2), 1990, pp. 154–66.

33 Weaver, 'Social Security Bureaucracy in Triumph and in Crisis', pp. 73–5.

34 Michael B. Katz, *The Undeserving Poor: From the War on Poverty to the War on Welfare* (New York, 1989), p. 106.

35 Allen J. Matusow, *The Unravelling of America: American Liberalism During the 1960s* (New York, 1984), pp. 119–20; Frances Piven and Richard Cloward, *Regulating the Poor: the Functions of Public Welfare* (revised edn, New York, 1993); Frances Fox Piven and Richard A. Cloward, *Poor People's Movements: Why They Succeed, How They Fail* (New York, 1977); Henry J. Aaron, *Politics*

and the Professors: The Great Society in Perspective* (Washington, DC, 1978), pp. 149–51. For discussion of the origins of policy see Richard H. Haveman (ed.), *A Decade of Federal Antipoverty Programs: Achievements, Failures and Lessons* (New York, 1977).

36 Robert Fisher, *Let The People Decide: Neighbourhood Organizing in America* (Boston, MA, 1984), pp. 96–109.

37 James T. Patterson, *America's Struggle Against Poverty, 1900–1980* (Cambridge, MA, 1981); James T. Patterson, *The Welfare State in America, 1930–1980* (Durham, NC, 1981); Sundquist, *Politics and Policy*, p. 112.

38 Margaret Weir *et al.* (eds), *The Politics of Social Policy in the United States* (Princeton, NJ, 1988).

39 Katz, *The Undeserving Poor*, pp. 112–13.

40 Aaron, *Politics and the Professors*, pp. 152–9.

41 Gelfand, 'Elevating or Ignoring the Underclass', p. 23.

42 *Ibid.*

43 John Myles, 'Postwar Capitalism and the Extension of Social Security into a Retirement Wage' in Weir *et al.* (eds), *The Politics of Social Policy in the United States*, pp. 265–92.

44 Starr, *Social Transformation of American Medicine*, pp. 112–14.

45 David Vogel, *Fluctuating Fortunes: The Political Power of Business in America* (New York, 1989).

46 Katz, *The Undeserving Poor*, 1989, pp. 138–73; Theda Skocpol, 'The Limits of the New Deal System and the Roots of Contemporary Welfare Dilemmas' in Weir *et al.* (eds), *The Politics of Social Policy in the United States*, pp. 293–312; William Schambra, 'Is New Federalism the Wave of the Future?' in Marshall Kaplan and Peggy L. Cuciti (eds), *The Great Society and its Legacy: Twenty Years of US Social Policy* (Durham, NC, 1986), pp. 24–31.

47 Paul E. Peterson and Mark Rom, 'Lower Taxes, More Spending, and Budget Deficits' in Charles O. Jones (ed.), *The Reagan Legacy: Promise and Performance* (Chatham, NJ, 1988), pp. 213–40.

3

US government and management of the economy

Chapter 2 addressed the role of government in relation to particular economic and social functions and attitudes to government in general. However, such themes capture only part of the role of government and this chapter looks at another dimension, namely its efforts to manage the economy. The broad economic trends are summarised. The post-war perceptions about government's responsibilities are discussed before a survey of federal measures during the 1950s and the more active and interventionist policies of the 1960s. As indicated in Chapter 2, the 1970s and 1980s brought reassessment of federal influence and the last section of this chapter outlines the greater economic problems. The shifts in federal policy and the development of new problems, notably over the budget, are considered.

At the end of the war there were real fears of a return to the depressed conditions of the 1930s, but in the event real national income increased by 3.7 per cent per annum between 1948 and 1973.[1] During this long boom, recessions in 1948–49, 1953–54, 1957–58, 1960–61 and 1970 were marked by a slackening in growth rates rather than falls in output or national income and the economy was more stable than before the war, though Romer's work suggests that this contrast may be an artefact of the earlier data.[2] Even in this expansive phase, there were difficulties. After a volatile period in the late 1940s, the rate of inflation first drifted up and then gathered pace from the mid-1960s. Unemployment rose in a 'ratchet fashion' during the 1950s: rising as the economy entered each recession, and subsequently declining, but settling at a higher level than before the downturn. There were contributory factors, such as the decline in underemployment as the farm workforce contracted, and the rise in total employment with a higher level of participation in the labour force. During the economic boom of the 1960s, the unemployment record improved considerably, falling from 6.7 per cent in 1961 to 3.5 per cent in 1969, with long-term unemployment falling substantially. Contributory factors were the drafting of more young men for service in Vietnam and the rising rates of college enrolments.

The levels of inflation and unemployment in the 1950s and 1960s were, however, modest compared to those experienced during the 1970s when the economy was in a far more uncertain state. National income growth was 2.1 per cent between 1973 and 1978, the severity of recessions progressively worsened and inflation accelerated.[3] Productivity growth was significantly reduced. As in the 1950s, unemployment 'ratcheted' up during the 1970s as the sluggish economy no longer absorbed the 'baby-boomers' and rising proportion of women workers so readily. The average duration of unemployment increased, though long-term rates remained rather low by international standards. Economic recovery set in from 1983, but initially it involved regaining earlier lost ground and the economy weakened between 1990 and 1992. This chapter considers the sources of the post-war boom and the reasons for the poorer performance since 1969. The nature of economic policy is examined, since economic shifts produced swings in perceptions of the economy and the priorities of economic policy.

The immediate post-war years were an uncertain period, but one which established some vital elements of the subsequent boom, particularly consumer and business confidence. There was a swift contraction in government spending, equivalent to nearly 30 per cent of national income between 1945 and early 1946.[4] Inflationary pressure followed the termination of wage and price controls. Nevertheless the feared slump never materialised, the recession of 1949–50 was mild compared to that following World War II. Rather a virtuous cycle was established through the revival of a pattern of high levels of investment, technological change and productivity growth. These processes had been dislocated during the Depression and new technologies developed in the 1930s and 1940s remained to be exploited fully.[5] Government and corporate research and development capabilities had been strengthened during the war. Consequently a high level of new investment and productivity growth underpinned the rise in real incomes between 1945 and 1969. Improvements in skills resulted from the expansion of education and training, and the transfer of labour out of the comparatively low productivity farm sector was an added influence. Finally, low primary-product prices supplied cheap resources and contributed to moderate rates of inflation.

Between 1945 and 1960 economic activity was led by the twin forces of private-sector investment and consumption. Trends in consumer spending can be gauged by dividing the components of personal consumption, excluding housing, between non-durables, durables and services, as in Table 3.1.

Growth was concentrated in the housing, automobile and consumer durables sectors, reviving the key areas of 1920s prosperity, and expenditure on services rebounded strongly too. The economic conditions favourable to high levels of consumption were re-established during World War II, though the full effects only became apparent after 1945. The war economy operated close to full employment and restrictions on civilian consumption

Table 3.1 *Distribution of real personal consumption in the US, 1929–90 (%)*

Sector	1929	1940	1950	1960	1970	1980	1990
Durables	8.7	8.1	10.9	9.5	10.1	10.7	13.5
Non-durables	43.0	49.2	45.8	43.5	39.5	35.1	32.4
Services	48.3	42.6	43.3	46.9	50.3	54.1	54.1

Source: US Bureau of the Census, *Statistical Abstract of the United States: 1993* (113th edn, Washington, DC, 1993), p. 442, table 690.

led to an accumulation of savings. Between 1941 and 1945 personal saving averaged 21 per cent of personal disposable income compared to an average of 3 per cent in the 1920s or 7 per cent from 1948 to 1969. After 1945 Americans drew down savings and took on debt in order to purchase consumer goods: the value of outstanding instalment credit increased from $2.4 million in 1945 to $42.8 million in 1960. After the initial reconversion phase, demand was maintained by population growth, plus rising real incomes as the expansion of white-collar employment, especially salaried jobs, provided greater stability in incomes and consumption. During the Korean War, after initial prevarication, the imposition of price, wage and credit controls in January 1951 moderated inflation and checked demand for durable goods between 1950 and 1953.[6] Demand for durable goods grew more slowly in the late 1950s, but the sustained rise in real incomes and further extensions of consumer credit maintained high levels of consumer spending through the 1960s.

Housing was particularly in demand since wartime migrations and limits on civilian construction had resulted in substantial suppressed demand. The number of new housing starts increased from 937,000 in 1946 to 1,692,000 in 1950 and residential construction accounted for 7.1 per cent of real GDP in 1950, well above its 1940 share of 4.2 per cent and even exceeding 1929 levels. The housing boom was supported by federal policies. Between 1945 and 1951 the Treasury compelled the Federal Reserve to maintain low interest rates in order to maintain the value of Treasury bonds. More direct influences were tax deductions on mortgage debt and the activities of the Federal Housing Administration, established in 1934, the Veterans' Administration and the GI Bill of Rights in 1944.[7] Neither agency built houses, but each insured mortgage loans made by financial institutions, in effect protecting private lenders against losses. The housing sector was further buttressed by New Deal deposit insurance schemes for commercial banks and the savings and loan industry. The reduced risk ensured a ready availability of funds for house-building: repayment periods were extended up to twenty-five or thirty years and loans were granted for larger proportions of property values. There was an improvement in the quality of the housing stock, with increases in the proportion of homes with running water and inside toilets. As well as new construction, there was a significant upgrading of rural housing due to higher farm incomes, public and private investments in utility supplies and the impact of rural depopulation, which reduced the numbers living in the poorest housing.

From mid-1950 to 1953 the economy was dominated by the consequences of US involvement in Korea and defence spending contributed to economic recovery. Unemployment had passed 5 per cent during the 1949–50 recession, but diminished rapidly as the economy mobilised once again. Federal expenditure doubled to $46.7 billion, transforming the budget surplus of 1950 into a substantial deficit, despite higher taxes. Inflation accelerated until checked by the reintroduction of controls on wages, prices, raw material supplies and credit. The abrupt fall in military spending at the end of the Korean War contributed to a new recession in 1953–54 which saw unemployment rise from 2.5 per cent, its post-war low, to 6 per cent.[8]

Government and the economy after 1945

Clearly, government exerted great influence over the economy after 1945 through its spending and various programmes. As Chapter 2 indicated, this was largely the outcome of the incremental expansion of specific programmes and the broader reaction to the crises of the Depression and war. Liberal ambitions for planning were thwarted by conservatives, so the government's overall impact was the product of numerous separate decisions and policies. The government promoted economic activity through tax reductions in the late 1940s, a more relaxed monetary policy, plus the various stimuli to the housing market and federal and local programmes such as road-building, defence and farm-price supports. Federal transfer payments accounted for a rising share of national income and wartime tax changes had increased federal leverage in the economy. In the aggregate government expenditure provided a baseline of economic activity and at times operated counter-cyclically as the combination of declining tax revenues and payments of unemployment compensation raised federal deficits during recessions. By the 1960s commentators and policy-makers discussed the role of government programmes as 'automatic stabilisers'.

There has been a debate over whether the post-war years saw a fundamental shift in economic management to deliberate counter-cyclical policies. The New Deal's eclectic search for economic recovery had proceeded via regulation and structural reforms rather than active fiscal policy. Federal deficits were relatively modest and conceived as strictly temporary since the orthodoxy of balanced budgets remained very influential. The 1937–38 recession triggered a particularly active debate over policy between advocates of long-run deficits and the fiscal conservatives in which the 'spenders' succeeded in gaining Roosevelt's support.[9] Yet the strength and durability of the President's commitment was uncertain, and Congress checked part of the subsequent proposals for higher expenditure so that policy remained in a state of flux at the end of the 1930s. When massive federal deficits during World War II finally generated full employment the 'spenders" case was vindicated, but the need for their remedies was less pressing since the crisis conditions had passed.

In 1945 there was a wide variety of economic opinions and plans. However, Stein argued that the older emphasis on balanced budgets had been replaced by a willingness to expand deficits during recessions and to compensate with surpluses during times of growth. He detected a surprising degree of national consensus by 1949 around the use of fiscal policy to moderate economic fluctuations.[10] Keynesian ideas of deficit spending were introduced and popularised within the economics profession in the United States by Paul Samuelson, thereby strengthening the theoretical basis for greater intervention. Such attitudes were most prevalent among liberal politicians and economists in the Administration plus a small, though influential, number of corporate liberals associated with the Committee for Economic Development (CED), though there were significant differences over the best means of achieving their objective. US Chamber of Commerce leaders propounded a pragmatic acceptance of some intervention too, though their membership appeared unconvinced; the smaller National Association of Manufacturers maintained implacable opposition to deficits and any federal planning. The merits of counter-cyclical spending were called in aid by the national security establishment in advocating higher defence expenditure, which points to the significance of such ideas in policy-making, but also to the variety of interests involved.[11]

The absence of a coherent business vision left room for more interventionist policies, but it was a confined space since business and congressional conservatism reined in those elements of the New Deal associated with planning, reform and social welfare. There was a general acceptance of the desirability of economic growth, a notion embodied in the Employment Act of 1946, but as the passage of that legislation indicated, appropriate goals and policies remained a matter of considerable debate. As a result the final form of the 1946 Employment Act advanced the principle of maintaining economic growth without making major spending commitments. The outcome has been described as a 'commercial Keynesianism' which focused narrowly on taxation and monetary policies rather than spending or extensive planning. It was, in Collins's view, a triumph for the corporate liberals' vision of limited state intervention over the forces of both New Deal radicalism and business conservatism.[12] Collins and Stein have highlighted the complexities of the policy debate, but their emphasis on consensus exaggerated the earlier influence of New Deal liberalism and hence the extent of its defeat. It was only one tendency in the New Deal coalition. 'Commercial Keynesianism' was consistent with Roosevelt's general aim of limited reform whilst awaiting the revival of private investment. Similarly, commercial Keynesianism did not replace all earlier measures and much of the regulatory framework of the 1930s survived to the 1970s and beyond.

The 1946 Employment Act established a new advisory body, the Council of Economic Advisers (CEA), located in the President's office and, therefore, free of Treasury control, and the Act marked a broad policy commitment to federal economic management. But the CEA's role and the vigour and precise tools with which policies would be pursued were open issues on which there was little consensus. Policy was by no means dominated by a commitment to Keynesian ideas. Truman and Eisenhower proceeded cautiously, concerned about inflation and anxious to moderate the growth in government spending.[13] Truman's CEA formulated a strategy of pursuing sustained economic growth, but made little impact on the President's policies, which placed considerable emphasis on restraining inflation.[14] For Stein the Eisenhower administrations between 1953 and 1960 provided the key test of commitment to a new fiscal approach, since Republicans were closely identified with the orthodoxies of balanced budgets and Eisenhower's ideal of a 'corporate commonwealth' envisaged a restricted federal role.[15] Nonetheless, Eisenhower accepted a federal responsibility for economic management and used deficits to counter the 1953–54 recession, which indicated the extent and strength of the new consensus. However, a good deal of Eisenhower's expenditure on infrastructure was designed to promote growth and development on its own account rather than via deficit spending. Eisenhower's second term was devoted to countering pressures for higher spending on the grounds that it was inflationary and an undesirable expansion of the federal role.[16] The final stages of Eisenhower's presidency were marked by recurring contests over the level of expenditure on defence and the space programme as the Administration endeavoured to control the federal budget.[17] Although deficits increased during the late 1950s, this was more a result of recession-induced falls in revenue and growth in welfare payments than any deliberate counter-cyclical programme.

The 'New Economics' of the 1960s

A more distinct departure in policy was evident in the early 1960s. With recessions in 1957–58 and 1960–61, there was a upward trend in unemployment from 2.9 per cent in 1953 at the end of the Korean War to 5.5 per cent in 1959. The average period of unemployment rose from eight to fourteen weeks. Assertions of a 'missile gap' and technological lag compared to the Soviet Union following the launch of Sputnik were used by the Democrats against the Republicans. As a result in 1961 President Kennedy was receptive to more pro-active Keynesian policies, the so-called 'New

Economics', which placed greater emphasis on maximising economic growth rather than smoothing out fluctuations. Rather than accepting deficits during recessions, the 'New Economics' propounded the idea that the economy was liable to operate below its potential or full employment level so there could be a case for intervention even during upswings. This approach specified targets for growth and unemployment and placed far greater faith in the capacity to identify and implement policies to 'fine-tune' the economy. The centrepiece of the new regime was a cut in business and personal taxes of $14 billion, authorised by Kennedy in 1963 shortly before his assassination and implemented by Johnson in 1964. Rather than simply raising revenue, taxation was to be used to promote growth. Such tax cuts found favour with the wider business community, despite its suspicion of the 'New Economics'.

There was a major economic expansion from 1961 to 1969: real Gross National Product increased by 3.6 per cent per annum. Unemployment remained high in the early part of the decade, but fell from 6.7 per cent in 1961 to 3.5 per cent in 1969, and the average duration declined from nearly sixteen weeks to eight weeks. The driving forces were a major surge of new investment and renewed growth in purchases of houses and consumer durables. This growth was acclaimed as a triumph of the 'New Economics', although the tax cuts added momentum to an established upturn rather than initiating recovery. With its emphasis on stimulating growth plus a commitment to new domestic programmes, the federal government ran deficits throughout the 1960s. Even at its peak the 'New Economics' had shallow roots since, by international standards, federal spending remained low, which limited the authorities' economic leverage. Moreover other policy concerns affected economic policy in diverse, often contradictory ways. Escalating involvement in Vietnam drove up military outlays by $30 billion (a 60 per cent increase) between 1965 and 1968, and as the economy operated close to capacity there was a greater tendency for wages and prices to rise in the private sector. From 1965 the rate of inflation quickened, but the Federal Reserve's moves to restrict credit were modest and President Johnson, anxious to maintain his military and domestic programmes, delayed tax increases.

Problems and policies after 1969

After 1969 economic performance deteriorated markedly as part of an international slow-down in growth and acceleration of inflation. The US economy experienced recessions in 1970, 1974–75, and 1980–82, which were more severe than previous post-war downturns. The only sustained growth occurred during the mid-1980s; even then growth remained below its post-war trend for much of the time. In the first half of the 1970s unemployment 'ratcheted up' rather as in the 1950s: the

Table 3.2 *Annual rate of change in the US consumer price index, 1961–92 (%)*

Year	All items	Food	Energy
1961	11.7	1.0	0.4
1964	1.3	1.3	−0.4
1965	1.6	2.2	1.8
1968	4.2	3.5	1.7
1970	5.7	5.7	2.8
1973	6.2	14.5	8.1
1974	11.0	14.3	29.6
1975	9.1	8.5	10.5
1976	5.8	3.0	7.1
1977	6.5	6.3	9.5
1978	7.6	9.9	6.3
1979	11.3	11.0	25.1
1980	13.5	8.6	30.9
1981	10.3	7.8	13.6
1982	6.2	4.1	1.5
1983	3.2	2.1	0.7
1985	3.6	2.3	0.7
1986	1.9	3.2	−13.2
1990	5.4	5.8	8.3
1992	3.0	1.2	0.5

Note: Energy includes household fuels, motor fuels and, to 1982, motor oil.
Source: Economic Report of the President, 1994 (Washington, DC, 1996), p. 348,
B-60.

average rate increased from 3.5 per cent in 1969 to 8.5 per cent in 1975 and
the average period of unemployment rose from eight weeks to fourteen
weeks. The position improved over the second half of the decade, but worsened again between 1980 and 1983 when the rate reached 9.6 per cent and
an average duration of twenty weeks. There was then a sustained improvement to 1989 in which unemployment fell to 5.3 per cent before a reversal
in a new recession. Another distinctive feature was the acceleration of inflation which began in the mid-1960s due to increased federal spending and
wage rises in a tightening labour market, but gathered far greater momentum in the 1970s, especially between 1972 and 1974 and from 1978 to 1980.
In the first period the annual growth rate of consumer prices soared from
3.2 per cent to 11 per cent; the rate declined to 5.8 per cent by 1976, but
increased to 13.5 per cent in 1980, led by energy and food price rises (Table
3.2).

The combination of recessions and inflation created a crisis of confidence in existing institutions and policies. In the testing conditions of the
1970s economic policy was marked by uncertainty and changes of emphasis between the objectives of growth, with lower unemployment, and the
control of inflation. The new Nixon administration in 1969 accepted the

target of rapid growth, later used Keynesian rhetoric and deployed tax reductions in 1971, which indicated the extent of consensus around the 'New Economics'. At least the aim of promoting growth had been translated into an assumption that government spending was broadly positive. It was anticipated that economic growth would enable commitments to be met, but inevitably expenditure remained highly susceptible to other policy concerns and the political cycle of elections. Johnson's reluctance to control inflation in 1968, the separate concerns which determined the course of military spending, and Nixon's desire for pre-election prosperity in 1972 all generated instabilities. Moreover when the economy faltered, the optimistic hopes of sustainable growth were dashed and unemployment and recessions triggered greater expenditure.

As the problem of inflation became more pressing, economic policy was characterised by efforts to stimulate growth while reducing inflation, with the latter objective receiving increasing emphasis. A rise in interest rates in 1969 contributed to the recession in the following year. Earlier deflationary policies had combined such credit squeezes with exhortations to business and unions to restrain price and wage increases. However, President Nixon's desire for a bold stroke produced a striking departure from earlier practice, in the form of the New Economic Policy in August 1971, which introduced a ninety-day freeze on wages and prices followed by a series of controls to 1973.[18] At the same time balance of payments problems were addressed through the devaluation of the dollar by ending its convertibility to gold. Although the initial freeze checked inflation, price controls were countered by expansionary monetary policy, and the ending of the price freeze was followed by a further acceleration of inflation, given added momentum by oil and food price rises. The later phase of price and wage controls was less effective. The Federal Reserve relaxed monetary policy to the approval of the Nixon administration and there was a feverish economic upswing in the election year of 1972 as consumption and investment soared.

The Ford and Carter administrations resumed the earlier anti-inflationary strategy of 'jawboning' employers and workers, but to little effect. At first the Carter administration was inclined to pursue expansionary fiscal and monetary policies in order to reduce unemployment, but a further surge of inflation halted this effort in favour of restraining inflation. A more powerful influence, however, was the policy of the Federal Reserve Board, under chairman Paul Volcker. In 1979 the Federal Reserve embarked on a restrictive monetary policy backed by high interest rates and the resulting recession, particularly higher levels of unemployment, restrained price and wage increases.[19]

Paul Krugman, an economist, termed the 1970s and 1980s an 'age of diminished expectations' on the basis that policy-makers and the public lost faith in the capacity of economic theory or policy-makers to achieve sustained growth.[20] Certainly previous policies were discredited in the light of the poor economic performance, but, rather than total disillusionment with theory, there was a frantic search for, and advocacy of, alternative economic programmes and panaceas. Persistent stagflation created a crisis of confidence in Keynesian economic policies and more broadly in federal economic management, even among policy-makers. Recessions and accelerating inflation raised fundamental questions about how the economy, particularly labour markets, operated and resulted in an array of economic models and analyses. For Keynesian economists there was the dilemma that measures to check inflation depressed demand, thereby worsening recessions. Advocates of 'free-market' economic philosophies produced various alternative policies. For monetarists, such as Milton Friedman, inflation was a product of the government's failure to recognise the significance of the money supply. Conservative economists and politicians attributed the weaker economic performance primarily to the expansion in the role of government. Rather than being regarded as a source of stability, increased federal expenditure was criticised for 'crowding out' private investment. A diverse array of 'supply-side' theories challenged the focus on demand and instead criticised government, usually federal, spending, taxation and regulation for their effects on consumption, investment, production costs and the supply of labour and incentives to work. A critique of regulation *per se*, which had developed without much impact from the late 1950s, also flourished by offering competition and reduced state intervention as solutions to the puzzle of stagflation. Slower productivity growth and inflation increased business resentment of regulation and made collective bargaining more combative, as well as ensuring that demands for income redistribution encountered maximum resistance.

In this climate there was a greater tendency to regard government as the source of economic difficulties, especially since public policies offered no clear remedies for stagflation. The various economic prescriptions also received encouragement from elements of political fragmentation. As well as the economic problems, the Watergate episode had led Congress to seek greater control over executive power, including taking a more active role in budgetary matters. Many strands of the economic programme associated with the Reagan presidency, such as monetarism, deregulation and tax cuts, moved into the forefront of public policy under Ford and Carter. However, Reagan embraced these varied remedies more directly as the philosophical basis for his first administration between 1981 and 1984. In political terms President Reagan capitalised on anti-government sentiment and emphasised individualism and the idea of returning to old virtues of self-reliance and a smaller federal role. The economic message was couched in terms of restoring growth and confidence as part of a broader assertion of American economic and military power. It promised an easy transition to better times, but, compared to earlier 'growthmanship', identified new tactics. The programme called for a reduction in total federal spending, a shift in the composition of spending in favour of defence at the expense of welfare and a return to balanced budgets. At the same time tax reductions were advocated as a means of stimulating investment, work effort and enterprise and, thereby, growth and employment. Inflation was to be tackled through monetary policy plus the anticipated deflationary effects of deregulation. 'Reaganomics' was a mix of broad ideals and images under whose banner various specific policies were advanced by often contending advisers whose influence waxed and waned. Its theoretical foundations were often suspect, such as establishing the link between specific taxes and incentives, but the broad thrust of policy and the pro-market rhetoric were clear.[21] Inevitably the implementation of policy was also problematic, given political conflicts over tax and spending and contradictions between the various objectives. Monetary policy aimed at restraining growth, but the tax cuts were predicated on their ability to supply a quick economic stimulus if balanced budgets and higher military spending were also to be realised.

In the short term the Administration's plans were dwarfed by the independent policies of Paul Volcker, chairman of the Federal Reserve which applied an intensive dose of tight monetary policy. The Federal Reserve restricted money supply, raised interest rates sharply in real terms and engineered recessions in 1980 and 1982. The strategy produced a sharp rise in unemployment, but in stark contrast to the previous decade the rate of inflation diminished sharply from 10.3 per cent in 1981 to 3.2 per cent in 1983 and was only 1.9 per cent in 1986. A contributory element was a slower rise in oil and food prices due to increases in supply and the check to demand administered by recessions.

There was economic recovery from 1983 though its early stages involved regaining ground lost at the start of the decade. The economic upturn was led by rising consumer spending, notably on cars and housing, followed by an expansion of investment, and there was a substantial federal stimulus in the form of a further rise in military expenditure. In this respect the sources of expansion were in line with earlier phases of growth, though consumption was sustained by a pronounced fall in the level of savings and a marked increase in credit-card use.[22]

Economic growth was accompanied, however, by unprecedented fiscal problems. The 1981 budget enacted a $162 billion reduction in individual and corporate taxes through the Economic Recovery Tax Act which went further even than the Administration had planned. The political appeal of tax cuts resulted in indexing personal tax exemptions to protect their real value, which lessened the potential for inflation-induced 'bracket creep' to generate rising revenues.[23] As in 1964 tax cuts were expected to produce the economic advantages of renewed economic growth, but through different mechanisms. Where Kennedy's CEA had looked to stimulate consumption,

Table 3.3 *US federal receipts, outlays and deficit, 1945–94 ($ billion)*

Year	Receipts	Outlays	Surplus/deficit
1945	45.2	92.7	−47.6
1950	39.4	42.6	−3.1
1960	92.5	92.2	+0.3
1970	192.8	195.6	−2.8
1980	517.1	590.9	−73.8
1982	617.8	745.8	−128.0
1983	600.6	808.4	−207.8
1985	734.1	946.4	−212.3
1987	854.1	1,003.9	−149.8
1989	990.7	1,143.2	−152.5
1990	1,031.2	1,252.7	−221.4
1992	1,090.5	1,380.9	−290.4
1993	1,153.5	1,408.2	−254.7
1994	1,257.7	1,460.9	−203.2

Source: Economic Report of the President, 1995, p. 365, table B-77.

Reagan's supply-side approach was designed to promote greater effort, more saving and increased investment in order to bridge the gap between reduced revenues and a balanced budget. It was assumed that Americans had curtailed their work effort due to the deterrent effect of existing tax rates and so, according to an economic hypothesis known as the Laffer curve, reduced taxes might produce more work and, thus, higher revenues. It was a belief which appealed to taxpayers and to the conservative ideals of individualism and less government, but the Laffer curve involved a considerable leap of faith. The other aspect of budget balancing was expenditure cuts, but the Administration was set on raising military spending and political opposition limited reductions in Social Security, so that the burden of reductions fell heavily on relatively small parts of the budget such as other welfare programmes and public investment. These were too small to yield major savings and certainly unlikely to offset higher defence expenditure. Despite the recovery, tax revenues declined rather than followed the precepts of the Laffer curve and expenditure, though falling as the recession passed, remained above 1980 levels.[24] The result was a far greater federal deficit (Table 3.3).

There had been substantial deficits immediately after World War II, but these had been reduced through a combination of higher taxes and revenues. Thereafter the federal government ran deficits in most years and sustained interest payments on its debt, but the deficits and interest remained relatively modest compared to total national income or federal spending. Broadly, deficits rose during recessions and diminished in economic upturns in line with the notion of government programmes acting as 'automatic stabilisers'. However the package of Reagan policies undercut the earlier tendencies for revenue to rise during the growth phase: tax rates were lower and the 'bracket creep' effect of inflation was less potent. In 1970 the gross federal debt was $380.9 million, which represented 38.7 per cent of GDP and by 1980 totalled $908.5 million or 34 per cent of GDP, which was broadly in line with its position since 1960. The policies and events of the 1980s fundamentally and spectacularly altered the scale of federal debt. By 1985 the federal debt was $1,816.9 million and in 1992 totalled $4,002.6 million; these figures constituted 45.8 per cent and 68.2 per cent of GDP respectively. Considerable political debate took place about the budget deficit, but political and policy differences created a stalemate. The Reagan administration set its face against higher taxes or lower defence spending and Congress and lobbyists defended programmes, such as Social Security and farm spending. The scope for major cuts was, therefore, limited and the burden fell most on a small number of programmes, including public assistance. In 1985 Congress passed the Gramm–Rudman–Hollings scheme which set annual targets for lower deficits designed to return to a balanced budget within six years. In the event reductions were modest as Congress and interest groups resisted cuts in specific programmes and all sides pinned their hopes on faster economic growth providing an eventual solution. With the Reagan administration set against raising taxes, borrowing was required and, in turn, interest payments absorbed a greater share of the annual budget. A good deal of the borrowing was overseas, which added to the pressure to maintain high interest rates in order to maintain the flow of funds and made the United States more reliant on the volatile international capital markets. Moreover, as the value of the dollar rose in the early 1980s, imported goods became cheaper which in turn contributed to the trade deficit.

The Reagan era offered a sense of policy direction even though the actual programmes were at times changeable, contradictory or only partially implemented. The Administration's policies were avowedly not Keynesian, but the mix of lower taxes, deficits and the emphasis on growth retained some links to earlier policies. In spite of the Administration's non-interventionist philosophy and deregulation, the 'automatic stabilisers' still operated and the expansion of military spending exerted a powerful economic stimulus. The restrictive monetary policy lowered inflation, but monetarism was trimmed and then abandoned as the economy recovered. The clearest break with the post-war consensus was the Federal Reserve Board's willingness to accept high levels of unemployment in the early 1980s in order to reduce inflation. Nonetheless, job creation continued to be a very successful feature of the US economy since the economy absorbed the 'baby-boom' generation, a higher proportion of women workers, and an increased inflow of migrants. Unemployment was primarily short-term and long-term unemployment rates were low by international standards, though in the early 1990s long-term unemployment did not rebound as much as after previous recessions. The main generator of new jobs was the service sector. Yet the conservative programme did not achieve higher levels of savings or improved productivity. By the end of the 1980s the problems of budget and trade deficits plus another recession renewed the search for a new mix of policies. President Bush finally enacted tax increases in 1990, but the economy drifted into recession and policy-making was characterised by renewed uncertainty, conservatives advocating a return to some of the ideas of the early Reagan era and liberals advancing federal initiatives over public investment and industrial policy. The new Clinton administration supplied a more positive rhetoric and image of government as a potential aid in restoring competitiveness through investment in infrastructure and education, but equally advocated limited taxation, especially on middle-income groups. In this sense the Reagan era and the perception of a decline in American international competitiveness had altered the terms of the debate over economic management. There were echoes of the early Kennedy and Johnson eras in the ideas of improving human capital through education and training, but a far more cautious approach to government's capacity to control the economy.

Notes

1 Edward Denison, *Accounting for Slower Economic Growth: The United States in the 1970s* (Washington, DC, 1979), p. 7.
2 Christine Romer, 'Is the Stabilization of the Post-War Economy a Figment of the Data?', *American Economic Review*, 76(3), 1986, pp. 314–34.
3 Angus Maddison, *Dynamic Forces in Capitalist Development: A Long-Run Comparative View* (Oxford, 1991), pp. 48–9.
4 Robert A. Gordon, *Economic Instability and Growth: The American Record* (New York, 1974), pp. 90–1.
5 Maddison, *Dynamic Forces in Capitalist Development*, pp. 40–4.
6 Hugh Rockoff, *Drastic Measures: A History of Wage and Price Controls in the United States* (Cambridge, 1984), chapter 6.
7 Kenneth T. Jackson, *Crabgrass Frontier: The Suburbanization of the United States* (New York, 1985), chapters 11 and 13.
8 Robert J. Gordon, 'Postwar Macroeconomics: The Evolution of Events and Ideas' in Martin Feldstein (ed.), *The American Economy in Transition* (Chicago, 1980), pp. 107, 121.
9 Herbert Stein, *The Fiscal Revolution in America*, (Washington, DC, 1990), chapter 6; Robert M. Collins, *The Business Response to Keynes, 1929–1964* (New York, 1981), chapters 2–3.
10 Stein, *The Fiscal Revolution*, p. 240. see also Nicolas Spulber, *Managing the American Economy From Roosevelt to Reagan* (Bloomington, IN, 1989), p. 25.
11 Richard B. DuBoff, *Accumulation and Power: An Economic History of the United States* (New York, 1989), pp. 98–9.
12 Collins, *The Business Response to Keynes*.
13 Iwan W. Morgan, *Deficit Government: Taxing and Spending in Modern America* (Chicago, 1995), chapter 3.
14 Robert M. Collins, 'The Emergence of Economic "Growthmanship" in the United States: Federal Policy and Economic Knowledge in the Truman Years' in Mary O. Furner and Barry Supple (eds), *The State and Economic*

Knowledge: The American and British Experiences (Cambridge, 1990), chapter 5.

15 Robert Griffith, 'Dwight D. Eisenhower and the Corporate Commonwealth', *American Historical Review*, 77, 1982, pp. 87–122.

16 Iwan W. Morgan, *Eisenhower Versus 'The Spenders': The Eisenhower Administration, The Democrats and The Budget, 1953–1960* (London, 1990); John W. Sloan, *Eisenhower and the Management of Prosperity* (Lawrence, KS, 1991)

17 Morgan, *Eisenhower Versus 'The Spenders'*.

18 Herbert Stein, *Presidential Economics: The Making of Economic Policy From Roosevelt To Reagan and Beyond* (New York, 1984), chapter 5.

19 Krugman argues that Federal Reserve policy was less a conversion to monetarism and more a pragmatic willingness to employ monetarist rhetoric to justify a general deflation, with the aim of restraining wage and price rises. Paul A. Krugman, *The Age of Diminished Expectations: US Economic Policy in the 1990s* (Cambridge, MA, 1990).

20 *Ibid.*

21 Morgan, *Deficit Government*, pp. 152–3.

22 Lewis Mandell, *The Credit Card Industry: A History* (Boston, MA, 1990).

23 Marc Allan Eisner, *The State in the American Political Economy: Public Policy and the Evolution of State-Economy Relations* (Englewood Cliffs, NJ, 1995), p. 295.

24 Paul E. Peterson and Mark Rom, 'Lower Taxes, More Spending, and Budget Deficits' in Charles O. Jones (ed.), *The Reagan Legacy: Promise and Performance* (Chatham, NJ, 1988), pp. 213–40; David A. Stockman, *The Triumph of Politics: How The Reagan Revolution Failed* (New York, 1986).

4

US regional economic change since 1945

So far the emphasis has been on national trends, but such aggregate data can conceal significant regional and local variations. US regions differ, but the extent and nature of these differences has altered since World War II. This chapter summarises the general regional trends and then considers the underlying reasons for the changes. There is an assessment of the economic development of the West and South, often labelled the 'Sunbelt', and the contributions of governments and market forces to growth. Then attention switches to the fortunes of the older industrial and urban areas of the North and Midwest where industrial decline and economic restructuring were more in evidence.

A striking feature of US society since 1945 has been the growing importance of the western and southern states. In 1940 the US economy was dominated by the Midwest and Northeast. US industry was primarily located in a 'manufacturing belt' of states running from Illinois to Massachusetts, New York and Pennsylvania.[1] The nation's financial and commercial markets were centred in New York and Chicago and the political influence of Washington, DC, had expanded during the Depression and World War II. In contrast the predominantly agrarian and extractive economies of the South and West relied on outside capital and markets as well as buying the products of the manufacturing belt. Southerners and Westerners resented what they saw as their colonial relationship with the Midwest and Northeast.

The terms of US regionalism were very different by the 1970s when political commentators twinned the West and South as a new 'Sunbelt', a term coined to capture a shift in economic, political and cultural influence away from the Midwest and Northeast. The standard definition of the Sunbelt encompassed all states south of the 37th Parallel, though northern California and Virginia were included on occasion.[2] The Northeast and MidWest were labelled the 'Rustbelt' or 'Frostbelt', terms associated with images of urban and industrial decline, the threats posed by high energy costs and a flight of capital, people and jobs.

The 'Sunbelt/Frostbelt' dichotomy became a major issue of public

Table 4.1 *US per capita income by region as a percentage of the national average,*
1940–90

Region	1940	1950	1960	1970	1980	1990
New England	121	106	109	108	106	119
Middle Atlantic	124	116	116	113	108	116
East–North Central	112	112	107	105	101	98
West–North Central	84	94	93	95	94	94
South Atlantic	69	74	77	86	92	97
East–South Central	55	63	67	74	78	80
West–South Central	70	81	83	85	94	85
Mountain	92	96	95	90	95	88
Pacific	138	121	118	110	115	108

Sources: 1940–70: US Bureau of the Census, *Historical Statistics of the United States, Colonial Times to 1970, Bicentennial Edition*, Part 2 (Washington, DC, 1975), p. 242, series F287–96; 1980–90: US Bureau of the Census, *Statistical Abstract of the United States: 1993* (113th edn, Washington, DC, 1993), p. 451, table 704.

debate in the 1970s because the dramatic rises in energy, food and raw material prices favoured the South and West. However it also reflected longer-term trends. The Census Bureau's regional divisions of Northeast, Midwest, South and West (Table 4.1) displayed a convergence in levels of per-capita income, though there were significant variations within regions.

As well as changes in per-capita income levels, there was a shift of population to the western states, contraction of farm employment and significant industrial growth. In 1946 the South and West accounted for just 23 per cent of all personal income derived from manufacturing in the United States, but by 1982 the two regions' share had risen to 43 per cent.[3] A more modest shift occurred in the distribution of income from services. Overall the economic structure of the regions converged and the penetration of national chain-stores, hotels, fast-food franchises, television and radio contributed to greater cultural similarity.

The 'Sunbelt' label captured certain important trends and similarities between the South and the West, but there were significant variations too. The West was initially more urbanised, had higher levels of per-capita income and by the 1920s possessed aircraft and car plants. The South was a low-wage region and its industrial base, though it included steel and engineering, was modest and concentrated on textiles and tobacco products. Given this initial diversity, the Sunbelt displayed considerable variation in the rates, timing and character of its development. Abbott defined separate western and eastern sunbelts, including some more northern states and excluding Arkansas, Louisiana, Mississippi, Alabama and Tennessee.[4] Other studies adopted similar western and southern coastal definitions of the Sunbelt.[5] California, Texas and Florida expanded more rapidly than other states from 1910 to 1950 in terms of population or employment in manufacturing and services.[6] During the 1970s California, Florida and Texas together accounted for 42 per cent of total US population growth. Florida and Texas accounted for nearly half of in-migrants to the South from 1965 to 1985 and for 45 per cent of southern employment gains between 1969 and 1986. The two states had higher per-capita incomes, were more urban and possessed more high-tech employment than other southern states.[7] Even within states there were contrasts. Rodwin and Sazanami focused narrowly on 'growth poles' in Los Angeles, San Francisco Bay, parts of Texas, Florida, North Carolina, Virginia and Maryland.[8] To be even more specific, growth centred in the metropolitan areas of Los Angeles, Houston, Dallas–Fort Worth, Phoenix and Atlanta.

Sources of Sunbelt development

The local contrasts and important differences between the South and West need to be kept in mind and each region could be treated separately. However this would involve some repetition since there were common features in the two regions' post-war development. The sources of Sunbelt growth lay in a series of interrelated influences with private-sector investment, government programmes and local boosterism as the key factors, though the force of each element varied at different times and places.

Wartime developments in the West and South

Post-war trends owed a good deal to the transforming impact of World War II on investment, incomes and industry in the West and South.[9] Wartime demand revived depressed agricultural, oil and mining sectors. The strategic imperatives for decentralised facilities and an enlarged western military presence encouraged an expansion of defence-related industries and military bases in the South and West. Both regions experienced new investment, industrial diversification and urban growth. Nash estimated new investment in the West at $40 billion during World War II and the Defense Plant Corporation built 344 plants in the West at a cost of $1,853,634,000 between 1940 and 1945.[10] In the South, also defined to include Texas, federal expenditure on military facilities totalled $4 billion and assistance to war-related industry amounted to a further $4.5 billion.[11] Federal expenditure in World War II was a spectacular opportunity for boosters to promote economic development, a chance which southern and western elites pursued avidly with offers of land, housing and road-building.

During the 1940s manufacturing employment increased by one-third in California and by 14 per cent in Texas.[12] The aircraft companies in southern California and Seattle expanded rapidly and by 1943 the industry employed nearly one-quarter of a million workers in southern California.[13] New munitions plants and aircraft production were established in

Dallas–Fort Worth, Marietta, Nashville and Miami and employment in southern shipyards and aircraft plants increased from 20,000 in 1939 to 500,000 in 1943.[14] In the West shipbuilding proliferated around San Francisco Bay, Portland, Los Angeles and, rather improbably, in Denver. The atomic bomb programme brought specialised investments including research and testing facilities in Los Alamos, New Mexico, and a plutonium plant in Hanford, Washington. Along the Gulf Coast and around Los Angeles oil and chemical industries received federal investment, including federally-financed development of new petrochemical products, such as synthetic rubber, and interstate pipelines. Federal expenditure created new industries: steelworks near Los Angeles, in Utah and along the Gulf Coast and aluminium smelting in the Pacific Northwest.[15] A dam near Las Vegas attracted a magnesium plant and the city's fledgling gaming and hotel industry prospered from western flows of service personnel.[16] In the South wartime demand for labour provided a powerful urban 'pull' for an underemployed, low-income rural population: 1.6 million southerners left the South between 1941 and 1945 and a further 4.8 million migrated within the South, primarily to cities.[17] Western agriculture experienced a similar drain, but western cities also drew massive inflows of migrants from outside the region.

Bases and defence plants were mothballed or laid off workers after 1945, but much of the wartime legacy proved permanent. Private companies who had operated defence plants had acquired local knowledge and contacts and the federal government's policy of disposing of surplus defence plants provided a foundation for industrial investment after the war, in effect reducing the cost of southern or western investment for business. Wartime petrochemical facilities passed into private hands and underpinned postwar growth in Houston, Baton Rouge, Beaumont and Port Arthur in the Southwest as well as around Los Angeles. A defunct wartime bomber plant at Marietta, Georgia, attracted Lockheed and in Dallas and Fort Worth wartime aircraft plants were acquired by aviation companies relocating from the Northeast after the war. Los Angeles, San Diego and Seattle retained aircraft manufacturing capacity and expertise which facilitated renewed growth in the early 1950s.

Post-war economic development: continuity and change

The established elements of the southern and western economies remained in place. Agriculture contracted in terms of employment, but its diversification and improved profitability contributed to economic growth in both regions. Similarly the resource-based industries, like oil and natural gas, expanded with new discoveries and further investments in processing, distribution and support services. Along the Gulf Coast the petrochemicals sector spawned oil-related service and supply activities such as toolmakers and drilling contractors. The pace of exploration and investment was influenced by prevailing prices and the oil, gas, coal and other minerals industries retained their 'boom and bust' character. The resource-based sector was particularly profitable between 1973 and 1981 due to the large increases in energy prices, and this was a major contribution to the 'Sunbelt' rhetoric of the period. Other primary or extractive industries remained important in the South and West. For energy-intensive industries, such as aluminium smelting, cheap hydroelectric power was the principal attraction of the South and West. The mining sector continued to be a substantial, though shifting presence in the West and South, with some associated manufacturing, notably iron and steel in Alabama. The western timber industry expanded to meet the demand for house-building in the region between 1945 and 1980 and forestry remained significant in the South. Some manufacturing followed a related extractive industry so that forestry was linked to the steady growth of paper-making in the Southeast and Pacific Northwest.

Manufacturing continued to expand along some well-worn tracks as part of the developing national economy. Labour-intensive industries remained important in the South. Textile mills had been present before the Civil War, and from the 1880s outside and local capital had shifted the centre of textile manufacturing away from New England to the South in search of lower wages and longer shifts. Although some mills later moved overseas in search of further savings, textiles retained a substantial presence and some mills shifted to synthetic fibres. The manufacture of clothing and carpets was important in some areas. Product-cycle theory suggested that as industries mature and become more competitive, lower-wage locations are likely to be chosen in order to reduce costs.[18] As older factories required renewal, there was scope to locate new facilities in the Sunbelt. Given regional wage patterns, such corporate strategy was more applicable to the South than to the relatively high-wage West. Against this logic, Wright argued that minimum wage laws integrated the South into national labour markets from the 1930s and that wage differentials for skilled labour were always small.[19] Surveys of business opinion indicated that labour costs were a minor consideration in new investments, though these results probably reflected reticence about emphasising low wages or the fact that the issue was subsumed under the broader label of a favourable business climate. Certainly the wave of open-shop laws in the mid-1940s signified a desire not to be integrated fully into national markets, and levels of union organisation remained lower across the Sunbelt compared to the Midwest and Northeast. In any case, though wage differentials narrowed, a southern location still offered lower wages as well as savings on other costs, such as taxes and land prices, which reinforced the attraction of cheaper labour. Lower wages were particularly advantageous for labour-intensive industries, but held attractions for any business, especially where a location in one of the border states permitted easy access to northern markets. In the 1960s electronics assembly plants moved south and during the 1970s and 1980s new smaller steel mills were sited in southern states.[20]

After 1945 industry in the Sunbelt became more diverse as increased western population and higher southern per-capita income expanded local consumer demand. Both Hirschman and Myrdal noted the scope for 'internal' growth as firms supplying southern and western economies substituted local manufacturing for 'imports' of industrial goods. Western labour was relatively expensive so market opportunities, perhaps along with high transport costs, were the prime consideration for opening plants. Cobb's careful review of the literature concluded that expanding consumer markets were consistently the primary reason for locating in the South, though lower wages must also be borne in mind.[21] Automobile firms and their suppliers had established branch plants in California by the 1920s and expanded during the 1950s and 1960s as well as beginning to open southern factories. Miami, Tampa, Dallas–Fort Worth, Los Angeles and other cities developed diversified manufacturing bases including food, beer, meat-packing, clothing and consumer industries. Houston's dependence on the oil industry diminished after 1947 as chemicals and metalworking supplied more jobs.[22] In Miami tourism's share of total employment declined from 35 per cent to 20 per cent between 1940 and 1960 while manufacturing's share rose from 3.3 per cent in 1940 to 9.4 per cent in 1950 and 13 per cent in 1960.[23] National chains were important in retailing, hotels and fast-food outlets. As regional economies expanded, local capital and entrepreneurs had greater incentives to engage in manufacturing, perhaps as a supplier to a major industry or to cater for growing local markets.[24]

If there was continuity in the shape of the resource-based and labour-intensive industries, the concept of the Sunbelt was based on a break with the past and the appearance of new, more capital-intensive manufacturing. Given their relatively high value and modest transport costs, 'high-tech' industries were comparatively footloose and not tied to the older manufacturing belt for coal supplies, materials, labour or access to markets. Nash characterised the post-war West as a 'Technological Economy' founded on scientific research and innovation, especially in computers and aerospace. Major electronics, software and communications industries developed in Silicon Valley around San José as well as in Phoenix and Denver. Silicon Valley's early growth was supported by the entry of major eastern electrical companies, but its sustained growth and innovative capacity rested on the high rate of local company formations, including firms such as Hewlett-Packard which became internationally important. For the South Wright and Schulman both identified a break with the traditional low-wage economy in favour of a development strategy based on high-wage and high-technology industries.[25] The 'high-tech' label can be misleading. Some labour-intensive industries became more mechanised and high-tech industries like electronics included plants engaged in low-wage assembly work and the high-tech nuclear power plants were drawn by cheap land. Nonetheless by one estimate the high-wage industrial sector expanded by 180 per cent in the South between 1940 and 1960, which was double the national rate.[26]

The idea of the Sunbelt incorporated an emphasis on the attractions of the physical environment along with favourable perceptions of an associated life-style. The milder winters and an outdoor life close to beaches or mountains and scenic views contrasted with northern winters and older urban landscapes. Such positive views of southern California existed well before 1941 and many service personnel gained first-hand experience of the West and South during the war.[27] Earlier images of southern climate and culture were less positive: for much of the year Sunbelt states were characterised by extremely inhospitable heat and humidity. In this respect the use of air conditioning made an important contribution to Sunbelt development by making factories, offices and homes correspond to the sunny, but comfortable, ideal.[28] With this greater control over the environment there was more likelihood that people would be willing to move to the South or West, but it also exerted greater pressure on local government to supply the standards of schools, communications and urban facilities which migrants expected. As well as those who migrated to work, the Sunbelt drew retired people either as permanent residents or as 'frostbirds', temporary residents during the winter. The rising real value of retirement pensions supported older people who chose to spend all or part of the year in warmer climes. Initially Florida and southern California were the principal retirement destinations, but the flow broadened across the Southeast and parts of the Southwest including the purpose-built Sun City and Sun City West in Arizona, which catered for people over fifty-five.

Although manufacturing received greater attention, employment growth was more rapid in retailing, banking and real estate as well as utilities and construction. Population growth, urbanisation and the expansion of industry all required investments in an infrastructure of transport, power and water supplies and communications which, in turn, increased employment in the service sector. In California services accounted for 70 per cent of employment by 1987 and between 1957 and 1979 the South gained 3.4 million non-manufacturing jobs, double the increase in manufacturing employment.[29] The spread of suburban shopping malls and city-centre office buildings were testimony to such employment. The most rapidly expanding Sunbelt cities were those which maximised their role as a link between local and national markets.[30] Atlanta, Houston, Denver, Los Angeles, Dallas–Fort Worth and Miami performed a commercial role as distribution centres and suppliers of financial, business and other services. These key commercial cities drew on economies of agglomeration in the provision of services plus 'import substituting' industrialisation as population and incomes increased. The commercial function was strengthened by airport construction and local and interstate highway programmes. Atlanta initiated a highway-building programme in the early 1950s, developed its rail links and expanded the local airport into the major regional and then an international hub. In New Orleans, Los Angeles, Houston, Miami and Tampa port developments and overseas trade and finance were additional sources of growth as Sunbelt states gained from the rapid expansion of trade with Asia and South America.[31]

Sunbelt development retained a colonial character in the sense that East-Coast and Midwestern companies and financial institutions were a major source of capital. In Houston or Denver, for instance, New York and Chicago banks were the principal lenders to major local enterprises, including oil companies. Local banks increased in size and influence, but their role was generally as a link to larger eastern financial institutions, identifying suitable projects and drawing in outside investment. There were exceptions, notably the Bank of America in the West, and the San Francisco capital markets were important by the 1950s. Dallas, Atlanta and Florida financial institutions acquired a wider role more slowly, but by the 1980s were active regionally and internationally. Smaller local banks traditionally supported the resource-based industries, but gradually broadened their activities into real estate, industrial and commercial lending.[32] The boom of the 1970s and early 1980s triggered rapid growth in the Sunbelt's financial sector, including savings and loan businesses and new venture-capital companies. There were inflows of Japanese and European investment into western real estate and services including acquisitions of film companies.

California and Texas exerted a wider regional influence through flows of investment, the provision of services and media influence into surrounding states.[33] There were specialised service jobs, such as those in Hollywood's film and television industry, and the general expansion of the leisure industries. Hotel investments from the 1940s created the Las Vegas Strip and the city's population totalled nearly three-quarters of a million by 1990.[34] Disneyland opened in Anaheim in 1955 and was financed and advertised by a television show and film revenues.[35] Amusement parks, dude ranches, museums, national parks and summer and winter sports resorts proliferated across the Sunbelt states as national expenditure on recreation increased. The opening of the Walt Disney World Resort in central Florida in 1971 and its subsequent expansion re-emphasised the importance of tourism in the Sunbelt.

The contribution of governments to the Sunbelt

So far the economic changes have been examined in terms of the expansion of existing industries attracted by resources or cheaper labour or the more footloose high-tech industries. The process can be seen as a continuation of a national pattern of economic development.[36] Mancur Olson argued that growth occurred rapidly in the post-war southern and western economies because market forces operated more freely than in the older industrial areas. The private sector had a major impact, but market forces were not the only aspect. Rather, Sunbelt development occurred in a manner reminiscent of Gerschenkron's thesis that government policies can overcome economic backwardness by addressing deficiencies in infrastructure, private-sector demand and capital. This influence operated at both the state and federal level and it intersected with local boosterism as business and commercial interests used government resources in pursuit of private and public goals.

The New Deal's principal legacy to the West was extensive dam-building which provided more secure water supplies for irrigation and potential industrial uses. The construction of dams continued apace after 1945 in the West due to a rivalry between the Bureau of Reclamation and the Corps of Engineers. The South benefited from the Tennessee Valley Authority which combined hydroelectric power generation and transmission with manufacturing.

Post-war federal policies promoted transport improvements, house-building, construction, urban renewal, education and scientific research. All were national programmes, but offset the inertia and economies of agglomeration which might have favoured a concentration of investment in the more developed parts of the country. Federal funds provided a means for overcoming deficiencies in southern and western infrastructure without imposing the full costs on the regions. Transport improvements were important for further integrating the South and West into the national economy and encouraging inward investment and tourism. The Federal Airport Act of 1946 provided federal funding. The West received above its population's share of airfield and interstate highway spending.[37] From the 1920s road-building was funded by local taxes plus matching federal funds so local initiatives in the post-war period received federal support. In 1956 the degree of federal assistance was increased to 90 per cent of the cost for a National System of Interstate and Defense Highways.[38]

The South and West participated actively in the expansion of college enrolments, vocational training and federally-financed research which provided an educated workforce as well as creating direct employment. In addition to military-related research, federal support flowed via the National Science Foundation and the National Institutes of Health. Federal and state governments were a major source of new jobs with Denver, Sacramento, Norfolk and San Antonio highly dependent on such work. Federal policies contributed to migration where military personnel stayed on after being posted to a southern or western state.

Military programmes made a substantial contribution to Sunbelt growth. Although below its wartime peak, defence expenditure remained high by pre-war standards and, more significantly, the regional distribution of defence expenditure shifted from the North and Midwest to the South and West after the Korean War.[39] Between 1946 and 1965 defence expenditure accounted for an average of 10.9 per cent of personal income in California, the state obtained between 18 and 24 per cent of total spending after 1952 and pools of defence-related research and manufacturing were sustained, notably in southern California.[40] Defence funding underpinned the formative post-war growth of the electronics industry in Silicon Valley where an area of fruit and vegetable growing and processing was transformed into a centre of high-technology research and development.[41] The Mountain states benefited from substantial shares of the defence budget in the 1950s, though their relative standing fell back thereafter. Colorado Springs attracted a series of major military installations including Fort Carson, the North American Air Defense Command and the Air Force Academy.[42] By 1987 nearly one-third of the city's workforce was employed by the military.[43] The wartime boost to western science and research was maintained as establishments such as the Los Alamos National Laboratory and the Sandia National Laboratories, both near Albuquerque, remained active.[44] A later stimulus to the aerospace and electronics industries came from the expansion of defence expenditure from 1978, including the Strategic Defense Initiative, 'Star Wars', which was substantially directed to the West.[45] There were centres of federally-supported research in the South, too, including atomic research at Oak Ridge, Tennessee, where a wartime facility was extended by the Atomic Energy Commission and undertook a diverse programme of research.

The South as a whole was no more dependent on defence spending than might have been expected from its share of population or national income, and defence expenditure in the South was slanted to salaries more than procurement or research, which limited its economic impact. Nonetheless the military was a good consumer of textiles and cigarettes and defence contracts supplied a flow of investment in high-tech sectors into the region. Lockheed's Marietta plant dominated employment in the area and Charleston gained a series of defence establishments. Huntsville's textile economy was transformed by the wartime army presence at the Redstone Arsenal which provided the base for Von Braun's work on missiles from 1950; the facility passed to the National Aeronautics and Space Administration (NASA) and became the Marshall Space Flight Center in 1960.[46] By the mid-1960s the ordnance and guided missile sector accounted for two-thirds of local employment.[47] Cape Canaveral was, in turn, a wartime naval airbase, an air-force test range and a rocket launch site; the Saturn rocket assembly facility at Michoud, near New Orleans, started out as a shipyard in 1942.

The role of local boosters

Market forces and government influences were linked by the activities of local advocates of economic development, boosters. Business and civic leaders outweighed liberal elements in the southern and western planning movements by 1945 and in this respect post-war boosterism was a departure from New Deal ideas, but part of a longer tradition of using governments to promote local interests.[48] Across the Sunbelt a Chamber of Commerce strategy for economic development emphasised attracting inward investment via highway and airport improvements plus tax incentives, subsidies and municipal bonds to finance the construction of factories for incoming industries.[49] The business lobby supported pro-development politicians and campaigned in favour of bond issues to finance industrial sites and expansion of utilities. Local efforts were supported by state development agencies, governors and congressional representatives.[50] This business mobilisation of local, state and federal resources was a key link in post-war development.

Boosterism had a long pedigree. In the West land companies, railroads, developers and local government had long supported development.[51] Los Angeles boosters attracted aircraft manufacturing in the 1920s, strengthened this base by promoting research work at Caltech and then reaped the benefits of wartime demand.[52] Gerald Nash identified Chambers of Commerce, regional entrepreneurs such as Henry J. Kaiser, leading western politicians and A. P. Giannini's Bank of America as key western boosters.[53] Kaiser typified the way in which links to federal agencies cultivated during the New Deal and war were used to attract federal spending and to advocate policies favourable to the West after 1945.

The lineage of southern boosters ran from Henry Grady in the 1880s to a 'commercial–civic elite' composed of lawyers, merchants and Chambers of Commerce who advocated better roads and attracting industry in the 1920s. There were pockets of industrial investment and the weakening of southern agriculture between the wars increased the incentives for southern elites to diversify their investments into industry and commerce. After the war development efforts continued with the aim of maintaining wartime expansion and the growth of population and economic activity.[54] By 1955 Vance concluded that the 'dominant psychology of the South is no longer agrarian; it is Chamber of Commerce'.[55] Bruce Schulman pointed to the emergence of an alliance from the late 1930s between New Deal liberals and southern politicians, 'Whigs', favouring growth based on high-technology industry and improved education. For the New Dealers economic change and higher wages held out the attractive political prospect of creating a southern liberal–labour coalition. In practice Schulman acknowledged that his southern Whigs were only one element of a widespread post-war boosterism including business executives, bankers, developers, real estate and construction interests, public utility companies and railways. Active development campaigns were led by the older conservative business elites who dominated Dallas, Houston, Atlanta and Oklahoma City, and just as avidly by the political reform movements with a younger leadership who advocated growth in Augusta and New Orleans.[56]

The booster strategy was exemplified by the Chamber of Commerce in Oklahoma City, which promoted a local airport and reservoir between the wars and lobbied successfully for a wartime airbase and an air-traffic control training school in 1946.[57] From 1947 the Chamber implemented an extensive development plan based on new roads, urban renewal and improved water supplies; a development corporation undertook 350 commercial and industrial projects between 1954 and 1964. Houston's well-established pro-development policy was based on minimal planning restrictions and developers played a key role in the proliferation of offices, shopping malls and housing.[58] The interconnections between business and government were apparent in the siting of NASA's manned space centre in Houston. It was built on land donated to Rice University by the president of Humble Oil and the project was supported by vice-president Lyndon Johnson and local congressman Albert Thomas, chair of the House Appropriations sub-committee.[59] Subsequently the university received NASA research funds and Humble Oil developed industrial and housing land near the space centre. A construction company, Brown and Root, undertook design and engineering work for the centre; the firm's chairman headed the Board of Trustees at Rice University and was a major supporter of Lyndon Johnson.[60] Other dimensions of 1960s boosterism were the redevelopment of city centres to create imposing new business districts and the enticement of major league sports franchises. Construction of the Houston Astrodome by a private corporation was financed, in part, by municipal bond issues between 1958 and 1962.[61] In Atlanta the city built a sports stadium in 1965 and in the next three years brought in national baseball, American football and basketball teams.[62] Urban boosters in California, Arizona and Colorado were similarly active between the 1950s and 1990s.

The enthusiasm and effectiveness of local boosters affected the timing and character of regional development. Where the booster spirit was weak, development proceeded cautiously. Johnson suggested that San Antonio's slower growth compared to Houston and Dallas reflected less whole-hearted commitment from a conservative business leadership.[63] In some towns dominant employers preferred not to entice new firms who would compete for labour. The steel centre of Birmingham was afflicted by this attitude, symbolically losing its major sports franchises during the 1950s.[64] Denver's business elite preferred to avoid smokestack industries, but actively courted electronics and plastics manufacturers and financed local tourist developments.[65] In any case a rival local group plus investments from Dallas undermined cautious elements in Denver.[66]

If the space centre was one example of the intersection of private and federal influences with local advocates for development, education provided another facet. Wright and Schulman argued that in the southern states a new development strategy based on high-tech industry was supported by the expansion and upgrading of training and higher education provision within the region.[67] Much vocational training remained directed to low-wage textiles, but major education and research centres were created. The prime example was the Research Triangle of Chapel Hill, Raleigh and Durham in North Carolina, based around three universities. North Carolina governor Luther Hodges led a successful campaign to attract government and private research facilities to the area, creating an enclave of highly-skilled technicians and scientists. Stanford University played a booster role in the early growth of Silicon Valley's electronics industry through the activities of Frederick Terman, an electrical engineering professor and later dean, who expanded the University's electrical engineering programme via government and business funding.[68] The nearby Berkeley campus of the University of California possessed major engineering schools. As a result the area generated a supply of research expertise and a flow of innovations which led to new business ventures. The Stanford Industrial Park provided a base for both new firms and inward investment by eastern companies. The Stanford example involved particularly dramatic post-war change, but the path had already been charted in southern California by Caltech and the University of Southern California.[69] Conversely, in Orange County industrial and research employment expanded first and triggered the creation of local colleges.[70]

Contrasts within the Sunbelt

Inevitably there were variations in the degrees of economic development across the West and South. Uneven development was promoted by patterns of defence spending which favoured California and Texas and specific locations such as Los Angeles, Orange County, Colorado Springs, Denver, Seattle, Huntsville, Marietta and Houston. Levels of urbanisation varied: in 1960 50 per cent of the South's population lived in urban areas, but the proportions ranged from 75 per cent in Florida and Texas to around 40 per cent in North and South Carolina, Mississippi and Arkansas.

Per-capita income figures suggested qualifications to the Sunbelt phenomenon since the South reduced, but did not end its relative lag. Four of the five regional development commissions created under the 1965 Economic Development Act covered Sunbelt states: the Four Corners in the West and the Ozarks, Appalachian and Coastal Plains in the South.[71] In states such as Arkansas, Alabama and Mississippi low-wage and resource-based industries still predominated with manufacturing retaining a rural, small-town base, and unemployment rates tended to be above the national average.[72] In South Carolina manufacturing employment exceeded that in agriculture by 1940 and in 1980 the state ranked third in the nation in terms of the proportion of its workforce engaged in manufacturing. Yet low wages persisted: Goldfield described South Carolina as a poor agricultural state transformed into a poor industrial state.[73] Although declining in relative terms, the low-wage sector remained more significant in the South than elsewhere.[74] Textiles, clothing, food-processing, leather goods, timber, paper, furniture and tobacco-processing supplied 7.2 per cent of southern employment in 1969 and 4.3 per cent by 1986. The oil and gas boom of the 1970s was in a traditional sector, though one which might be counted as high-wage. According to Glickman and Glasmeier, in the South high-tech industries were 'no more than a thin veneer over an older industrial base', accounting for only 2.41 per cent of total southern employment by 1969 and 2.59 per cent in 1986. Within the high-tech category were electronics and defence plants devoted to assembly operations which utilised low-skilled, often female labour. Indeed by the 1970s foreign competition had increased the incentive for US firms to choose a southern location in order to reduce costs, and the anti-union tradition remained a potent force.[75]

The pace and form of Sunbelt growth created its own problems. Urban and agricultural demands for water created conflicts over access to supplies in the arid West and compelled a wider search for additional sources. Planning policies maximised growth, but increased the likelihood of over-crowding, pressure on the environment, pollution and problems of waste disposal. Moreover where boosterism emphasised low taxation, there were constraints on public services.[76] Houston experienced problems with water pollution and subsidence and in Florida the pace of development pressed on fragile wetlands. Los Angeles's traffic congestion and smog became a byword, but longer-distance commuting was prompted by steep increases in house prices, especially after 1970, coupled with neighbourhood campaigns to resist further encroachment in established residential areas.[77] In Silicon Valley overcrowding and escalating house prices encouraged relocation of manufacturing plants to lower-wage areas.[78]

Although the Chamber of Commerce development strategy remained pre-eminent, it was challenged from the mid-1960s. Suburbanites offered greater resistance to metropolitan expansion as middle-class neighbourhoods tried to protect themselves against development. Abbott identified Seattle, Portland and Denver as cities where middle-class residents tried to preserve their amenities, modifying the pro-growth consensus.[79] Previously development projects had frequently fragmented or destroyed minority neighbourhoods and low taxation had contributed to deficient services.[80] In many Sunbelt cities the greater political influence of black, Chicano and Hispanic communities produced demands by the 1960s for redistribution of the proceeds of growth, though their political representatives were often avid boosters. A broader critique of the growth ethic arose from environmentalists who attacked the impact of strip mining, nuclear power, the pace of dam-building and threats to wilderness areas. In California stricter environmental and anti-pollution laws were passed while in the Mountain states environmental pressure groups blocked attempts to transfer land from federal to state governments. The pendulum did not swing far since the booster spirit was rekindled among developers, business and financial institutions in the 1980s. Nonetheless even the deregulatory spirit of the Reagan administration did not fully override environmental groups. The momentum of growth was checked in the mid-1980s when falling energy prices brought a new downturn in the 'boom and bust' cycle of the oil, coal and gas industries.[81] The timber industry encountered problems from the depletion of reserves and competition from imports, leading to sawmill closures across the Pacific states.[82] The Sunbelt did not entirely escape the impact of foreign competition and de-industrialization. The closure of textile mills across the South in the 1970s and 1980s was accompanied by shutdowns in the 1980s.[83] Electronics firms shifted production facilities to lower-wage southern or overseas locations, and the possibility of declining defence expenditure with the end of the Cold War introduced a further threat to southern and western prosperity.

The manufacturing belt

The other side of post-war regional change was the relative decline of the midwestern and northern economies, the 'Manufacturing Belt'. Their earlier dominance was remarkable. In 1900 and even in the mid-1950s US manufacturing industry was dominated by three Census regions: East–North Central, Middle Atlantic and New England. Despite a steady fall in their shares of industrial employment, these areas remained the heartlands of US manufacturing for most of the post-war years. The East–North Central region included the automobile cities of Detroit, Flint and Toledo, steelmaking around Chicago, Cleveland and Youngstown, and tyre manufacturing in Akron. These major industries supported a diverse range of metalworking trades and machine-tool firms, particularly in Detroit, Dayton and Columbus. Along with meat-packing, farm machinery, soap, chemicals and electrical plants, the region hosted many of the leading industrial corporations of the early twentieth century. The Middle Atlantic encompassed the Pennsylvania coal and steel towns plus the diverse metalworking, engineering and chemical industries around Philadelphia and New York. The New England economy of 1945 was led by textiles, footwear and a varied engineering sector. Financial and commercial centres in New York, Chicago and Boston added a further dimension to the economic significance of the Midwest and North.

During World War II the East–North Central region's industries and population expanded rapidly, primarily to produce vehicles, machinery and other military supplies. Nine of the ten leading states for wartime prime defence contracts were in the Midwest and North, accounting for over 60 per cent of the value of all contracts.[84] The pattern was similar during the Korean War, but thereafter the fastest growth accrued to western states.[85] New York, New Jersey, Massachusetts and Connecticut remained major recipients of defence contracts, but Ohio, Michigan and Pennsylvania lost ground. Only in New England was the influence of defence contracts comparable to the West and South.

In the Midwest the core of automobile-related industries, electrical, metalworking, and consumer goods producers concentrated on supplying lucrative consumer markets during the 1950s and 1960s.[86] However other industries contracted. In the Middle Atlantic states textiles, steel and ship-building were in decline in the 1950s, along with coal-mining. Chemicals and electrical equipment expanded and there was some new investment by businesses moving out of New York state into New Jersey. Even a diverse local economy like Trenton, New Jersey, experienced persistent job losses and plant closures in manufacturing from the 1950s which were only partly offset by higher government and service employment.[87] Unemployment in the Middle Atlantic states ran ahead of the national average after 1960. New York's manufacturing workforce declined from 2 million in 1948 to 1.5 million in 1981, with the clothing industry declining steadily.[88] The New England economy was more dependent on manufacturing than any other Census region during the 1950s, but its leading industries were waning.[89] The cotton textile industry, rejuvenated by wartime demand, resumed its long-term contraction as production shifted to the South and overseas; woollen textiles followed a similar course.[90] In 1940 textiles accounted for 40 per cent of employment in New England; the industry shifted into silk and rayon, but by the 1970s employed only 10 per cent of the region's workers.[91] A similar decline occurred in the region's footwear, leather and paper industries. The fate of these older industries destroyed the economic base of towns such as Fall River, Lawrence, Lowell, New Bedford and Brockton.

During the 1950s New England's unemployment rate exceeded the national average, but a gradual revival occurred through the region's other principal sector, engineering and machinery manufacturing, particularly in the Connecticut Valley. While less grandiose than the West Coast aerospace centres, aviation was represented by engine and component producers including Pratt and Whitney in Connecticut and a General Electric plant in Massachusetts; nuclear submarine production was based in Groton, Connecticut.[92] Consequently, compared to the East–North Central or Middle Atlantic, New England was more subject to the swings in defence orders. The defence industries contributed to the region's revival during the

1960s, compounded the problems of recession in the early 1970s and contributed strongly to recovery later in the decade.

While the decline of manufacturing employment was discernible in many parts of the Midwest and North from the 1950s, its pace accelerated after 1970 and assumed catastrophic proportions in the East–North Central and Middle Atlantic states between 1978 and 1982. The East–North Central region alone experienced a loss of 990,000 manufacturing jobs, equivalent to 19.3 per cent of the region's total manufacturing jobs; this accounted for half of the net loss of jobs in the country as a whole. The contractions were concentrated in Michigan and Ohio as slack demand plus a rising volume of imports cut a swathe through the automobile industry and its associated component suppliers, as well as the steel producers. Farm machinery companies suffered from the agricultural crisis, especially in grain areas, in the 1980s.

In part the initial dominance of the Manufacturing Belt was the outcome of an earlier mix of influences which applied with less force after 1945. Markusen suggested that given the high degree of regional concentration of industry in 1945, there was potential for a redistribution in response to changed conditions.[93] In the late nineteenth and early twentieth centuries rapid innovation and high profits in industries such as cars and steel had promoted rapid expansion of production in a few centres such as Detroit. The oligopolistic structure of these industries deterred new entrants, especially where price agreements or other strategies restricted price competition, and the Depression of the 1930s deterred new investment. After 1945, however, the combination of renewed growth, especially in western and southern consumer markets, the availability of former defence plants and increased competition in some industries encouraged the opening of new plants outside the Manufacturing Belt. Moreover the business climate of the older industrial states consisted of higher wages, a more unionised workforce, and higher rates of taxation than in the South. In response corporations established new facilities in the South and West. The car and tyre firms, for instance, added new southern factories between 1945 and 1962 so that the main growth in their Detroit and Akron operations came in research, marketing and administration. From the 1970s the crisis in American heavy industry, especially automobiles, fell most heavily on the older factories of the Manufacturing Belt. Apart from New England and parts of New York State, defence spending provided less of an economic stimulus to economic growth in the Midwest and North than elsewhere.

In other areas the balance of regional advantage was less clear-cut. The older industrial areas possessed a well-educated and highly-skilled workforce and well-established colleges. New England had the elements underpinning one facet of Sunbelt growth, namely the mix of defence contracts and corporate and university links in electronics. The Massachusetts Institute of Technology (MIT) maintained its position as the leading non-industrial recipient of defence-related research and development funds.[94] The electronics firm Raytheon was established on the basis of wartime research at MIT, and by 1986 research projects at MIT's Lincoln Laboratory had resulted in the creation of forty-eight companies.[95] Digital Equipment Corporation (DEC) and Wang had links to Boston universities.[96] The size and quality of the Boston area's universities and colleges generated innovations and entrepreneurs as well as supplying skilled workers, especially in electrical engineering. New England was a high-income area possessing good internal and international transport connections which facilitated the growth of export-oriented industries.[97] The most striking development was the cluster of electronics firms in the Greater Boston area so that Route 128, the city's orbital road, was compared to Silicon Valley. Although their products and origins differed, Route 128 and Silicon Valley both benefited from the military patronage which supported research and development work in electronics. In both areas a few major firms developed, but the cutting edge of innovation was supplied by small firms thrown up by a high rate of new ventures. New England's engineering sector provided a ready source of machine-tools, components and specialist services which aided new entrants. The result, like Silicon Valley, was a network of generally small firms linked by contractual ties which, coupled with the academic element, provided a reinforcing cycle of local expansion. New England electronics firms resembled their West Coast cousins in locating production operations elsewhere so that manufacturing employment in the region contracted steadily after 1945, although Wang, Digital, Apollo and Raytheon all had operations in Lowell.

The example of New England indicated that institutions in older industrial areas could be innovative and adaptable. The contrast between New England and the Middle Atlantic and East–North Central states is, therefore, intriguing. The other two regions possessed similar reserves of skilled labour plus major universities and technical schools. Midwestern colleges benefited from the prosperity of local manufacturing in the 1950s and 1960s, but their graduates tended to leave the region. New York, New Jersey and Pennsylvania possessed prestigious colleges and major corporate research facilities, but supported existing industries rather than being a source of new ventures. In contrast to electronics, the capital costs of entry to other industries restricted the opportunities to develop small businesses and, as with more mature industries, there was less emphasis on major innovations. With more limited access to defence research funding, there was also less scope for moving in alternative directions. Consequently the close connections with local manufacturing left midwestern and eastern educational institutions vulnerable to the contraction of their main patrons in the car, steel and machinery industries. In this respect the nature of local industry and corporate strategies shaped the character of surrounding institutions and their innovative capacity.

The Midwest and North did not lack boosters. Chambers of Commerce were active lobbyists, along with national politicians anxious to protect their constituency interests. As in the West and South federal funds were used to build airports and highways. In New England mill closures created concern about industrial decline, which city and state governments sought to counter from the 1930s by attracting new industry, supplying buildings and improving local infrastructure. Maine pioneered new forms of state-supported lending to business in 1949. In New England the American Research and Development Corporation, a venture-capital firm, was formed in 1946 by a consortium of Harvard, MIT, the local Federal Reserve Bank and insurance firms, and later supported DEC.[98] The Bank of Boston also assisted high-tech newcomers. In the Midwest local efforts were made from the 1940s to promote private investment in inner-city areas and the 1950s and 1980s saw extensive city-centre office building.[99] There was a well-established planning movement in cities such as Cincinnati and Indianapolis; the latter, for instance, resembled Sunbelt cities in its use of city-centre redevelopment, including luring a national sports franchise in 1984. Business–government partnerships developed in cities such as Pittsburgh, where a high-tech council was created to encourage new firms.[100] City and state authorities used planning techniques and industrial parks to promote economic development. In the 1970s local governments across the Midwest and North redoubled their efforts to aid declining manufacturing industries as well as seeking new investment by reducing taxes and wages.[101] Regional organisations of politicians and businessmen coordinated promotional efforts. During the 1950s local and national bodies, including Congress and the Council of Economic Advisers, studied the region's difficulties. Midwestern and East-Coast politicians highlighted the regional patterns of defence expenditure which favoured the Sunbelt. Northern and midwestern cities were generally more active than those in the Sunbelt in using federal aid for the purposes of urban renewal, and local development planning was promoted under the 1961 Area Redevelopment Act and then by Economic Development Region status for New England in 1965. The greater crisis of the late 1970s led to the creation of a Northeast–Midwest Congressional Coalition with the aim of promoting federal programmes favourable to older industrial areas.[102]

While midwestern and northern boosters employed similar tactics to those of the Sunbelt, they operated in a harsher climate, which reduced their effectiveness.[103] Most significantly, the Chamber of Commerce spirit was countered by the more immediate effects of corporate policies intent on reducing or relocating industrial employment rather than attracting it. In addition pro-growth forces were less unified and faced greater resistance. Divisions between central cities and suburbs were more clear-cut than in the Sunbelt. Older cities had limited opportunities for annexation so the loss of population, tax revenues and employment to the suburbs had a greater impact on northern and midwestern cities. Resources for redevelopment were more restricted and the planning process operated within greater physical and political constraints. The range of interest groups was greater among business groups and in terms of organised interests such as unions, professions and neighbourhood associations.

As in the Sunbelt, economic change in the North and Midwest was by no means a uniform process.[104] New York, Chicago and Boston lost manufacturing jobs, but remained major commercial and financial centres. There was considerable suburban growth, including the expansion of professional and service employment, and the booster coalition of builders, developers and financial institutions was very evident in such locations. Often new employment was concentrated in suburban areas, around airport and highway developments such as Chicago's O'Hare Airport and in research and service work. While textiles and heavy industry contracted in Philadelphia, biotechnology and insurance businesses provided new jobs; Pittsburgh countered part of the decline of steelmaking with increased service employment. Often smaller cities fared better than the major metropolitan areas. Some were government centres, and other small towns possessed some of the Sunbelt attributes attractive to footloose industry, namely less unionised labour, fewer urban problems and improving transport links. Columbus, for instance, developed high-tech industries; centres of the electronics and computer industries developed around Worcester and in southern New Hampshire by the 1970s; IBM had facilities in several northern states. In the Midwest Japanese automobile-makers and their component suppliers and steel producers located on greenfield sites in rural areas and small towns just outside the traditional centres of the US car industry.[105] Such locations combined access to markets with non-union labour. Although in its early stages, the Japanese investments suggested a revival of the Manufacturing Belt's core industries, though in new places and with different employment characteristics. US firms opening smaller steel mills in the Plains states and recent Japanese mill investments in the Midwest added to this reorganisation.

New England's surprisingly good economic performance between 1978 and 1986 resulted from the combination of a stimulus from the rising real spending on defence and the success of the area's computer firms in exploiting business demand for minicomputers. With export growth and a construction and real-estate boom, New England contrasted starkly with the crisis conditions elsewhere in the Manufacturing Belt. The real-estate boom of the 1980s included redevelopment of several older mill sites for shops, offices and housing as well as Lowell's historic site. There was substantial growth in the business and financial services, insurance and construction sectors. Existing firms expanded in the Boston and Hartford financial markets and some financial services companies and corporate headquarters relocated from New York, notably into Connecticut. New

Hampshire, however, used low taxation to draw businesses out of neighbouring Massachusetts. As in the Sunbelt, low-wage, service employment was a less remarked facet of New England's revival. Harrison argued that the contraction of older, unionised industries, immigration and increased employment of young and women workers created a lower-wage workforce through which firms recast the region's economy as one based on services.[106] His appraisal in the early 1980s pictured a region of more unstable employment and less upward mobility. Subsequently regional wages increased, but Harrison's pessimism directed attention to the varied nature of service employment beyond the high-tech sphere. New England's economic resurgence became shaky in the late 1980s as the speculative real-estate and construction boom collapsed creating financial problems; minicomputer sales slowed and defence-related industries faced an uncertain future.

Summary

Overall regional change after 1945 presented a diverse picture. There was a distinct and rapid transfer of population and employment, particularly in manufacturing, to the West and South at the expense of the Midwest and North. There was some support for the idea that involved a process of convergence as firms responded to differences in wages and other costs by relocating their manufacturing operations. Aspects of the regional transformation were evident before 1940, notably growth in California and the troubles of the New England economy, and World War II accelerated the migration of people and industry to the West and away from southern agriculture. The more dynamic post-war industries either already had a presence in the Sunbelt, as in the case of aircraft, or were more footloose and less tied to the traditional industrial centres. Population growth and higher incomes increased the attractiveness of western and southern markets as locations for production and distribution, in effect substituting local or internal production for 'imported' products from the Midwest and North. There was a cyclical aspect to regional change. Sunbelt growth was accelerated by the stimulus to the resource-based industries during periods of high energy prices, notably in the 1970s. Market forces were not, however, the sole influence. Federal transport programmes and defence expenditure provided a powerful force for development in the West and South by supplying capital and a source of demand in a form less tied to either specific locations or the established industries of the North and Midwest. Defence spending was a crucial support for the aerospace and electronics industries and aided the creation of the expanding local markets which attracted other investments. Federal expenditure and corporate investment each had their own discrete motivations, such as strategic concerns or factor costs, but were also influenced by the activities of local boosters. The latter involved a varied cast, though business interests were the dominant element, and the effectiveness of such local initiatives had a major role in attracting wartime and post-war investment. Their impact depended on the interplay with the general forces favourable to investment in new regions; by contrast the booster spirit in the North and Midwest struggled against a current of people and investment flowing out of the region. The more recent contraction of manufacturing in the Midwest and North stemmed largely from the impact of foreign competition on US heavy industry. While a regional approach captures profound changes, there was an uneven character to post-war economic development which cut across simple regional categories. The limitations of the Sunbelt label, embodied in the contrasts between Los Angeles and Memphis or Birmingham, implied that the forces shaping Sunbelt growth operated to varying degrees. The revival of New England's economy from the 1950s or the growth of manufacturing in the rural Midwest revealed similar forces at work in parts of the North and Midwest. Conversely the impact of 'de-industrialisation' on the heavy industries was felt in California as well as in Michigan or Illinois and there was convergence in terms of urban and industrial problems, such as pollution and congestion, not just in levels of per-capita income.

Notes

1 For a distinction between New England and the other 'foundry' states see Joel Garreau, *The Nine Nations of North America* (New York, 1981).

2 See Richard M. Bernard and Bradley R. Rice (eds), *Sunbelt Cities: Politics and Growth since World War II* (Austin, TX, 1983), pp. 6–7.

3 Richard M. Bernard (ed.), *Snowbelt Cities: Metropolitan Politics in the Northeast and Midwest since World War II* (Bloomington, IN, 1990), p. 5, table 1.3.

4 For a critique of the Sunbelt concept and a personal definition see Carl Abbott, *The New Urban America: Growth and Politics in Sunbelt Cities* (Chapel Hill, NC, 1981), chapter 1.

5 For the Sunbelt as a coastal feature of South and West see Larry Sawers and William K. Tabb (eds), *Sunbelt/Snowbelt: Urban Development and Regional Restructuring* (New York, 1984), p. 12.

6 Harvey S. Perloff, *Regions, Resources and Economic Growth* (Baltimore, MD, 1960), chapter 16.

7 Norman J. Glickman and Amy K. Glasmeier, 'The International Economy and the American South' in Lloyd Rodwin and Hidehiko Sazanami (eds), *Deindustrialisation and Regional Economic Transformation: The Experience of the United States* (Boston, MA, 1989), pp. 64–6, 72.

8 Rodwin and Sazanami (eds), *Deindustrialisation and Regional Economic Transformation*, pp. 18–19.

9 Gerald D. Nash, *The American West Transformed: The Impact of the Second World War* (Bloomington, IN, 1985); James C. Cobb, *Industrialization and Southern Society, 1877–1984* (Lexington, KY, 1984), p. 64; Bernard L. Weinstein and Robert E. Firestine, *Regional Growth and Decline in the United States: The Rise of the Sunbelt and the Decline of the Northeast* (New York, 1978), pp. 48–9.

10 Nash, *The American West Transformed*, pp. 17, 20–5.
11 David R. Goldfield, *Cotton Fields and Skyscrapers: Southern City and Region, 1607–1980* (Baton Rouge, LA, 1982), p. 183.
12 Perloff, *Regions, Resources and Economic Growth*, p. 256.
13 Nash, *The American West Transformed*, p. 20.
14 A. J. Youngson, 'The Acceleration of Economic Progress in the Southern United States' in *Possibilities of Economic Progress* (Cambridge, 1959), chapter XI.
15 Nash, *The American West Transformed*, p. 17; Bruce J. Schulman, *From Cotton Belt to Sunbelt: Federal Policy, Economic Development and the Transformation of the South, 1938–1980* (New York, 1991), p. 98.
16 Richard White, *It's Your Misfortune and None of My Own: A History of the American West* (Norman, OK, 1991), p. 500.
17 Schulman, *From Cotton Belt to Sun Belt*, p. 82.
18 On the product cycle see Raymond Vernon, 'International Investment and International Trade in the Product Cycle', *Quarterly Journal of Economics*, 80, 1966, pp. 190–207. For a variant see Ann Roell Markusen, *Profit Cycles, Oligopoly and Regional Development* (Cambridge, MA, 1987).
19 Gavin Wright, *Old South, New South: Revolutions in the Southern Economy Since the Civil War* (New York, 1986).
20 Christoph Scherrer, 'Governance of the Steel Industry: What Caused the Disintegration of the Oligopoly?' in John L. Campbell *et al.* (eds), *Governance of the American Economy* (Cambridge, 1991), p. 194.
21 James C. Cobb, *The Selling of the South: The Southern Crusade for Industrial Development, 1936–1980* (Baton Rouge, LA, 1982), pp. 209–27.
22 Joseph A. Pratt, *The Growth of a Refining Region* (Greenwich, CT, 1980), pp. 100–1.
23 Bernard and Rice (eds), *Sunbelt Cities*, pp. 74–5.
24 Abbott, 'The Metropolitan Region', pp. 84–5.
25 Wright, *Old South, New South;* Schulman, *From Cotton Belt to Sunbelt.*
26 Goldfield, *Cotton Fields and Skyscrapers*, p. 184.
27 Kevin Starr, *Inventing the Dream: California through the Progressive Era* (New York, 1985); Kevin Starr, *Material Dreams: Southern California through the 1920s* (New York, 1990).
28 Raymond Arsenault, 'The End of the Long Hot Summer: The Air Conditioner and Southern Culture', *Journal of Southern History*, 50(4), 1984, pp. 597–628.
29 Michael B. Teitz and Philip Shapira, 'Growth and Turbulence in the Californian Economy' in Rodwin and Sazanami (eds), *Deindustrialisation and Regional Economic Transformation*, p. 87; Robert J. Newman, *Growth in the American South: Changing Regional Employment and Wage Patterns in the 1960s and 1970s* (New York, 1984) p. 5.
30 Abbott characterises such cities as specialising in trade and financial services: Abbott, *The New Urban America.*
31 Edward F. Haas, 'The Southern Metropolis, 1940–1976' in Blaine A. Brownell and David R. Goldfield (eds), *The City in Southern History: The Growth of Urban Civilisation in the South* (London, 1977), p. 161.
32 Walter L. Buenger and Joseph A. Pratt, *But Also Good Business: Texas Commerce Banks and the Financing of Houston and Texas, 1886–1986* (College Station, TX, 1986), pp. 154–72, 225–8.
33 Abbott, 'The Metropolitan Region", *Interpretations*, pp. 80–1.
34 Carol A. O'Connor, 'A Region of Cities' in Clyde A. Milner II *et al.* (eds), *The Oxford History of the American West* (New York, 1994), p. 561.

35 Judith A. Adams, *The American Amusement Park Industry* (Boston, MA, 1991), chapter 5.
36 Mancur Olson, 'The South Will Fall Again', *Southern Economic Journal*, 49, 1982–83, pp. 917–32.
37 Carl Abbott, 'The Federal Presence' in Milner *et al.* (eds), *The Oxford History of the American West*, p. 494.
38 Mark H. Rose, *Interstate: Express Highway Politics, 1941–1956* (Lawrence, KS, 1979), chapter 7.
39 Roger E. Bolton, *Defense Purchases and Regional Growth* (Washington, DC, 1966), pp. 98–9; Ann Markusen *et al.*, *The Rise of the Gunbelt: The Military Remapping of Industrial America* (New York, 1991); but note that the study showed that the Sunbelt and the Gunbelt are not identical.
40 James L. Clayton, 'The Impact of the Cold War on the Economies of California and Utah', *Pacific Historical Review*, 36, 1967, p. 456; Markusen *et al.*, *The Rise of the Gunbelt,* chapter 2; James L. Clayton (ed.), *The Economic Impact of the Cold War: Sources and Readings* (New York, 1970).
41 AnnaLee Saxenian, 'The Urban Contradictions of Silicon Valley: Regional Growth and Restructuring of the Semiconductor Industry' in Sawers and Tabb (eds), *Sunbelt/Snowbelt*, p. 192.
42 Markusen *et al.*, *The Rise of the Gunbelt*, chapter 8.
43 Ann Markusen and Joel Yudken, *Dismantling the Cold War Economy* (New York, 1992), p. 170.
44 Abbott, 'The Federal Presence', p. 492.
45 On Silicon Valley in the 1980s see AnnaLee Saxenian, *Regional Advantage: Culture and Competition in Silicon Valley and Route 128* (Cambridge, MA, 1994); Bennett Harrison, *Lean and Mean: The Changing Landscape of Corporate Power in the Age of Flexibility* (New York, 1994), chapter 5.
46 Markusen and Yudken, *Dismantling the Cold War Economy*, pp. 190–1; Schulman, *From Cotton Belt to Sunbelt*, p. 148.
47 Mary A. Holman, *The Political Economy of the Space Program* (Palo Alto, CA, 1974), p. 205; Walter A. McDougall ... *The Heavens and the Earth: A Political History of the Space Age* (New York, 1985), chapter 18.
48 Roger Lotchin, *Fortress California, 1910–1961: From Warfare to Welfare* (New York, 1992); Roger Lotchin, 'World War II and Urban California: City Planning and the Transformation Hypothesis', *Pacific Historical Review*, 62, 1993, pp. 143–71; Abbott, *The New Urban America*, pp. 108–42.
49 Cobb, *Industrialization and Southern Society,* pp. 38–9.
50 Cobb, *The Selling of the South*, pp. 74–8.
51 Mansel G. Blackford, *The Lost Dream: Businessmen and City Planning on the Pacific Coast, 1890–1920* (Columbus, OH, 1993).
52 Markusen *et al.*, *The Rise of the Gunbelt*, chapter 5.
53 Nash, *The American West Transformed*, p. 201–4. On Kaiser see Mark S. Foster, *Henry J Kaiser: Builder in the Modern American West* (Austin, TX, 1989).
54 Haas, 'The Southern Metropolis; Cobb, *The Selling of the South*, pp. 65–6; Abbott, *The New Urban America*, chapters 4–5.
55 Schulman, *From Cotton Belt to Sunbelt*, p. 124.
56 Bernard and Rice, *Sunbelt Cities,* pp. 21–2; Cobb, *Industrialization and Southern Society*, p. 102.
57 Richard M. Bernard, 'Oklahoma City: Booming Sooner' in Bernard and Rice (eds), *Sunbelt Cities*, pp. 213–34.
58 William D. Angel, 'To Make A City: Entrepreneurship on the Sunbelt

Frontier' in David C. Perry and Alfred J. Watkins (eds), *The Rise of the Sunbelt Cities*, Urban Annual Affairs Reviews, 14, 1977, pp. 109–28.

59 David G. McComb, *Houston: A History* (Austin, TX, 1981), p. 142.

60 Robert Dallek, *Lone Star Rising: Lyndon Johnson and his times, 1908–1960* (New York, 1991).

61 McComb, *Houston: A History*, pp. 187–9.

62 Bradley R. Rice, 'Atlanta: If Dixie Were Atlanta' in Bernard and Rice (eds), *Sunbelt Cities*, p. 38.

63 David R. Johnson, 'San Antonio: The Vicissitudes of Boosterism' in Bernard and Rice (eds), *Sunbelt Cities*, pp. 235–54.

64 Cobb, *Industrialization and Southern Society*, p. 81; Stanley B. Greenberg, *Race and State in Capitalist Development: Comparative Perspectives* (New Haven, CT, 1980); Robert Norrell, 'Caste in Steel: Jim Crow Careers in Birmingham, Alabama', *Journal of American History*, 73, 1986–87, pp. 69–694.

65 Lynne Pierson Doti and Larry Schweikart, *Banking in the American West: From the Gold Rush to Deregulation* (Norman, OK, 1991), p. 167–170.

66 Peter Wiley and Robert Gottlieb, *Empires in the Sun: The Rise of the New American West* (Tucson, AZ, 1982), pp. 122–4, 129.

67 Wright, *Old South, New South*; Schulman, *From Cotton Belt to Sunbelt*.

68 AnnaLee Saxenian 'The Genesis of Silicon Valley', in Peter Hall and Ann Markusen (eds), *Silicon Landscapes* (Boston, MA, 1984), pp. 20–34; Stuart W. Leslie, *The Cold War and American Science: The Military-Industrial-Academic Complex at MIT and Stanford* (New York, 1993), pp. 50–5, 63–9, chapters 2 and 6.

69 Mike Davis, *City of Quartz: Excavating the Future in Los Angeles* (London, 1990), p. 55.

70 Allen J. Scott, *Metropolis: From The Division of Labor to Urban Form* (Berkeley, CA, 1988), chapter 9.

71 Robert Estall, *A Modern Geography of the United States* (London, 1978), pp. 441–4.

72 William W. Falk and Thomas A. Lyson, *High Tech, Low Tech, No Tech: Recent Industrial and Occupational Change in the South* (Albany, NY, 1988); Thomas A. Lyson, *Two Sides To The Sunbelt: The Growing Divergence Between the Rural and Urban South* (New York, 1989); David R. Goldfield, *Promised Land: The South Since 1945* (Arlington Heights, IL, 1987), pp. 146–8.

73 Goldfield, *Cotton Fields and Skyscrapers*, p. 191.

74 Low-wage industry constituted 42 per cent of southern manufacturing jobs compared to 29 per cent in the US as a whole: Norman J. Glickman and Amy K. Glasmeier, 'The International Economy and the American South' in Rodwin and Sazanami (eds), *Deindustrialisation and Regional Economic Transformation*, pp. 69–70.

75 Cobb, *Industrialization and Southern Society*, p. 65; Goldfield, *Promised Land*, p. 149.

76 Goldfield, *Promised Land*, pp. 197–201.

77 Davis, *City of Quartz*, chapter 3.

78 Harrison, *Lean and Mean*, pp. 114–17.

79 Abbott, *The New Urban America*, pp. 214–22.

80 For case-studies see Robert D. Bullard (ed.), *In Search of the New South: The Black Urban Experience in the 1970s and 1980s* (Tuscaloosa, AL, 1989).

81 White, *'It's Your Misfortune and None of My Own'*, pp. 558–67.

82 William G. Robbins, 'The Western Lumber Industry: A Twentieth Century Perspective' in Nash and Etulain (eds), *The Twentieth Century West*, pp. 244–9.

83 John Gaventa and Barbara Ellen Smith, 'The Deindustrialization of the Textile South' in Jeffrey Leiter *et al.* (eds), *Hanging By A Thread: Social Change in Southern Textiles* (Ithaca, NY, 1991), pp. 181–96. Edward J. Soja, 'Economic Restructuring and the Internationalization of the Los Angeles Region' in Michael Peter Smith and Joe R. Feagin (eds), *The Capitalist City: Global Restructuring and Community Politics* (Oxford, 1987), pp. 182–3.

84 Markusen *et al.*, *The Rise of the Gunbelt*, p. 13, table 2.1.

85 *Ibid.*

86 Bolton, *Defense Purchases and Regional Growth*, p. 125; Markusen and Yudken, *Dismantling The Cold War Economy*, pp. 27–8, 44–7, 172, 192–4.

87 John T. Cumbler, *A Social History of Economic Decline: Business, Politics, and Work in Trenton* (New Brunswick, NJ, 1989), chapters 8–10.

88 Morton Schoolman and Alvin Majid (eds), *Reindustrializing New York State: Strategies, Implications and Challenges* (Albany, NY, 1986), pp. 55, 79, 92.

89 Robert Estall, *New England: A Study in Industrial Adjustment* (London, 1966), pp. 7–8.

90 Seymour E. Harris, *The Economics of New England: Case Study of An Older Area* (Cambridge, MA, 1982).

91 Bennett Harrison, 'Regional Restructuring and 'Good Business Climates': The Economic Transformation of New England Since World War II' in Sawers and Tabb (eds), *Sunbelt/Snowbelt*, pp. 48–9.

92 Estall, *New England*, pp. 162–3.

93 Ann Markusen, *Regions: The Economics and Politics of Territory* (Totowa, NJ, 1987), pp. 77–8, 103–4.

94 Leslie, *The Cold War and American Science*.

95 *Ibid.*, p. 41.

96 Nancy S. Dorfman, 'Route 128: The Development of a Regional High Technology Economy', *Research Policy*, 12, 1983, pp. 299–318.

97 Jane Sneddon Little, 'The Dollar, Structural Change, and the New England Miracle', *New England Economic Review*, Sept./Oct. 1989, pp. 47–57.

98 Bennett Harrison and Jean Kluver, 'Deindustrialization and Regional Restructuring in Massachusetts' in Rodwin and Sazanami (eds), *Deindustrialization and Regional Transformation*, p. 109. John S. Hekman and John S. Strong, 'The Evolution of New England Industry', *New England Economic Review*, March/April 1981, p. 45.

99 Jon C. Teaford, *Cities of the Heartland: The Rise and Fall of the Industrial Midwest* (Bloomington, IN, 1993), pp. 214–15.

100 For some examples of local planning initiatives see Bernard (ed.), *Snowbelt Cities*.

101 For a discussion see Ann R. Markusen and Virginia Carlson, 'Deindustrialisation in the American Midwest: Causes and Responses' in Rodwin and Sazanami (eds), *Deindustrialization and Regional Transformation*, pp. 32–56.

102 Markusen, *Regions*, pp. 162–7.

103 For twelve case studies of midwestern and northern cities in the post-war period see Bernard (ed.), *Snowbelt Cities*.

104 Richard D. Bingham and Randall W. Eberts (eds), *Economic Restructuring of the American Midwest: Proceedings of the Midwest Economic Restructuring Conference of the Federal Reserve Bank of Cleveland* (Boston, MA, 1990).
105 Martin Kenney and Richard Florida, *Beyond Mass Production: The Japanese System and Its Transfer to the United States* (Oxford, 1993).
106 Harrison, 'Regional Restructuring and 'Good Business Climates' in Sawers and Tabb (eds), *Sunbelt/Snowbelt*, pp. 63–8.

5

Work in the United States since 1945

The US workforce has become larger and more diverse since 1945. It has also faced changes in the economic environment and in the policies of employers and governments which have affected the character of work and labour relations. This chapter looks at the changing composition of the workforce. The trend to increased employment of women is discussed in terms of the types of work undertaken, employers' attitudes to women workers and the extent to which gender affects employment; Chapter 9 takes up the related issue of female incomes. The other principal theme in this chapter is the state of US labour unions and the various explanations for their recent decline.

From 59.3 million in 1947, the civilian labour force, including those registered unemployed, increased to over 128 million by 1993. The long-term shift away from farming continued. The numbers in agriculture declined from 7.8 million in 1947 to a little over 3 million in 1993 and agriculture's share of the total workforce fell from 13.2 per cent to 2.4 per cent. Trends in non-farm employment are summarized in Table 5.1. The most significant expansion occurred in the broad services category, which accounted for some 12 per cent of non-farm workers in 1946 and over 27 per cent by 1990. Service employment rose annually, albeit unevenly, with average increases exceeding 50 per cent during each of the three decades after 1950. It encompassed a wide variety of occupations including hospital and health-service work, education and personal and business services. Manufacturing's share of the workforce peaked in the early 1950s after a century of expansion. Productivity gains accounted for the slower growth of manufacturing employment for much of the period, but there was a steep contraction in the number of industrial jobs after 1979. The mining sector experienced sharp cyclical swings in employment during the 1970s and 1980s in line with movements in energy prices, but was smaller in 1990 than in 1945. Employment in transport and communications and public utilities fluctuated during the 1950s and 1960s with, for instance, declines in railway employment offset by growth in airlines and telecommunications. From the late 1970s deregulation affected much of the transport, communications and public utilities sectors and employment growth accelerated at first, but trends diverged between industries as recessions and

Table 5.1 *Total US non-farm employment and distribution by sector, 1950–90 (%)*

	1950	1960	1970	1980	1990
Total (000s)	45,197	54,189	70,880	90,406	109,419
Distribution (%)					
Mining	2.0	1.3	0.9	1.1	0.6
Construction	5.2	5.4	5.1	4.9	4.7
Manufacturing	33.7	31.0	27.3	22.4	17.4
Transport, communication and public utilities	8.9	7.4	6.4	5.6	5.3
Wholesale trade	5.8	5.8	5.7	5.9	5.6
Retail trade	14.9	15.2	15.6	16.6	17.9
Finance, insurance, and real estate	4.2	4.8	5.1	5.7	6.1
Services	11.8	13.6	16.2	19.7	25.5
Government	13.3	15.4	17.7	18.0	16.7

Source: Ronald E. Kutscher, "Historical Trends, 1950–92, and current uncertainties", *Monthly Labor Review*, November 1993, p. 7, table 3.

mergers brought lay-offs. Construction remained a major source of employment subject to its own cyclical rhythms and with above-average rates of unemployment. Wholesale trade followed average growth rates, but the larger retail trade sector expanded more rapidly. The size of the work-force in the diverse finance, insurance and real estate group increased annu-ally from 1946 to 1990, but declined during the next two years. Government employment rose, principally at the state and local level which had 3.3 million workers at the end of the war and almost 16 million in 1993.

Trends in unemployment

In all sectors experienced workers were least likely to be out of work. There were distinct differences in unemployment rates between sectors. The highest rates occurred in agriculture, construction and on the durable goods side of manufacturing. Mining was characterised by high levels of unemployment except during the 1970s. By contrast unemployment was below average in the various service sectors, though the wholesale and retail trades fared poorly after 1975. In terms of unemployment, both the 1950s and 1970s were characterised by upward trends though, as Table 5.2 indi-cates, unemployment rates were higher and more volatile after 1969. The rate of unemployment was affected by the increased labour participation of women and by the arrival of the 'baby-boom' generation in the labour market. The largest group of unemployed were white men, but the propor-tion of white women out of work rose from 1960 and that of black men and women increased from the mid-1970s. The unemployment rate, rather than the absolute number, was consistently higher for African-Americans, Hispanics and people aged between sixteen and nineteen. To an extent

Table 5.2 *Unemployment by race and gender in the US, 1950–93 (%)*

	White			Black	
	All	Men	Women	Men	Women
Mean, 1950–69	4.6	3.8	4.8	8.5	8.8
Mean, 1970–93	6.7	5.7	6.2	13.1	13.3
Mean, 1950–93	·5.8	4.9	5.6	11.0	11.3
Range	2.9–9.7	2.5–8.8	3.1–8.6	4.8–20.3	4.1–18.6
Standard deviation					
1950–69	1.1	1.1	0.9	2.7	1.9
1970–93	1.3	1.3	1.1	3.2	2.2
1950–93	1.6	1.5	1.2	3.8	3.1

Source: Economic Report of the President, 1994 (Washington, DC, 1994) p. 314, table B-40.

various elements intersected with, for instance, the Hispanic population having a younger age distribution, but the persistence of differential rates of unemployment implied continuity in discrimination in labour markets.

Usually white-collar work was associated with more regular work patterns, but although a higher proportion of women held white-collar jobs, female unemployment rates exceeded male rates from 1945 to 1981, despite the male predominance in such highly cyclical work as construction. The higher female rate during the 1950s and 1960s reflected an expansion in the supply of women workers and a greater frequency of short-term unemployment for women since they were far more likely to hold part-time and temporary jobs. After 1981 there were new patterns. For the first time female unemployment rates temporarily fell below male rates in 1982 and 1983 and then again from 1990 to 1993. The contraction of heavy industry in the early 1980s hit areas of traditional male work, though women in manufacturing were more likely to be unemployed. The main contrast came in the burgeoning service employment where young women obtained greater access. The greater incidence of part-time work for women may also have been a contributory factor, though this had peaked in 1982 and women showed a greater tendency to retain full-time jobs, so the lower female unemployment since 1990 might mark a new trend.[1] It was most pronounced in the 16–20 age group and among black women who had lower unemployment rates than black men from 1953 to 1955, 1957 to 1961 and in most years after 1979.

There were significant racial differences in unemployment, although similar cyclical fluctuations. White male unemployment declined in the 1960s and tended to rise compared to the national average in later years. By contrast white female unemployment fell less than male unemployment during the 1960s, but increased less thereafter. Unemployment rates for

Table 5.3 *Occupations of employed workers in the US, 1940–90*

Occupation	1940	1950	1960	1970	1982	1990
White-collar	27.8	33.3	43.3	48.3	53.7	57.2
Blue-collar	46.1	46.6	36.5	35.3	29.7	30.6
Service	10.5	9.4	12.2	12.4	13.8	10.6
Farm	15.6	10.7	7.8	4.0	2.7	1.7

Sources: US Bureau of the Census, *Historical Statistics of the United States, Colonial Times to 1970, Bicentennial Edition,* Part 1 (Washington, DC, 1975), p. 139, series D182–98; US Bureau of the Census, *Statistical Abstract of the United States: 1984* (104th edn, Washington, DC, 1985), p. 417; US Bureau of the Census, *Statistical Abstract of the United States: 1993* (113th edn, Washington, DC, 1993), p. 426.

black women usually rose compared to the national average during economic upswings and fell less during recessions. Black men fared less well over the course of the 1950s, saw a relative improvement in their unemployment rate during the 1960s, but encountered faster growth in unemployment from 1970 to 1984.

The growth of white-collar employment

Sectoral shifts were accompanied by more rapid expansion of white-collar occupations than blue-collar ones (Table 5.3), though there were significant differences in terms of gender in the rate of transformation. In 1990 44 per cent of male workers were blue-collar workers compared to only 13 per cent of women. Between 1960 and 1990 the proportion of female workers holding white-collar jobs increased from 55 to 74 per cent with the main decline being in service employment. Among men the proportion in white-collar work was 37 per cent in 1960 and only 44 per cent in 1990, and the main fall occurred in farm work.

The expansion of white-collar work and the growth of the service sector have been seen as evidence of a new post-industrial society, characterised by work which was more intrinsically satisfying and provided greater autonomy than blue-collar, especially industrial, employment. Workers now provided services rather than produced goods. Among the presumed consequences was the creation of a less class-conscious, more educated workforce and white-collar jobs were associated with higher-status and more regular employment than factory work. Given the expansion of white-collar employment, prospects of advancement were good through the 1950s and 1960s, full-time employees possessed considerable job security and unemployment rates were lower than in other sectors.

The transition to a less work-centred existence was promoted by greater availability of paid holidays, but actual hours of work each week altered much less than they had done in the first three decades of the century. There was a modest fall in average weekly hours worked in manufacturing from 43.5 in 1945 to 39.5 in 1975, but then a rise to 40.8 hours in 1990. The major reduction in weekly hours occurred in the retail trade as a result of a higher incidence of part-time employment.

The idea of a post-industrial society became more credible in the early 1980s as blue-collar industrial employment contracted while financial and service occupations expanded. Often, however, contrasts between blue-collar and white-collar work are overdrawn. At least in the favourable economic climate of the 1950s and 1960s blue-collar earnings increased and there was wider access to pensions. Distinctions between types of work were blurred since many white-collar occupations serviced manufacturing, and by the 1980s corporate emphasis on human resource management advocated forms of participation by all types of worker in a bid to improve productivity. The white-collar workforce was far from homogeneous in income, status, stability of employment or working practices since the category encompassed professionals, technical, managerial and administrative staff, clerical workers and sales staff. Much office work offered modest earnings, was subject to its own routines and, to varying degrees, to the automation and close supervision associated with assembly-line operations.[2] Fast-food outlets applied assembly-line principles to the preparation, sale and consumption of meals. There was limited autonomy in the burgeoning service sector where certain jobs involved a particularly personal form of commitment since in dealing with other people, especially customers, the worker's appearance and manner had a major influence. In retailing, catering and hotel work, for instance, national chains used standard layouts, and ways of addressing customers were expected which limited workers' autonomy, whereas in local shops or restaurants individuality carried more weight, but in both settings the quality of personal service was important.

Women and employment

The number of women in paid work increased from the 1890s and the gender balance of the US workforce continued to shift after World War II (Table 5.4). Women more often worked after marriage and returned to work after having children so the turn-of-the-century pattern of a female workforce primarily composed of single women, widows and divorcees changed fundamentally (Table 5.5). Women constituted 45.7 per cent of all workers in 1993 compared to 28.1 per cent in 1947 and the total number of women workers increased from 16 million to 54.6 million over this period. The changes highlight the question of how work is defined since, in part, increased participation in paid employment provided a more visible measure of female work compared to less well-documented forms of part-time, seasonal and household-based work. There were contrasting trends

Table 5.4 *Female employment in the US, 1890–1987*

Year	Total (000s)	Distribution (%)		
		Single	Married	Widowed/divorced
1890	3,712	68	14	18
1900	4,997	66	15	18
1910	7,640	60	24	15
1920	8,347	77	23[a]	
1930	10,632	54	29	17
1940	13,007	49	36	15
1950	16,553	32	52	16
1960	23,240	23	56	21
1970	31,543	22	59	18
1980	45,487	25	55	19
1987	56,554	25	55	20

Note: From 1960 the widowed/divorced category also includes women separated from their husbands
[a] Includes married, widowed and divorced women.
Sources: US Bureau of the Census, *Historical Statistics of the United States*, Part 1, p. 133, series D49–53; US Bureau of the Census, *Statistical Abstract of the United States: 1993*, p. 399, no. 632.

Table 5.5 *Female labour force participation rates by marital status, 1900–90 (as % of women in each category)*

Year	Single	Married	Widowed/Divorced	All Women
1900	44	6	33	19
1910	51	11	34	25
1920	46	9	n.a.	23
1930	51	12	34	24
1940	46	16	30	26
1950	46	23	33	29
1960	43	32	36	35
1970	51	40	37	40
1980	64	50	44	52
1987	67	58	47	58

Note: From 1960 the widowed/divorced category also includes women separated from their husbands
Sources: US Bureau of the Census, *Historical Statistics of the United States*, Part 1, p. 133, series D58–62; US Bureau of the Census, *Statistical Abstract of the United States: 1993*, p. 399, no. 632.

in labour-force participation rates, the extent to which men and women worked. In the late 1940s around one-third of all women worked compared to 87 per cent of all men; by 1993, however, 58 per cent of women were in employment while the proportion for men had fallen to 75 per cent. These figures take no account of the higher incidence of part-time working among women. The aggregates also masked important variations. In 1994 the average participation rates for black and white women were both around 59 per cent, but this was the result of different experiences. Black women had a higher labour-force participation rate, 46 per cent, than white women at 33 per cent in 1950, but it increased far less rapidly than that for white women with the main divergence occurring after 1970. The least rapid rise in participation was for teenage black women.

There are various interpretations of the growth in female employment. To some extent it was the continuation of earlier trends. As Tables 5.4 and 5.5 indicate, female employment expanded from the 1890s with perhaps a check during the Depression of the 1930s. The development of female work in clerical and white-collar jobs was well established before 1940. However Chafe identified World War II as a key phase on the basis that labour short-ages drew more women into employment, including the armed forces, and wartime patriotism and the example of women undertaking different work countered the ideology of domesticity as a woman's proper role.[3] Hartmann pointed to incentives for servicemen's wives to supplement low incomes.[4] One million more women were employed in manufacturing in 1946 than in 1940 and there was a shift towards industries such as aircraft, automobiles and munitions and out of agriculture, domestic service, retail-ing, waitressing and other types of service work. Female clerical employ-ment expanded rapidly. African-American women experienced less change since they were already more likely to work and were allowed fewer oppor-tunities in war industries, but they moved away from domestic service. In contrast to Chafe's emphasis on change, Kessler-Harris highlighted the temporary nature of wartime labour markets and played down the notion of fundamental changes in attitudes towards female employment.[5] Despite federal decisions in favour of the principle of equal pay, women earned less than men and separate job classifications maintained lower rates of pay. Hartmann explored the ways in which increased employment coexisted with more restrictive ideologies of 'women's place' and married women with young children remained less likely to take outside employment than other women.[6] At the end of the war there were social pressures to return to earlier roles as newspapers, magazines, film and television advocated a family life based on female domesticity; psychological writings of varying degrees of sophistication extolled the value of full-time motherhood.[7] After 1945 contraction of defence industries plus the priority given to re-employment of returning war veterans displaced women from heavy manufacturing industries.[8] In the car industry, where the United Automobile Workers' Union broadly supported female employment, women constituted 25 per cent of the workforce in 1944, but only 8 per cent two years later, despite female workers' efforts to retain their place.[9] The number of women in clerical posts fell by 500,000 between 1945 and 1947, though women clerks retained some wartime gains through a revision of the frontier of female employment to include a larger share of routine cler-ical duties.[10]

The decline of employment in certain areas and the assertion of the domestic ideal occurred alongside continued entry of married women into paid employment. By 1950 married women had overtaken single women for the first time as the largest component of the female workforce and, as average fertility rates declined, the proportion of younger married women in employment rose during the 1960s. The ideology of domesticity was then at odds with actual behaviour. This paradox was not new since the proportion of women, both single and married, in paid employment had increased from 1890 and some, especially working-class, women had always balanced the contending demands of paid work and domestic responsibilities, but there was a distinct change in patterns of female employment.[11] Goldin emphasised incremental change in which post-war developments can be understood in terms of the contrasting experiences of different cohorts of women. The rising fertility rate and increased family size during the 'baby boom' indicated that many men and women embraced some of the post-war images of family life. Since the 'baby boom' primarily involved younger women and men who married earlier and had larger families, it reduced the supply of young, single women in the labour market. Goldin identified a cohort of older, married women who were well equipped to take advantage of this situation, especially in white-collar occupations, because they possessed good education and had completed their families, having earlier limited their fertility.[12]

Alternative explanations emphasised influences in the immediate post-war years. Easterlin suggested that young couples possessed relatively high incomes during the 1940s and the 1950s which enabled them to choose to have larger families in which women performed a domestic role rather than taking paid work.[13] More broadly, the increased tendency for married women to enter the workforce in the late 1940s has been explained in terms of their contribution to the family economy. From this perspective, married women entered the workforce in greater numbers to obtain additional income to meet the costs of mortgages, consumer goods or other items on the household budget, including the expense of raising and educating children, during an inflationary era. Some women worked to finance their husbands' further education since the veterans eligible for educational support from the GI Bill of Rights were overwhelmingly male. The portrayal of female employment in terms of sustaining overall family income retained contact with the domestic ideology, though it extended the definition of family income beyond simply male income.[14] It is possible, however, that women explained their paid work in terms of the domestic ideology without being entirely committed to it. Women valued paid work for its associated status, social contacts and recognition and such factors should be set against economic motivations or an undue emphasis on static or uncontested notions of domesticity.

Matthaei emphasised the role of advertising in expanding the range of consumer products which people regarded as required purchases, though housing and the replacement of older equipment after the war were rational responses to the end of wartime constraints. For Goldin the avail-ability of consumer goods provided an incentive to work, but also, by sub-stituting for home-made goods and services, created more scope for married women to take paid work whilst maintaining their domestic roles. Some middle-class women made the transition from employing servants to wielding new household appliances in person, thereby undertaking addi-tional tasks, but less affluent women perhaps had more scope for reducing their burden in housework.[15] Neither the availability of consumer goods or convenience foods fundamentally altered domestic roles, but rather created an additional pressure for working wives to juggle the responsibilities of home, assumed to be more manageable with the new gadgets, and paid employment. In this sense the gender element of domestic ideology remained a powerful force despite the expansion of female employment.

On the demand side, employers' attitudes altered. Previously firms who employed women expected high rates of turnover among a largely young workforce, but the 'baby boom' created uncertainty about the availability of younger female workers. In the 1940s firms made greater efforts to recruit married women by making part-time working more readily avail-able, removing marriage bars, and ascribing more positive attributes to older female employees. African-American women were accepted into cler-ical work from the 1950s. The labour market evolved in ways favourable to increased employment of women since among the post-war growth sectors were retailing, food services, secretarial and clerical work, teaching and nursing (see Table 5.1).[16] All were sectors where women already had a sub-stantial presence. The post-war rise of consumption strengthened demand for women workers in retailing and other service industries and the 'baby boom' increased the need for teachers and other child-related services which often involved female employment. There were, then, simply more jobs in which female employment was accepted and accorded higher status than factory work. Regional shifts in manufacturing activity opened up additional employment opportunities in southern and western states. As unemployment rates declined, employers had additional incentives to utilise female workers and real wages for women increased. In certain areas, notably secretarial and clerical work, the boundaries of female and male work were redefined as employers sought cheaper female labour, sometimes labelled 'pink-collar' workers, and men switched to managerial or higher-level administrative occupations associated with better pay and promotion prospects. In the case of bank tellers, real-estate agents and air hostesses, firms sought cheaper female workers who were perceived as possessing advantages in dealing with the public.[17] Often female employment dis-played aspects of women's prescribed domestic roles which could be writ large within the bounds of conventional ideals about gender.

Influences on female employment shifted in the 1960s as later marriage and lower fertility expanded the pool of younger female workers, in spite of longer time spent in education. The general prosperity of the 1960s, even with the upward drift of inflation, might have been expected to reduce the incidence of married women working. However, Easterlin detected a deterioration in the real incomes of young couples which, he argued, stimulated female employment at the expense of childbearing. This explanation looks more convincing for the 1970s when inflation, recessions and rising unemployment exerted a tighter economic squeeze on younger couples, producing greater disincentives for women to leave employment. Goldin argued that the significance of family income declined compared to the early 1900s so higher female employment constituted a response to higher real wages available for women. In fields such as social work, health services and teaching, African-American women increased their employment in the 1960s, though often catering primarily to minority communities. White women were more likely to obtain access to the higher-paid professions.[18] Wider access to colleges opened up better employment prospects and the most striking gains in employment during the 1960s accrued to college-educated women in professions such as law and medicine; there were increases too in business and engineering, though from such a low base that the total number of women in these occupations remained small.[19]

Demand-side factors were accompanied by changes in women's attitudes to work, notably a tendency to remain in the labour market for longer periods or to return earlier in the family life-cycle. Goldin argued that the pattern of earnings in non-manual white-collar work altered so that gaps in work experience were potentially more costly in terms of lost or foregone future earnings. In effect more of a career structure developed as greater training and more recognition of seniority resulted in higher earnings. However, the degree of change should not be exaggerated since in many occupations, notably temporary secretarial work, flexibility in the form of part-time work or the ability to move in and out of employment offered advantages in accommodating the domestic demands on women. The key may be that such work met the needs of different cohorts of women: for some the temporary element meshed with child care and other responsibilities, but for permanent workers or older women who returned to full-time work the greater career structure had advantages. More problematic were promoted posts and professions where any period out of full-time work resulted in a loss of experience and seniority which were serious disadvantages.

While women worked in greater numbers by 1990, especially after marriage, certain aspects of women's employment remained remarkably constant. The labour market continued to display gender divisions so that, in the words of one study of occupational patterns, a 'woman's place is with other women'.[20] Women workers were concentrated in teaching, nursing, secretarial work, sales and the food and textile industries, as was the case in 1940 or 1900. A study of eleven major occupations between 1940 and 1970 found little change in patterns of segregation by gender compared to a pronounced fall in racial segregation.[21] Even within broad occupational categories, such as clerical work or in the professions, there were often further sub-divisions, with female employment concentrated in lower-grade jobs rather than positions associated with greater status or opportunities for promotion. The persistence of gender segregation reflected various trends. The entry of women into predominantly male occupations either occurred very gradually or else proceeded extremely rapidly, resulting in the 'feminisation' of the occupation as in areas of clerical work. By contrast movement of men into predominantly female areas of employment remained slight. In the 1970s labour-market trends affected the gender balance of employment. A smaller proportion of men, particularly those over fifty-five, were in work as the expanded coverage and real value of pensions facilitated earlier male retirement, particularly among lower-income men.[22] There was contraction in traditionally male-dominated sectors such as mining or steel from the 1950s and in the automobile and other heavy industries in the late 1970s and early 1980s. By contrast, though areas of traditional female employment, like textiles and footwear, declined, the expansion of other industries, such as food-processing and light assembly work, provided compensation and women benefited from sustained growth of retailing and service work.

Labour unions

Over 14 million Americans belonged to labour unions in 1945, the result of twelve years of growth and, excluding agricultural workers, this constituted 35 per cent of the workforce, which was high by American standards. Both the American Federation of Labor (AFL) and the Congress of Industrial Organizations (CIO) had a substantial presence among mining, construction and manufacturing workers in northeastern and midwestern states, which translated into local political influence in northern cities and a role in national affairs. During the Depression workers had displayed greater willingness to try unions as a source of protection and such 'union consciousness', in Lichtenstein's phrase, was backed by an assertiveness in industrial disputes which underpinned membership growth, despite high levels of unemployment. The existing labour movement supplied finance, organisers and a pro-union ideology. There was a split within the AFL between craft-based unions and those in mining, clothing and other industries who advocated the organisation of less skilled workers. The latter, after pursuing their aims through a grouping within the AFL, were expelled and formed a separate organisation, the CIO, in 1937 headed by the miners' leader, John L. Lewis. The political reflection of 'union consciousness' was permissive federal legislation. From the codes of the National Recovery Administration, 1933–35, to the far more significant creation of the National Labor Relations Board in 1935, the New Deal facilitated union organisation and promoted collective bargaining. After the US Supreme Court declared the Wagner Act constitutional in 1937, an economic upswing and the outbreak of war persuaded managements in automobiles, steel and other industries to concede union recognition. There were advantages to unions from inclusion in the New Deal coalition, primarily in terms of the massive increase in membership and influence compared to contraction and the state's support for managerial prerogatives between 1920 and 1933.

The momentum was sustained during World War II through the activities of the National Defense Mediation Board and the War Labor Board. Wartime expansion of employment, particularly in heavy industry, and the spread of union security agreements sustained membership growth which, coupled with the automatic deduction of union dues from pay packets, strengthened unions' financial resources considerably. A framework of federal labour law developed which enabled unions to pressure employers into recognising, via a system of elections, independent unions as legitimate representatives.[23] On balance unions benefited substantially from New Deal labour relations policies to 1945, gaining far greater leverage in their dealings with employers.[24] Resistance from employers remained widespread and intense, but unions provided a way for many workers to achieve greater security of employment and more influence over working conditions.[25] Between 1945 and 1975 the dominant theme of industrial relations literature was that New Deal and wartime policies had created a stable, pluralist and even consensual system of collective bargaining in which employers conceded unions a permanent place. The principal critique of labour unions implicitly accepted the system's strength, but portrayed unions as overly bureaucratic institutions unwilling to respond to local or individual demands and constituting a conservative force in relation to the new social movements of the 1960s. Developments since 1970 suggest that the earlier industrial relations system was far less firmly rooted than its proponents assumed and far more of an achievement than its detractors argued.

With agriculture, where unions had virtually no presence, contracting, the pool of potential union recruits increased rapidly after 1945, but union fortunes were mixed. Total membership rose unsteadily from 14.3 million at the end of the war to 16.8 million in 1955 and 19.3 million in 1970, with the fastest growth occurring during economic upswings in the early 1950s and late 1960s (Table 5.6).

Union membership fell rapidly in the early 1980s and by 1991 was down to 13.9 million, below its immediate post-war level.[26] If the unions' relative rather than absolute position is examined, the 1970s and 1980s were still the

Table 5.6 *US membership of labour unions, 1940–91 (excludes Canadian members)*

| Year | Total (000s) | As % of | |
		Non-farm workforce	Total labour force
1940	8,717	26.9	15.5
1945	14,322	35.5	21.9
1950	14,300	31.5	22.3
1955	16,802	33.2	24.7
1960	17,049	31.4	23.6
1965	17,299	28.4	22.4
1970	19,381	27.4	22.6
1975	19,611	25.5	20.7
1976	19,634	24.5	20.3
1978	20,246	23.6 22.7	19.7
1980	n.a.	24.7 22.7	n.a.
1985	n.a.	18.0 17.9	n.a.
1989	n.a.	n.a. 16.3	n.a.
1990	n.a.	16.1	n.a.
1991	13,933	12.3	11.9

Sources: US Bureau of the Census, *Historical Statistics of the United States*, Part 2, p. 178, series D948–49, D951; US Bureau of the Census, *Statistical Abstract of the United States: 1984*, p. 439, table 726; Mary E. Frederickson and Timothy P. Lynch, "Labor: The Great Depression to the 1990s" in *Encyclopedia of American Social History*, volume II, (New York, 1993), p. 1488. Michael Goldfield, *The Decline of Organized Labor in the United States* (Chicago, 1987), pp. 10–11, tables 1–2; Michael A. Curme, Barry T. Hirsch and David A. Macpherson, "Union Membership and Contract Coverage in the United States, 1983–1988", *Industrial and Labor Relations Review*, 44(1) 1990, pp. 5–33.

main point of contraction, but earlier signs of uncertainty were evident. As a proportion of the total labour force, union membership peaked at 25.5 per cent in 1953, was fairly stable through the 1960s, but declined to around 20 per cent in the late 1970s.[27] As a percentage of non-agricultural employment, the unions' highest post-war share was 35.5 per cent in 1945 and the proportion was 33.2 per cent a decade later; it was still 27.4 per cent by 1970, but by 1990 union members represented only 16.1 per cent of the non-farm workforce, back to the levels of the late 1930s.[28] There were contrasting tendencies in different sectors. Troy's estimates, based on his own data rather than the Census data used so far, indicated that in 1945 the highest rates of unionisation were in construction, mining and transport, primarily railways.[29] Thereafter union density, that is the proportion of workers who are union members, declined consistently in mining and construction: in mining union density was 83 per cent in 1947, but had diminished to 36 per cent by the mid-1960s and 15 per cent twenty years later. In manufacturing, the most spectacular area of growth during the 1930s, union density peaked around 1953, followed a fluctuating, but downward course over the next two decades, and dropped precipitously during the 1980s. From 40 per cent in 1947, union density in manufacturing had declined to 32 per cent in 1980 and was barely 25 per cent five years later. Union density in transport followed a similar course. The centres of union expansion during the New Deal weakened, therefore, accounting for much of the unions' post-war decline. The principal growth for unions after the war occurred in public service where, by Troy's estimate, union density rose from 12 per cent to 39 per cent between 1947 and 1975.

Explanations for the fortunes of US labour unions since 1945 take several forms and the mix of relative, but until the 1970s not absolute, decline means none of the influences constituted a complete barrier to union organisation. Broad economic explanations identified structural changes unfavourable to union growth. The size of the workforce in the highly-unionised districts of the mining industry contracted from the 1950s while new investments went into less organised areas, and the later energy boom was associated with exploration in new, less unionised regions and more capital-intensive operations such as strip mining. The longer-term expansion of manufacturing into western and southern locations required unions to move beyond their regional heartlands into often hostile territory. Unions had a presence across the Sunbelt states, especially in California, and recent studies have questioned the notion that southern or western workers were disinterested in organised labour. Nonetheless employers and local elites mobilised considerable resistance to union organisation so that the changing location of US manufacturing weakened labour unions.[30] By 1947 more than thirty states, primarily in the South, had passed 'right-to-work' laws which restricted boycotts, picketing and closed-shop agreements. These restricted the impact of Operation Dixie, a southern union-organising drive conceived in 1937 and launched after the war. However, regional change was not the sole influence since the fall in membership occurred across regions, including within the most unionised states. Across the Midwest traditionally anti-union employers moved to counter unions' wartime gains and right-to-work laws were passed in Indiana and Illinois.[31]

The manufacturing sector, in which 67 per cent of workers were in unions in 1945, accounted for a declining share of the workforce. Productivity improvements reduced the numbers of blue-collar industrial workers in the 1950s and 1960s, particularly in the older, heavy industries, which again struck at union strongholds. The fastest growing manufacturing industries, such as electronics, were characterised by lower levels of union organisation and large corporations, like IBM, operated extensive corporate welfare systems and their sustained growth and market position offered stability of employment for workers at least to the 1990s. Smaller electronics businesses had an individualistic and entrepreneurial ethos which worked against acceptance of, or worker interest in, unions. The structural changes assumed a more acute form when massive lay-offs created a haemorrhage of union membership in the late 1970s and early 1980s. Manufacturing was the main source of the absolute fall in total union membership during the 1980s. The steelworkers' union, for instance, lost over half of its membership in the decade to 1983.[32]

A variety of characteristics have been attributed to white-collar workers, a major growth sector after 1945, to suggest why they might be less likely to join labour unions. Among the influences cited are the absence of a union tradition, a tendency to identify with either management or middle-class status rather than unions, and a preference for organising in a more individual fashion or via staff associations. There were exceptions to this general picture. McColloch pointed out that as the character of some white-collar work became more routine union membership rose; indeed by the 1980s many professional and white-collar occupations appeared as bastions of worker organisation through unions or professional bodies.[33] Although beginning from a low base, there was a rapid expansion of membership among workers in hospitals, the fire service, police, sanitation workers and education. The American Federation of State, County and Municipal Employees and the American Federation of Government Employees recruited successfully in the 1960s. According to one estimate, from less than 5 per cent of all union members in 1945, the public sector increased to 29 per cent in 1983.[34] The growth of public-sector unionism was responsible for the rise in overall union membership in the 1960s, countering declines in the industrial sector. Growth was aided by President Kennedy's executive order 10988 in 1962, which permitted unionism and collective bargaining among public-sector workers, and the adoption of similar state laws, in some cases before 1962 and taking diverse forms, encouraged organisation among state and local government workers. There was similar expansion in education by the American Federation of Teachers and the National Education Association. Far more barren territory for unions was the service sector, the other major area of employment growth, where unions accounted for only 9 per cent of service workers in 1947 and barely 14 per cent three decades later. On the one hand, there were relatively high-income occupations with an individualistic ethos and, on the other hand, low-wage service jobs were filled by part-time and temporary workers, often in small firms. Both types of worker were hard to organise. Consequently unions were largely excluded from some of the most rapidly growing sectors. The expansion, for instance, of restaurants and fast-food outlets occurred most rapidly in the South and West and in suburban areas and the chains and franchise systems resisted union organisation.[35] The accompanying shift to a younger workforce and greater part-time and temporary employment undermined existing food-service unions. In transport and distribution, the Teamsters union developed from a largely midwestern organisation into an effective national union with a southern presence by using its considerable economic leverage in key areas to obtain recognition in new districts. The union's highly-centralised structure made for an effective bargaining agent, but local activity, especially any opposition, was suppressed ruthlessly and, coupled with the personal domination of Jimmy Hoffa, led to the union's entanglement with corruption and an antagonistic relationship with other unions.

Lichtenstein argued that World War II was a critical point in the CIO unions' transition from 'fluid', active organisations into accommodating bureaucracies.[36] CIO union leaders, such as Philip Murray, Walter Reuther and Sidney Hillman, advocated a new 'social unionism', including improved health care, public housing and economic planning which aimed to extend New Deal welfare reforms and supported the strand of New Deal thought favourable to planning. However Piven and Cloward, Moody and Lichtenstein have all concluded that 'social unionism' gave way to a revival of the earlier tradition of 'business unionism' based on maximising wages through narrowly-defined collective bargaining.[37] The creation of permanent organisations to conduct workers' affairs within workplace contractualism embodied and consolidated the earlier gains, but in line with Michels's 'iron law of bureaucracy', such organisations and their routines risked a loss of spontaneity.

Post-war developments had a distinctive political flavour as a result of the legacy of federal industrial relations laws which defined 'responsible' or acceptable union behaviour and carried the risk of future, less favourable decisions. The executive and, to a greater extent, Congress were increasingly critical of unions; both institutions had a major role in defining notions of 'responsible' union behaviour and the scope of industrial relations. The business 'right-to-manage' campaign and public dissatisfaction over the high level of strikes created a new political mood and a Congressional alliance of Republicans and conservative Democrats sponsored more restrictive labour legislation. President Truman vetoed one bill in 1946, but in the following year Congress passed the Taft–Hartley Act, despite another Presidential veto. The Act narrowed the definition of 'responsible' unionism, emphasising the conditional nature of the federal support extended under the Wagner Act. Among the provisions of the Taft-Hartley Act were a ban on the closed shop, greater scope for employers to express opposition to union organisation and an extension of the list of unfair labour practices to include secondary boycotts. The Act also prohibited supervisory staff from organising unions, thus capping employers' post-war campaign against foremens' unions. Where unions had an established presence, Taft–Hartley's impact was limited, but the provisions of the law posed a formidable barrier to new organising drives when employers were determined to resist unions.

Political pressures on the unions, combined with internal rivalries, were reflected in the effects of post-war anti-Communism. Although limited in numbers, Communist organisers and officials were influential in several CIO unions, including that of the electrical workers and the West Coast longshoremen. As the Cold War developed, anti-Communism provided a further lever against labour unions; part of the Taft–Hartley Act required union officials to sign affidavits declaring that they were not members of the Communist Party. National leaders, particularly in the CIO, were anxious to avert the threat of more intrusive legislation and to counter claims that it was un-American. The issue coloured union disputes, both within individual unions and in AFL attacks on the CIO, weakening organising efforts. Rivalries were sharpened in the 1948 election campaign when Henry Wallace's Progressive candidacy attracted more left-wing support while the CIO leadership supported Truman. Between 1948 and 1950 the CIO expelled ten unions, containing about 20 per cent of total membership, on the basis of their Communist associations. The expulsion gave the CIO little respite from charges of Communism, but removed the union's more radical edge.[38] The repressive climate of the Cold War contributed to the trimming of ideas of 'social unionism' and the move to a narrower business unionism dealing with wages and working conditions. Perhaps most significant was the weakening of bi-racial unionism because the Communists had been to the fore in rejecting racial divisions. Another problem confronting unions was corruption. The AFL expelled the International Longshoreman's Association in 1953 following New York state hearings on corruption, and the Teamsters union was expelled in 1957. Congress added further to the definition of 'responsible' unionism, passing the Landrum–Griffin Act in 1959 following congressional hearings on corruption and financial malfeasance in unions, which damaged the image of unions and indicated the dangers in the centralisation of control which existed. The extent to which these events really represented the turning aside from an alternative path is debatable. Business unionism was well entrenched in the AFL and Brody suggested that even within the CIO the progressive drive had weakened by the 1940s.[39] Wartime prosperity, in Brody's view, made workers and unions 'satisfied' and 'apathetic' and the emphasis on economic issues in the immediate post-war period reflected workers' concerns over wages as management reduced overtime working and tightened up piece-rates.[40] Certainly labour unions concentrated on lobbying through established political channels, but their campaigns still constituted a broadly liberal force in support of health care, expansion of the welfare state and counter-cyclical economic policies. In 1955 the AFL and the CIO merged into a single national organisation, the AFL–CIO, which consolidated their position as a national institution and reflected the passing of the older generation of union leaders whose disagreements had led to the CIO's breakaway in the 1930s.

On a wider level the relative decline of unions has been ascribed to a decline in the earlier union consciousness. Economic growth, rising real incomes and low unemployment rates in the 1950s and 1960s perhaps made workers regard unions as less significant for achieving stable employment or better conditions. Opinion-poll results indicated declining public support for unions, though in a long-running Gallup poll the fall in approval for unions was quite modest compared to the decline in union membership. [41] The contrasting trends in union density across different sectors, especially increases in the public sector, suggested that workers' perceptions varied. On the whole the attitude of government towards unions was more permissive and public-sector workers regarded union membership positively for collective bargaining.

Industrial relations

The progenitors of the post-war system included the pre-1935 textile industry and the provisions on the railways and in parts of government service where the civil-service tradition had fostered pensions and defined working practices. The basic framework of industrial relations was based on 'workplace contractualism' involving the formulation of job classifications, shop-floor rules, seniority systems and grievance procedures as well as the union role in wage bargaining. Each element was an advance on the earlier arbitrary, management-dominated labour relations system. The central elements were 'job control', that is defining conditions relating to a post rather than to the individual worker, grievance procedures and an emphasis on seniority. As Brody emphasised recently, such 'workplace contractualism' provided workers with a defence against arbitrary treatment.[42] A system of arbitration and a growing body of case law were further steps in the direction of rules of appropriate behaviour.[43] Another feature was pattern bargaining, which involved establishing wages and conditions through bargaining with one of the leading firms in an industry and then seeking to apply the terms, or the master contract, as a pattern across all companies. For unions pattern bargaining offered economies in prosecuting disputes and a degree of equity; thus, the steel, car or tyre workers could direct negotiations and, if necessary, strike activity at one leading firm and then seek to enforce the contract across the industry. This process avoided involving all workers in a dispute simultaneously, but carried a high risk of disputes when contracts were renewed. For managers pattern bargaining carried potential advantages if it reduced the competitive significance of wage costs.

Although the post-war system was rooted in inter-war and wartime developments, the transition into the 1950s was by no means straightforward. Workers' dissatisfactions were apparent in a wave of strikes in the late 1940s which included major defeats for several unions; employers seized the opportunity to try to repel labour's earlier gains and the reinvigorated anti-Communism placed unions on the defensive and often at odds amongst themselves. Despite these factors, unions managed to extend the scope of bargaining and the generally prosperous state of business in the 1950s and 1960s alleviated some of the antagonism in industrial relations. Harris's careful study of management thinking on labour relations in the 1940s concluded that the dominant strategy was a new and more sophisticated approach which he dubbed 'realism', exemplified by General Motors, rather than the previous total hostility.[44] From this perspective, management tolerated unions providing their influence could be confined to specific issues, and, where possible, reduced, through the assertion of managerial prerogatives, the 'right to manage'. Gordon, Edwards and Reich identified a 'core' of major industries, such as automobiles, steel, rubber and electrical products in which unions had made inroads during the 1930s and 1940s and where major corporations adopted labour relations policies which embodied the 'realism' described by Harris.[45] These industries were characterised by higher levels of union membership, above-average earnings, a wider range of fringe benefits and more stable employment than the rest of US manufacturing. The assumption that employers used the industrial relations system to achieve stability should be approached cautiously. A good deal of the system rested on recurring tests of strength between unions and employers at local or national level over the boundaries of industrial relations and particular wage levels or terms and conditions. Moreover industrial managers were more assertive and enjoyed higher public esteem after the wartime boom than they had in the depressed 1930s. In effect managements pressed their own definition of acceptable or responsible unionism. While realism remained the principal managerial strategy, it was a recipe for contests as much as for consensus. Strikes were sufficiently frequent to indicate that neither employers nor workers regarded industrial relations as unproblematic. The steel industry was characterised by recurring, lengthy and often bitter contests, primarily over wages, throughout the 1950s and 1960s as managers endeavoured to obtain concessions and workers resisted and sought wage increases.

During the 1950s and 1960s national pattern bargaining operated in the automobile, steel, coal, meat-packing, electrical products, oil and trucking industries; there were regional agreements in some sectors such as dock work.[46] In the steel industry several firms negotiated through a single bargaining agent. Bargaining in different industries was often interlinked; terms in steel carried over to other metalworking industries and in the automobile sector United Automobile Workers (UAW) contracts provided targets which unions in the tyre and component industries aimed for.[47] Workers benefited from the application of seniority and the existence of grievance procedures which limited managerial power.[48] In return managers gained control over the direction of production and labour on the shop floor and unions concentrated on collective bargaining for their members rather than promoting wider social reform. The strict application of seniority and the proliferation of internal job ladders and promotion procedures were further signs of the influence of 'workplace contractualism'. These developments provided a considerable degree of security and scope for advancement for workers who acquired seniority. Another strand in the development of 'workplace contractualism' was the expansion of the regulated industries, such as airlines, utilities and trucking, where governments established a degree of stability and predictability and an approach to industrial relations favourable to clear rules and regulations.

Pattern bargaining was never as rigidly applied as the above account implies. There were variations in wages and conditions between firms and local areas and in the strength of union locals and their degree of control at the shop-floor level. Schatz described the situation in the electrical products industry as 'a crazy quilt pattern of bargaining' involving several different unions.[49] Nor was pattern bargaining the sole form of industrial relations. In construction, the retail trade or the police service bargaining was highly localised and craft unions remained powerful in the building trades and on the railways.[50] In the case of railways and aviation as well as their own employees, specific federal laws regulated collective bargaining. Where pattern bargaining operated its coverage was by no means complete and various contractual issues, primarily non-wage elements, were addressed at different levels from the plant to centralised union and management organisations, so local influences remained important.[51]

The more powerful unions succeeded in adding additional elements to contracts; fringe benefits had come into wider use during World War II as a means of circumventing limits on wage increases and post-war inflation maintained their attraction. The 1946 coal settlement included a royalty to fund medical and hospital funds and in 1950 General Motors agreed to a pension scheme. Company pension schemes and medical insurance became more common as firms, influenced by a tighter labour market and generally good profits, reinstituted a broader version of the welfare capitalism which a handful of companies had adopted between 1910 and 1929, but had abandoned during the Depression. Striking evidence of the new climate of industrial relations were the adoption of wage formulas, including automatic cost-of-living agreements and annual increases in anticipation of productivity gains; these appeared in General Motors' contract with the UAW from 1948. The UAW obtained a Supplementary Unemployment Benefit scheme in 1955 in which company funds made payments to workers as a supplement to their Social Security benefits during lay-offs. The arrangement indicated a greater commitment to stable industrial relations, though it emphasised both the employers' rather narrow conception of the employment link and the continued instability of employment, even in one of the most profitable industries of the post-war period. The influence of union bargaining extended more widely through the demonstration effect either through other workers seeking similar terms or through employers offering comparable or better terms and conditions with the aim of averting labour organisation. However critics argued that such developments signalled a strategy of maximising contractual gains for existing union members rather than maximising membership or interest in a broad reform agenda. The evidence of corruption and links to the underworld in unions such as the Teamsters, Longshoremen and in construction further distanced union leaders from their members as well as creating a damaging public image.

Ironically the New Deal legacy of stronger unions and the workplace contractualism, especially the emphasis on seniority, constrained union organisation among women workers and African-Americans. The principle of seniority provided stability, but left later entrants to the workforce in a relatively less privileged position. More fundamentally, the existence of job and wage discrimination on the basis of gender or race restricted opportunities. Even in the case of a union, such as the UAW, where the national leadership advocated equality, positive sentiments could be slow to yield significant changes, especially where shop-floor workers defended such practices. Inevitably the picture was mixed with the United Packinghouse Workers of America's national campaigns on civil rights challenging southern locals, but the union was conservative over women's rights. For meat-packing, steel or coal workers, the long-term contraction of employment offered a reason to deter potential alternative workers.[52] Nonetheless, although the concentration of women in part-time work hindered organising, female union membership, which had fallen at the end of the war, increased so that by the 1970s women constituted one-third of total union membership. To some extent the internal tensions reflected generational change as the older leadership valued the positive aspects of the industrial relations system that had emerged from the 1930s and 1940s while younger workers made new demands. Such challenges were evident in the various African-American caucuses within unions in the 1960s and early 1970s and in new women's groupings. Divisions were also apparent in workers' litigation under the Equal Employment Opportunity Commission (EEOC) against their national unions as well as employers in discrimination cases. Cobble detected such intergenerational differences over aims and tactics among waitresses and Deslippe found similar tendencies in meat-packing.[53]

Many large firms avoided pattern bargaining as, for instance, in telecommunications, and recently Jacoby emphasised the strength and durability of anti-unionism among large employers.[54] Firms in the metalworking, tobacco and textiles sectors continued their tradition of aggressive anti-unionism and, in newer, growth-industries, firms, such as Eastman Kodak and IBM, deployed high wages and welfare benefits with the aim of making union membership less attractive by supplying a corporate version of 'workplace contractualism'. Such firms employed industrial relations consultants to advise on strategies to inhibit union organising.[55] As production shifted to the South and West, managements were less willing to accept union organisation in the new plants, especially where non-union labour was significantly cheaper. New, smaller steel mills in the South had lower union densities than those of the older, northern plants; the UAW organised southern car plants, but was less effective in relation to component suppliers.[56] There were signs of tension in the industrial relations system in the 1960s: managements became more likely to contest National Labor Relations Board (NLRB) elections, and the rate of union success in elections declined from the 1950s and more precipitously during the 1970s and 1980s.[57] As the inflation rate rose in the late 1960s, contract negotiations were more confrontational, especially over productivity and cost-of-living elements. The industrial relations environment was bleaker as the rate of economic growth was checked by severe recessions in 1970, 1974 and between 1978 and 1982 while inflation accelerated. As average real earnings declined, workers sought higher pay-rises, especially where inflation eroded real wages in the course of a long-term contract. Business, on the other hand, attempted to control wage costs more closely. There was greater incentive to do so as the wage differential between union and non-union labour widened during the 1970s and the cost of Social Security taxes, pensions and other fringe benefits had risen.[58] Government too emphasised wage restraint in its efforts to control inflation; in 1971 the Nixon administration applied a wage freeze followed by a system of wage controls and the policy was followed by intense efforts by workers to recoup wages.

An increasingly well-organised business campaign, initially centred on the construction sector, mobilised large and small firms in support of reforming labour laws.[59] Business applied lobbying and public-relations strategies used by environmental and consumer groups and gained public support by arguing that the problems of international competitiveness owed much to regulation.[60] The other side of the coin was a decline in local community support for unions.[61] The effects of recessions were compounded in many 'core' industries by the impact of foreign competition in the form of increased imports, often in response to slack domestic demand, and later by factory investments by overseas firms. Many Japanese and European entrants in the automotive, tyre and electronics industries established non-union operations in areas with little tradition of union organisation. Some American corporations adopted a similar approach; General Motors, for instance, established non-union plants in the South in the 1970s.[62] American companies became more concerned about their declining international competitiveness, especially as the earlier pattern of incremental innovation gave way to more rapid changes in vehicle design. Even within the Midwest new firms challenged prevailing pattern-bargaining arrangements and sited plants away from the established industrial and union centres. In meat-packing from the 1970s Iowa Beef Processors adopted new processing methods, located plants in more rural areas of the Midwest and employed non-union labour paid below national wage levels.[63] The firm's success led the older firms to adopt similar methods, reducing employment and closing plants. Manufacturers sought remedies to the immediate crisis through reducing their workforces, attempting to limit wage rises and even demanding wage reductions. These forces were evident in the automobile industry, where plant closures and automation reduced employment.[64] Between 1979 and 1981 Chrysler's financial crisis persuaded the UAW to defer the automatic element in wage increases, to concede a six-month wage freeze and to give up seventeen days of paid holidays. Pattern bargaining then operated in reverse with Ford and General Motors demanding and obtaining similar concessions in the new 1982 contract; the industry's component suppliers came under similar pressure to reduce labour costs. Between 1982 and 1985 there was a phase of 'concession bargaining' across other sectors including airlines, meat-packing, farm equipment, steel and trucking. In meat-packing the earlier trend to lower wages accelerated and, for example, in 1983 most of the Armour plants were sold to a rival firm which reopened with non-union workers.

The process received greater momentum from the deregulation of trucking, telecommunications and airlines which disrupted the established economic structure of limited competition, high profits and high wages and extensive fringe benefits. There was an inflow of new entrants, many employing non-union labour. Within five years the phase of expansion gave way to failures and reorganisations in the face of sluggish growth in demand. In the subsequent restructurings companies reduced employment, sought lower wages and reduced benefits as well as further reorganising work practices. The Teamsters' bargaining, which had been highly centralised under the National Master Freight Agreement, became fragmented and localised during the 1980s. Organised labour was then on the defensive across the private sector, but their weaknesses were reinforced and extended into the public sector by Ronald Reagan's dismissal of all striking Professional Air Traffic Controllers' Organization (PATCO) members in 1981, since their contracts did not permit strikes.[65] The episode involved fateful misjudgement and poor tactics by the union leadership, but signalled a major change in federal policy and in the balance between employers and unions. Further evidence came in the decisions of the NLRB in the early 1980s which revised several earlier precedents favourable to unions and placed greater emphasis on the rights of individual workers and of management.[66] The potential for an emphasis on workers' rights rather than union rights was present from the early development of the industrial relations system of the 1930s and 1940s. From this perspective unions were one mechanism for workers to assert their rights, but not necessarily the only conceivable institution, and in the new climate of the 1980s this interpretation carried greater force.

The example of overseas manufacturers, especially the Japanese car and steel producers, led to the belief that more fundamental restructuring of employment practices was essential to restore US competitiveness. This strategy, which Barbash labels 'quid-pro-quo' bargaining, in itself indicated the extent to which the post-war industrial relations system had retained an adversarial character and had operated within a limited remit.[67] The new corporate strategy fractured that stability. Japanese production systems included more flexible work practices and the use of forms of group working and worker participation. The result was far higher labour productivity. In return workers with core Japanese firms expected long-term employment, though this might involve periodic retraining. There were fewer managers, less complex or flatter managerial hierarchies and producers made greater use of contractual links to suppliers rather than performing work 'in house' through vertical integration. Workers for the 'periphery' of suppliers encountered far less favourable terms and conditions of employment. Such employment practices challenged the basic principles of 'job control' by reducing the range of job categories and their associated terms and conditions. As Japanese automobile, steel, tyre and electronics firms established US operations, increasing numbers of American workers were subject to elements of these work practices. Usually the new factories had company unions and were located in rural areas or less unionised states; co-operative ventures between US and overseas firms recognised independent unions.[68]

US producers had addressed some of these issues in the early 1970s, notably following the 1972 Lordstown strike at a new General Motors factory which was taken as a sign of worker alienation. However by the end of the decade overseas competition provided a fresh impetus. Firms seeking to emulate the Japanese model revised contracts, usually with the acquiescence of workers who hoped to save at least a proportion of their jobs, or else firms opened factories in greenfield sites. The opening of General Motors' Saturn plant in 1985 signalled an attempt at co-operation with the UAW over more flexible work practices while the New United Motors Manufacturing, Inc. (NUMMI) plant, a joint venture between General Motors and Toyota, displayed more managerial control. In practice the new corporate strategies were diverse and displayed considerable continuity with established methods.[69] Some developments occurred within a climate of plant closures and wage concessions which limited their capacity to offer job security or to alter worker attitudes. Among component suppliers to the automobile industry the level of unionisation declined from over 80 per cent to 60 per cent, little above 1940 levels, between 1974 and 1983.[70] Moreover the forms of worker participation which were introduced often involved more driving forms of management, resulting in what Parker labels 'management by stress' rather than a complete departure from earlier practices. Milkman's study of a General Motors plant identified further 'deskilling' among production workers and Babson emphasised the tensions involved in changing work practices.[71] Nonetheless the potential for cost savings and higher productivity led managements to extend their use of such schemes. The responses of unions varied. At times unions embraced ideas of worker participation in order to promote their role; the UAW obtained agreements on job retraining as a counter to reduced employment. Politically, unions joined managements as advocates of protectionism to check the effects of import competition, and at the company level concessions were made in the hope of retaining some employment which made collective bargaining even more localised.

Notes

1 Donald R. Williams, 'Women's Part-time Employment: A Gross Flow Analysis', *Monthly Labor Review*, April 1995, pp. 36–44.
2 Mark McColloch, *White Collar Workers in Transition: The Boom Years, 1940–1970* (Westport, CT, 1983).
3 W. H. Chafe, *The American Woman: Her Changing Social, Economic and Political Roles, 1920–1970* (Oxford, 1972).
4 Susan M. Hartmann, *American Women in the 1940s: The Home Front and Beyond* (Boston, MA, 1982).
5 Alice Kessler-Harris, *Out To Work: A History of Wage-Earning Women in the United States* (Oxford, 1982).
6 Hartmann, *American Women in the 1940s*; Daniel Nelson, *Farm and Factory: Workers in the Midwest, 1880–1990* (Bloomington, IN, 1995), pp. 144–5.
7 Elaine Tyler May, *Homeward Bound: American Families in the Cold War Era* (New York, 1988); Leila J. Rupp, 'The Survival of American Feminism: The Women's Movement in the Postwar Period' in Robert H. Bremner and Gary W. Reichard (eds), *Reshaping America: Society and Institutions, 1945–1960* (Columbus, OH, 1982), pp. 34–39.
8 Kessler-Harris, *Out To Work*.
9 Nancy Gabin, 'Wins and Losses: The UAW's Women's Bureau after World War II, 1945–1950' in Carol Gronemann and Mary Beth Norton (eds), *'To Toil The Livelong Day: America's Women at Work, 1780–1980* (Ithaca, NY, 1987), pp. 233–49; Ruth Milkman, *Gender At Work: The Dynamics of Job Segregation by Sex during World War II* (Chicago, 1987), chapters 6–7.
10 Hartmann, *American Women in the 1940s*, p. 90; Margaret L. Hedstrom, 'Beyond Feminisation: Clerical Workers in the United States from the 1920s through the 1960s' in Gregory Anderson (ed.), *The White-Blouse Revolution: Female Office Workers since 1870* (Manchester, 1988), p. 155.
11 Hazel Kyrk, 'Who Works and Why', *The Annals of the American Academy of Political and Social Science*, 251, 1947, pp. 44–52.
12 Claudia Goldin, *Understanding the Gender Gap* (New York, 1990).
13 Richard A. Easterlin, *Birth and Fortune: The Impact of Numbers on Personal Welfare* (New York, 1980), chapters 2–4.
14 See Julie A. Matthaei, *An Economic History of Women in America: Women's Work, the Sexual Division of Labor, and the Development of Capitalism* (New York, 1982), pp. 248–54.
15 Ruth Schwartz Cowan, *More Work For Mother: The Ironies of Household*

Technology from the Open Hearth to the Microwave (New York, 1983), pp. 192–3, 208–16.

16 Rochelle Gatlin, *American Women since 1945* (London, 1987), p. 38, table 2.1; Dorothy Sue Cobble, *Dishing it Out: Waitresses and their Unions in the Twentieth Century* (Urbana, IL, 1991), p. 207.

17 Barbara F. Reskin and Heidi I. Hartmann (eds), *Women's Work, Men's Work: Sex Segregation on the Job* (Washington, DC, 1986), p. 8; Georgia Panter Nielsen, 'Flight Attendant Labor Organizations' in William M. Leary (ed.), *Encyclopedia of American History and Biography: The Airline Industry* (New York, 1992), pp. 173–8.

18 M. V. Lee Badgett and Rhonda M. Williams, 'The Changing Contours of Discrimination: Race, Gender, and Structural Economic Change' in Michael A. Bernstein and David E. Adler (eds), *Understanding American Economic Decline* (Cambridge, 1994), p. 318.

19 Suzanne M. Bianchi and Daphne Spain, *American Women in Transition* (New York, 1986), pp. 119–21.

20 *Ibid.*, p. 165.

21 Reskin and Hartmann (eds), *Women's Work, Men's Work*, p. 19. Mary King, 'Occupational Segregation by Race and Sex, 1940–1988', *Monthly Labor Review*, 115(4), 1992, pp. 30–7.

22 Donald O. Parsons, 'The Decline in Male Labor Force Participation', *Journal of Political Economy*, 88(1), 1980, pp. 117–34.

23 For a recent collection on the changes see Howell John Harris and Nelson Lichtenstein (eds), *Industrial Democracy in America: The Ambiguous Promise* (Cambridge, 1993).

24 For a review see Howell John Harris, 'The Snares of Liberalism? Politicians, Bureaucrats and the Shaping of Federal Labour Relations Policy in the United States, 1915–1947' in Steven Tolliday and Jonathan Zeitlin (eds), *Shop Floor Bargaining and the State* (Cambridge, 1985), chapter 5.

25 David Brody, 'Workplace Contractualism in Comparative Perspective' in Harris and Lichtenstein (eds), *Industrial Democracy in America*, pp. 176–205, reprinted in David Brody, *In Labor's Cause: Main Themes on the History of the American Worker* (New York, 1993), pp. 221–50; Steven Tolliday and Jonathan Zeitlin, 'Shop-Floor Bargaining, Contract Unionism and Job Control: An Anglo-American Comparison' in Nelson Lichtenstein and Stephen Mayer (eds), *On The Line: Essays in the History of Auto Work* (Urbana, IL, 1989), pp. 219–44; Sanford Jacoby, *Employing Bureaucracy: Managers, Unions, and the Transformation of Work in American Industry, 1900–1945* (New York, 1985).

26 US Bureau of the Census, *Statistical Abstract of the United States: 1993*, p. 393, no. 621; p. 435, no. 687.

27 Goldfield, *The Decline of Organized Labor in the United States*, p. 10, table 1.

28 Frederickson and Lynch, 'Labor: The Great Depression to the 1990s'.

29 For membership data by sector see Leo Troy, 'The Rise and Fall of American Trade Unions: The Labor Movement From FDR to RR' in Seymour Martin Lipset (ed.), *Unions In Transition: Entering the Second Century* (San Francisco, CA, 1986), pp. 87–9.

30 Robert H. Zieger (ed.), *Organized Labor in the Twentieth Century South* (Knoxville, TN, 1991); Jeffrey Leiter *et al.*, *Hanging By A Thread: Social Change in Southern Textiles* (Ithaca, NY, 1991); Rick Halpern, 'Organized Labor, Black Workers, and the Twentieth Century South: The Emerging Revision' in Melvyn Stokes and Rick Halpern (eds), *Race and Class in the American South since 1890* (Oxford, 1994), pp. 43–76.

31 Daniel Nelson, *Farm and Factory: Workers in the Midwest, 1880–1990*, pp. 155–61.
32 Troy, 'The Rise and Fall of American Trade Unions, p. 92, table 8.
33 McColloch, *White Collar Workers in Transition*.
34 Troy, 'The Rise and Fall of American Trade Unions, p. 83.
35 Cobble, *Dishing it Out*.
36 Nelson Lichtenstein, *Labor's War At Home: The CIO in World War II* (Cambridge, 1982).
37 Frances Fox Piven and Richard A. Cloward, *Poor People's Movements: Why They Succeed, How They Fail* (New York, 1977), chapters 2–3; Kim Moody, *An Injury to All: The Decline of American Unionism* (London, 1988).
38 Ronald W. Schatz, *The Electrical Workers: A History of Labor at General Electric and Westinghouse, 1923–60* (Chicago, 1993), chapter 7.
39 David Brody, 'The New Deal and World War 2' in John Braeman *et al.* (eds), *The New Deal: The National Level*, volume 1 (Columbus, OH, 1975), pp. 267–309, reprinted in Brody, *In Labor's Cause*, pp. 175–219.
40 Schatz, *The Electrical Workers*, pp. 150–6.
41 Seymour Martin Lipset, 'Labor Unions In The Public Mind' in *Unions In Transition*, pp. 287–321.
42 David Brody, 'Workplace Contractualism: A Historical/Comparative Analysis' in *In Labor's Cause*, pp. 221–50.
43 See Lichtenstein, *Labor's War At Home*.
44 Howell John Harris, *The Right To Manage: Industrial Relations Policies of American Business in the 1940s* (Madison, WI, 1982).
45 David M. Gordon, Richard Edwards and Michael Reich, *Segmented Work, Divided Workers: The Historical Transformation of Labor in the United States* (Cambridge, 1982).
46 Moody, *An Injury to All*, pp. 2–3.
47 Moody, *An Injury to All*, p. 2 says that pattern bargaining existed in steel in that UAW bargained with the major producers under the Basic Steel Agreement and that settlement there set 'a pattern for steel-fabricating, aluminium, copper and can companies'.
48 Tolliday and Zeitlin, 'Shop-floor bargaining", pp. 219–44.
49 Schatz, *The Electrical Workers*, chapter 9.
50 Moody, *An Injury to All*, pp. 25, 194.
51 David B. Lipsky and Clifford B. Donn (eds), *Collective Bargaining in American Industry: Contemporary Perspectives and Future Directions* (Lexington, KY, 1987), pp. 316–17.
52 See Robert J. Norrell, 'Labor Trouble: George Wallace and Union Politics in Alabama' in Zieger (ed.), *Organized Labor In The Twentieth Century South*, pp. 250–72; Denis Deslippe, '"We Had An Awful Time With Our Women": Iowa's United Packinghouse Workers of America', *Journal of Women's History*, 5(1), 1993, pp. 10–32.
53 Cobble, *Dishing It Out*; Deslippe, '"We Had An Awful Time With Our Women"'.
54 Sanford M. Jacoby, 'Norms and Cycles: The Dynamics of Nonunion Industrial Relations in the United States, 1897–1987' in Katharine G. Abraham and Robert B. McKersie (eds), *New Developments in the Labor Market: Toward a New Institutional Paradigm* (Cambridge, MA, 1990), pp. 19–57.
55 *Ibid.*
56 Christoph Scherrer, 'Governance of the Steel Industry: What Caused the Disintegration of the Oligopoly?' and 'Governance of the Automobile

Industry: The Transformation of Labor and Supplier Relations' in John L. Campbell *et al.* (eds), *Governance of the American Economy* (Cambridge, 1991) pp. 193–4, 221–2.

57 Richard B. Freeman *et al.*, 'The Evolution of the American Labor Market' in Martin Feldstein (ed.), *The American Economy in Transition* (Chicago, 1980), p. 368.

58 Richard B. DuBoff, *Accumulation and Power: An Economic History of the United States* (New York, 1989), p. 126.

59 Moody, *An Injury to All*, chapter 6.

60 David Vogel, *Fluctuating Fortunes: The Political Power of Business in America* (New York, 1989), pp. 233–7.

61 Gordon L. Clark, *Unions and Communities under Siege: American Communities and the Crisis of Organized Labor* (Cambridge, 1989).

62 Harry C. Katz, 'Automobiles' in Lipsky and Donn (eds), *Collective Bargaining in American Industry*, p. 21.

63 John Portz, 'Economic Governance and the American Meatpacking Industry' in Campbell *et al.* (eds), *Governance of the American Economy*, pp. 281–5.

64 Katz, 'Automobiles', pp. 13–50.

65 David Morgan, 'Terminal Flight: The Air Traffic Controllers' Strike of 1981', *Journal of American Studies*, 18(2), 1984, pp. 165–83.

66 Vogel, *Fluctuating Fortunes*, pp. 269–70.

67 Jack Barbash, 'Trade Unionism From Roosevelt To Reagan' in *The Annals of The American Academy of Political and Social Science*, 473, 1984, pp. 11–22.

68 For a good account see Martin Kenney and Richard Florida, *Beyond Mass Production: The Japanese System and its Transfer to the US* (New York, 1993).

69 Tetsuo Abo (ed.), *Hybrid Factory: The Japanese Production System in the United States* (New York, 1994); Kenney and Florida, *Beyond Mass Production*.

70 Katz, 'Automobiles', p. 19, table 2.1.

71 Mike Parker, 'Industrial Relations Myth and Shop-floor Reality: The Team Concept in the Auto Industry' in Harris and Lichtenstein (eds), *Industrial Democracy in America*, pp. 249–74; Steve Babson, 'Restructuring the Workplace: Post-Fordism or the Return of the Foreman?' in Robert Asher and Ronald Edsforth (eds), *Autowork* (Albany, NY, 1995), pp. 227–56.

6

Agriculture and the rural United States

The earlier discussions of demographic and regional change and the labour force all involved the contraction of the US agricultural population. The transformation of agriculture has been one of the fundamental features of the post-war economy. Technological and structural changes are dealt with in the first part of this chapter, which then turns to the question of rural poverty. The second part of the chapter looks at federal farm policies which have shaped agriculture, but which have been fraught with paradoxes and uncertainties in the light of the sector's sustained technological change and productivity growth.

General Trends

US agriculture, like that in Europe and Japan, was transformed after 1945.[1] At the end of the war there were over 24 million people living on farms, but by 1990 the number had declined to only 4.5 million. Farm residents constituted 17.5 per cent of the total population in 1945, but only 1.9 per cent in 1990. Although the absolute number of farm families fell in all regions, the contraction was most marked in the South, which contained over half of the country's farm population in 1950, but accounted for only 28.7 per cent by 1987. The result was a massive rural depopulation, particularly among African-Americans in the South, and a steady reduction in the number of farms. Over the same period the Midwest's share of the farm population rose from one-third to half.[2]

The number of farms declined. During the 1950s and 1960s roughly one-quarter of the farms in existence at the start of each decade had disappeared by its close. Thereafter the rate of exits slowed, but was still 17 per cent in the 1970s and 12 per cent in the 1980s. Average farm size increased as surviving operators purchased additional land and the tendency for farmers to rent extra acreage brought even greater centralisation in the management of land. Rapid technological change transformed farming into an increasingly capital-intensive business of large-scale commercial farms sustained by an 'agribusiness' sector of farm machinery, chemical and food companies. Smaller producers were squeezed out by the cost of the new technology and tenants and farm labourers were displaced

Table 6.1 *Trends in US agriculture, 1945–90*

Year	Farm population (million)	% of total	Number of Farms (million)
1945	24.4	17.5	5.8
1950	23.0	15.2	5.3
1955	19.1	11.5	4.6
1960	15.6	8.7	3.9
1965	12.3	6.4	3.3
1970	9.7	4.7	2.9
1975	8.8	4.1	2.5
1980	6.0	3.2	2.4
1985	5.4	2.2	2.2
1990	4.6	1.9	2.1

Sources: US Bureau of the Census, *Historical Statistics of the United States, Colonial Times to 1970, Bicentennial Edition,* Part 1, (Washington, DC, 1975), p. 457, series K1–2, K109, K430; US Bureau of the Census, *Statistical Abstract of the United States: 1993* (113th edn, Washington, DC, 1993), p. 652, table 109; US Bureau of the Census, *Statistical Abstract of the United States: 1992* (112th edn, Washington, DC, 1993), p. 644, table 1077.

as farming required less labour. Along with climate and international markets, the political processes which shaped public policy had a profound influence on the economic and social change in agriculture.

Crisis and transformation in agriculture before 1945

In certain respects the post-war trends were foreshadowed before 1945. Large-scale and capital-intensive operations existed primarily in midwestern grain areas where mechanisation was well developed, and in the diverse farming of California which relied on extensive irrigation. Even in the labour-intensive South, there were large landowners. The 'agribusiness' system was present: Land Grant colleges and state agricultural experiment stations contributed to education and research. For producers of staples such as grain or cotton, the inter-war period was a time of considerable difficulty, especially when prices fell steeply between 1929 and 1933. The farmers responded by expanding output in an effort to maintain income, but this merely added to surplus stocks and downward pressure on prices. As waves of rural bank failures restricted the supply of credit, mortgage foreclosures escalated. The policy response was an extension of the federal government's role in agricultural commodity and credit markets. Financial support to farmers was expanded under the new Farm Credit Administration from 1933 and federal loans substituted for declining lending by banks and insurance companies. A variety of price and income supports were introduced. Producers of the principal surplus crops received 'non-recourse' loans from the Commodity Credit Corporation (CCC) which, in effect, provided a guaranteed minimum income with higher returns to farmers if market prices rose above the loan rate. Additional payments were made to farmers who removed land from cultivation and conservation payments, inspired by the problems of the Dust Bowl, encouraged the withdrawal of land from the production of surplus crops as well as promoting better farming methods. Federal programmes raised commodity prices and average farm incomes after 1933 and reduced the total acreage under staple crops, but surpluses were increasing by the end of the 1930s. The Department of Agriculture's concept of an 'ever-normal granary' envisaged permanent arrangements for accumulating reserves against future shortfalls which contrasted with the original emphasis on short-term responses to emergency conditions.

The problem of surpluses reflected contradictory elements in New Deal farm programmes. Acreage reductions reduced output only if yields remained constant, but farmers abandoned less productive land and worked their remaining acres more intensively, so yields improved. Federal credit, price and income measures raised returns to farmers above their market level and reduced the costs and uncertainties associated with investing in more productive methods. Although the timing and extent of change varied considerably depending on the commodity, the New Deal programmes, by shifting the balance in favour of mechanisation, foreshadowed subsequent technological changes and a shake-out of rural population. In general higher commodity prices benefited all producers, and in the absence of intervention smaller farmers might well have fared worse given their limited resources and lower productivity, but undoubtedly the New Deal farm policy primarily benefited larger commercial farmers and landowners. Federal credit agencies chiefly assisted those applicants judged to possess the best commercial prospects and the major producers' greater resources offered more scope for mechanisation and diversification. From the federal policy-makers' perspective, substantial acreage reductions required maximum participation by the commercial operators who controlled the largest holdings, so such farmers received the bulk of the benefit payments which increased their capacity to invest in the new technology. This pattern fulfilled the New Deal's aim of promoting higher incomes and greater efficiency, but contributed to the problem of surpluses. Alternative policies favourable to subsistence production, co-operatives or tenants might have improved the prospects for the mass of farmers, perhaps through more co-operative ventures, but federal programmes for such people had limited budgets and their own modest resources left little room for manoeuvre.

World War II stimulated further mechanisation and diversification, but provided a release for the surplus commodities and labour which had accumulated during the 1930s. In response to the labour requirements of military service and industrial work, the farm population fell by 6.1 million between 1940 and 1945, a 20 per cent reduction, with the greatest decline occurring in the South.[3] Farmers reacted by seeking draft deferments for farm workers and making greater use of women, children and the elderly.[4] Along the eastern seaboard West Indian labour was imported and in the West Mexican workers were brought in under the Bracero Agreement of 1942.[5] Nonetheless farmers complained about disruptions to established labour systems as the 'pull' of more lucrative employment drove up wage rates. Street's study of the cotton economy detected no general shortage of labour, but concluded that uncertainty over labour supply and rising wages made even southern farmers more 'machinery-minded'.[6] Increased demand and a rise of 138 per cent in average agricultural prices prompted farmers to expand production by some 17 per cent during the war.[7] Federal policies emphasised maximising production. The Emergency Price Control Act in 1942 extended price supports for a broad range of produce at 90 per cent of parity for two years beyond the end of the war.[8] This reassurance against an immediate post-war deflation encouraged mechanisation and increased production, though farmers remained extremely cautious about taking on debt. By 1946 the parity ratio, a comparative measure of the ratio of farm to non-farm prices, stood at 109 compared to 81 six years earlier and farmers had used their higher incomes to reduce their debts. Despite supply shortages, the use of farm machinery increased, including tractors, combine harvesters and corn-picking and milking machines. As labour productivity rose, the trend towards more capital-intensive farming moved forward several steps. Diversification away from staples went further too in response to the demand for oil crops, notably soy beans, to replace previously imported supplies and for meat and dairy produce. Burgeoning urban markets, particularly in the South and West, stimulated the growth of truck farming of fruit and vegetables as well as poultry and egg production.

A gathering pace of change

Confirmation that pre-war trends to larger units and mechanisation would continue, and accelerate, came after 1945. Many areas of farming were affected by mechanical, chemical and organisational innovations which raised productivity dramatically.[9] Research and development work by machinery and chemical companies and by federal and state agencies had produced considerable advances in scientific knowledge and the stock of both proven and potential technology, and with the ending of rationing manufacturers increased production of equipment, fertilisers and other chemicals and feeds. Corporate and public research programmes and agricultural training and education expanded further after 1945 and supplied the basis for a new agricultural revolution and transformation of rural society.[10] Overall Cochrane estimated that labour inputs declined by 26 per cent during the 1940s and by a further 35 per cent in the following decade.[11]

A vocal lobby in favour of mechanisation and diversification had existed in the South from the 1880s without making much impact on agricultural practices, but by the 1940s farmers' attitudes had altered. It may well be that the experience of the Depression and war, especially on staple-crop producers, had created a greater openness to new methods and alternative crops and a more receptive approach to technological change. Certainly the state of credit and labour markets in the late 1940s was favourable to the acquisition of labour-saving technologies. With low debts and increased savings farmers were well placed to undertake new investment. In 1946 Federal Land Banks were a major source of funds and, compared to the previous decade, engaged less in re-financing bad debts and more in lending for equipment purchases. Banks and life insurance companies expanded lending after 1946, having retrenched during the Depression, and surpassed the value of federal credit by 1951. Private financial institutions followed the federal agencies' example by supplying cheaper credit and extended repayment periods. Bank and insurance-company lending was, in any case, often reliant on federal support to farm mortgages. Farm wages continued their wartime rise and while many migrants returned to farms during 1945, net out-migration resumed in the following year, strengthening concerns about the availability and cost of labour in the future. For southern farmers, in particular, such events confirmed their closer integration into a national labour market in which workers were likely to be more mobile and more expensive. Against a background of excellent sales, there was good reason to be more 'machinery minded' and farmers possessed the resources to put their ideas into practice. Between 1945 and 1950 over one million extra tractors came into use; the number of corn-picking machines more than doubled and the increase in combine-harvester numbers was nearly as great.[12]

Change in the southern cotton economy

Developments in cotton-growing were particularly significant since its labour-intensive culture had long been a mainstay of southern agriculture. The region was highly susceptible to the effects of mechanisation and became the principal source of migrants from farms after 1945. Sharecropping and tenancy arrangements in the South had been designed to ensure a regular supply of labour throughout the year for planting, weeding or chopping and harvesting cotton. During the 1930s planters in the newer cotton areas of Texas and California introduced tractors and substituted wage-labour for tenants. The outflow of labour to urban employment during the 1940s accelerated the process of change, with the proportion of farms with tractors increasing from 11.7 per cent to 23.4 per cent in the South between 1945 and 1950.[13] Harvest labour requirements remained substantial, but in 1941 International Harvester's decades of research finally yielded an effective spindle-type cotton-picking machine.

Although only a few machines were sold during the war, the firm opened a new factory in 1948. In 1949–50 California growers responded to farm-workers' strikes by increasing their adoption of machine-picking from 13 per cent of the state's 1949 crop to 51 per cent two years later.[14] Elsewhere spindle-machines were adopted slowly: only 5 per cent of the national crop was machine-picked in 1950.[15] The early machines were too expensive for small farms and were unsuitable on hilly terrain where hand-picking remained more economical. Hand-picking persisted longest in the Southeast and elsewhere old and new systems coexisted for a time. On large plantations machines were used at the height of the harvest for maximum effect with hand-picking deployed earlier and later.[16] However, mechanisation gathered momentum, particularly in the Mississippi and Arkansas Deltas, in the mid-1950s. The machine-picked proportion of the cotton crop increased from 23 per cent in 1955 to 50 per cent in 1959 and reached 72 per cent by 1963.[17]

A feature of technological change in the cotton economy was the sequence of interrelated innovations which resulted in a sustained process of innovation, culminating in a package of new methods and a far more capital-intensive system of farming. At each stage mechanisation of one operation encouraged efforts to innovate in other parts of the production process. Although comparatively late, the impact of cotton-picking machines on demand for labour was profound. The hand labour for chopping (weeding) cotton was replaced by tractor-pulled flame weeders which burnt off weed growth and there was increased application of weed-killers and pesticides. Chemical defoliants were adopted to force leaf drop before machine-picking in order to produce cleaner cotton; first marketed in 1949, defoliants were in general use by the 1960s. The effects of mechanisation were evident in rapidly diminishing numbers of tenants, sharecroppers, mules and horses on southern farms as landowners switched from cropping and other forms of tenancy to wage-labour. From 718,723 at the end of the war, the number of tenants fell to 245,230 in 1959 while the number of croppers declined from 446,556 to 121,037 over the same period.[18] The older pattern of small, separate cropper farms gave way to the vast acreages of neo-plantations operated by an owner or manager supervising a small staff of wage-earners with machinery.

Technological changes in farming

In other regions tractors, ploughs and other farm equipment became larger, more powerful and more sophisticated through a series of piecemeal innovations and machinery was applied to a wider range of farm tasks. Earlier developments, such as hybrid corn, were adopted more widely and other new plant varieties were developed, selecting favoured characteristics such as yield, disease-resistance, size and colour. The pattern of interrelated

Table 6.2 *US annual average agricultural yields per acre, 1945–89*

Years	Wheat (bushels)	Corn (bushels)	Cotton lbs
1945–49	16.9	36.1	273
1955–59	22.3	48.7	428
1965–69	27.5	77.4	485
1975–79	31.4	95.2	481
1985–89	35.3	111.5	624

Sources: US Bureau of the Census, *Historical Statistics of the United States*, Part 1 (Washington, DC, 1975), p. 500, series K448, K453, K458; US Bureau of the Census, *Statistical Abstract of the United States: 1981*, (102nd edn, Washington, DC, 1981), p. 686; US Bureau of the Census, *Statistical Abstract of the United States: 1989* (109th edn, Washington, DC, 1989), p. 646; US Bureau of the Census, *Statistical Abstract of the United States: 1993* p. 669.

changes to facilitate mechanisation, evident in cotton-growing, occurred for other commodities: tomatoes, for instance, were 'redesigned' to be smaller, firmer and less juicy in order to accommodate machine-picking. Livestock farmers followed the same course, employing new vaccines, drugs and animal feeds. For instance, poultry-raising was transformed into a large-scale, more productive business via selective breeding and the addition of vitamins and antibiotics to feeds. A larger proportion of farmers applied chemicals and the average quantities used increased: the volume of chemicals applied rose from 15.1 million short tons in 1946 to 20.9 million in 1951 and 39.5 million short tons in 1970.[19] The chemical industry developed new synthetic nitrogenous fertilisers which came into widespread use. Commercial weedkillers and pesticides were deployed in greater quantities, including crop-dusting and spraying from aircraft, a practice dating from the 1920s. New scientific developments went well beyond the traditional use of fertilisers and selective breeding. Corporations, agricultural colleges and government-supported laboratories generated new compounds more frequently, reflecting the general expansion of public and private research capabilities during the 1930s and 1940s. Of equal importance was the increased faith among scientists, manufacturers and farmers in the efficacy of chemicals to solve problems plus the favourable post-war climate for investment. Such developments contributed to the reduction in labour requirements and to a rapid growth of crop and livestock yields after World War II (Table 6.2).

Diversification had its roots in the inter-war crisis affecting staples and acreage reductions and the Soil Conservation programmes which encouraged alternative crops and even reversion to grassland. After 1945 rising incomes shifted demand away from staples, like wheat, to increased consumption of meat, with beef and later chicken to the fore. In the South and West urban growth provided larger markets for milk and truck crops, fresh vegetables and other produce which was driven for sale locally.

Improvements in transport and in techniques for preserving, drying and freezing produce, especially perishable crops, enabled farmers to supply national markets. Overall US farmers produced more livestock, poultry, fruit, peanuts and soybeans. The latter originally provided a hay crop and source of animal feed, but shortages of imported oils and fats during World War II prompted spectacular increases in soybean production. From the early 1950s southern farmers expanded soybean acreage, especially in Arkansas, Mississippi and Louisiana. Soybeans met the tenets of mainstream farm policy in that they had agricultural and industrial uses and yields improved steadily, but demand was sufficient for market prices to be invariably well above their support price.

Structural changes in agriculture

Earlier signs of the competitive advantage of larger commercial farmers were confirmed by post-war developments. Despite variations in timing, average farm size rose throughout US agriculture in a cycle of technical change, increased economies of scale and further innovation. Commercial operators were best placed to pursue this strategy due to their access to credit, and rising land values created capital gains which facilitated borrowing. There was every incentive to adopt new technologies quickly since the earliest innovators reaped the largest returns, and failure to innovate could leave a farmer as a high-cost producer and even force an exit from the industry. Equally the cycle of innovation could become a treadmill involving substantial debt and, thus, vulnerability to a 'cost-price squeeze' if costs rose faster than prices for an extended period. This was not a new risk, but became more common as the rising volume of purchased inputs created greater potential for cost pressures. The trend in farm size implied the existence of increasing economies of scale, but the available evidence is equivocal since precise measurements are elusive. Studies suggested that many farms were far larger than the optimum required to maximise economies of scale.[20] Major operators may have been influenced by new management techniques which allowed bigger acreages to be overseen effectively, encouraging a definite trend towards renting extra land so that even slight cost or efficiency advantages could be multiplied by the larger acreage. Trucks, telephones and radios simplified the direction of widely-scattered workforces. Detailed information on costs, inputs, yields and sales furnished the means for more precise planning and by the 1960s computerised systems were in use. Suppliers of feeds, chemicals and other products actively promoted 'scientific' farming methods as did extension agents, farm journals and the Soil Conservation and Agricultural Conservation Programme. There were financial incentives for expansion in the form of appreciating land values and tax concessions. Corporate farming became more common in the 1960s, particularly in Florida,

Table 6.3 *Selected indices of US agricultural inputs, 1950–90 (1982 = 100)*

Year	Farm labour	Equipment	Chemicals	Feed, seed & livestock	Other purchases	Total inputs
1950	237	52	43	44	78	94
1960	163	69	58	74	99	97
1970	119	78	76	87	90	93
1980	108	102	131	102	116	106
1990	87	64	90	105	97	97

Source: Economic Report of the President, 1994 (Washington, DC, 1994), p. 381, table B-98.

California and Utah, in response to favourable tax rules and many family farms assumed a corporate form.[21]

The trend towards more capital-intensive methods and larger farms involved increasing reliance on purchasing supplies of machinery, feedstuffs, fertilisers, pesticides and other chemicals. Table 6.3 indicates this development.

Below the leading operators was a diverse array of farmers about whom it is difficult to generalise. Some, especially those with access to capital and credit, pursued the grand strategies of mechanisation, applying chemicals and renting additional land, but they were vulnerable during periods of low returns or high interest rates. The well-established co-operative movement enabled farmers to obtain savings in buying in supplies or hiring equipment and co-operatives had a valuable marketing function, particularly in dairying, through the establishment and promotion of brand-names and quality standards. One strategy for farmers of all sizes was to become, in effect, a satellite of a major food business by supplying produce under contract. Such an arrangement provided security against which to borrow and might itself be a source of capital, credit and advice from a manufacturer or retailer. In some cases manufacturers undertook full vertical integration, combining production and marketing. A rapid expansion of poultry production among small farmers was facilitated by feed companies and processors who supplied credit, chicks, feed and even buildings.[22] The proportion of all crops under marketing contracts increased from 15 per cent in 1960 to 23 per cent in 1980 and the share was far higher for processed vegetables, potatoes and citrus fruits.[23] Co-operative and satellite arrangements underpinned major businesses such as California Sunkist Growers or Richard Simplot's Idaho potato enterprise which was contracted to the McDonald's fast-food empire.[24]

In part large and small farmers pursued different strategies, but achieved similar overall costs, though with wide variations in their resulting incomes. Perhaps the most common approach among smaller farmers was a mix of gradual mechanisation, including the purchase of second-hand equipment, and the minimisation of indebtedness. In this way resources could be husbanded enough for the farm to be passed to the next generation. Grim's study of one community of black farm-owners after 1940 revealed a variety of strategies including even more labour-intensive methods during the 1950s, a piecemeal move into mechanisation and forms of communal working to share scare resources.[25] On family farms mechanisation maximised the family's capacity to operate independently, but the corollary was long hours of work and low incomes. Such methods combined capital investments with a form of intensive working which could make family farms competitive in terms of production costs with major operators. The strategy relied on a high degree of family labour on the farm with women and children undertaking many tasks. Elbert's study of family farmers revealed the critical role of women in basic farm duties and in contributing capital and off-farm income, and yet farm women were often excluded from key managerial decisions.[26] New industrial and service employment in the South and rural Midwest offered greater opportunities for supplementing farm income through off-farm employment; such alternative work remained limited in the Plains states. Despite such survival strategies, the number of family farms declined as new generations proved less willing to accept the demanding terms required for survival, regarded urban occupations as more prestigious or sought a more diverse urban society. The average age of the rural population rose steadily, exceeding that of urban-dwellers from 1960.[27] On the retirement or death of parents land was often rented out or passed into other hands. The timing of the 'push' varied by crop according to the timing and rate of mechanisation, so in cotton and rice the attrition among small farmers was in full force by the 1950s while in tobacco districts mechanisation occurred a decade later. There were racial differences too. In the 1940s a higher proportion of African-Americans than whites lived on farms, but the position was reversed by 1960. The proportion of African-Americans resident on farms fell from 21 per cent in 1950 to one per cent thirty years later.[28] Black farm-owners had held on to their land grimly through the 1930s, but their numbers declined from 160,980 in 1945 to 55,600 in 1969. With smaller acreages and inequalities in access to public and private credit, survival was difficult even with intensive labour.[29]

The rural poor

Although agricultural employment contracted, there remained a force of seasonal, often migratory agricultural labour primarily deployed at harvest. The capital-intensive California agricultural economy relied on Mexican-American labour to pick fruit, vegetables and other crops. Low pay was maintained through the importation of workers so that a 'dual' system combined mechanisation and cheap day-labour. Cobb emphasised the continuing dependency of African-Americans in the Mississippi Delta on local white farmers and officials for employment and welfare provision.[30] Union-organising campaigns, notably among California farmworkers, were successful in the 1960s as the ending of the Bracero programme reduced the flow of imported labour, but militancy led growers to turn to machinery for harvesting.[31] In the 1960s new minimum wage laws raised wage rates, but again accentuated the trend towards mechanisation.

Rural poverty remained concentrated in the Ozarks, Appalachia and parts of the Deep South so that the distribution of depressed rural areas characterised by low incomes and above-average unemployment in 1990 was strikingly consistent with its 1900 or 1930 pattern. Rural problems were studied intensively in the 1950s and legislators, officials and academic researchers generally concluded that a decline among poor, marginal farmers and farm-workers was the inevitable and desirable outcome of improved efficiency. State and federal agencies promoted just such a transformation. The dissolution of the Farm Security Administration, the main source of aid to small farmers and tenants, symbolised the direction of policy since its successor in 1946, the Farmers' Home Administration (FHA), placed even greater emphasis on lending in line with commercial prospects. FHA support enabled some farmers to acquire additional land, equipment and buildings, to undertake conservation or irrigation work, or to diversify, but total funding was modest. Small farmers benefited from general price supports, but their limited landholdings restricted the payments received as well as their capacity to reduce acreages without jeopardising their income.[32] The incidence of poverty was higher among small farmers than any other occupational group during the 1950s and 1960s, though the extension of the Social Security system to include farm-workers in 1955 provided an additional source of support. In 1954 President Eisenhower highlighted small farmers' problems, but a US Department of Agriculture (USDA) report concluded that there were simply too many farmers and policy efforts should be directed at accelerating the exodus. The resulting Rural Development Programme aimed to promote 'off-farm' employment through education and training as well as financing improvements in rural health services. During the 1960s new federal agencies were located in depressed rural areas such as Appalachia, the Ozarks and the Four Corners region which covered parts of Arizona, New Mexico, Utah and Colorado. Such areas were experiencing farm poverty, often combined with the decline of mining or the timber trade. The emphasis was still on providing training for alternative employment and the Rural Development Act of 1972 was in the same vein. Such programmes contributed to improvements in education and health provision and there was industrial investment, though largely in lower-wage activities. Even so, in 1963 43 per cent of farmers lived below the official poverty line, more than double the rate for the rest of the population. Twenty years later only 21 per cent of farm-family incomes were below the poverty line, but the non-farm figure was just 12 per cent.[33]

Federal farm policy since 1945

Farm programmes operated in a very different climate after 1945, but public policy remained a critical influence. In the West extensive federal landownership added a further dimension. The New Deal framework of price supports, non-recourse loans and credit remained in place and had been extended to more commodities during the war. There was a cast of interested, often argumentative, parties including farmer organisations, state agricultural officials, the USDA, economists, food-processors, machinery and agricultural chemical companies, local and national politicians and a burgeoning consumer movement. Generally the USDA bureaucracy flourished, extending its remit into all aspects of food production and consumption. Despite declining numbers farmers retained considerable political influence due to the rural slant of state and national legislatures, the seniority of key southern congressmen into the 1960s and effective lobbying by farmers and related agribusiness interests. The foremost farmer organisation in 1945 was the American Farm Bureau Federation (AFBF), which primarily represented larger commercial producers. The voice of smaller farmers was the Farmers' Union, while the Grange, a farmer organisation, continued its nineteenth-century co-operative tradition and social role. In addition to such general organisations, commodity groups representing suppliers of specific produce exercised considerable influence through detailed lobbying.[34]

Policy debates were complicated by the contending impulses inherent in farm programmes. Price and income supports were intended to stabilise commodity markets; their existence increased the value of farm assets and affected farmers' investment decisions. This provided a powerful incentive to maintain the programmes, but their operation was affected by the normal uncertainties associated with fluctuating harvests and international markets. At the same time the goal of greater efficiency and the high level of price supports generated sustained innovation and higher productivity which contributed to the problem of surpluses. At times the usual state of the 'ever-normal granary' appeared to be one of escalating and expensive stocks. The system of price supports and parity prices established a particular target, but involved payments for production rather than direct subsidies. This arrangement left farmers a degree of autonomy which blurred the image of dependency on the state, but made production controls a critical issue for regulating prices, incomes and subsidies. All parties acted pragmatically in pursuit of often divergent interests and the effect was generally to constrain changes of policy.

A collapse of prices and demand was widely anticipated when the war ended, though farmers had the guarantee of 1942 against an immediate deflation. In the short term the readjustment proved comparatively easy as high domestic incomes plus exports to Europe and Asia, including food assistance programmes, ensured excellent returns to farmers until 1949. Farmers supported the ending of rationing and price controls and generally gained during the ensuing inflation. Cattle producers effectively forced the removal of controls on meat prices by refusing to market cattle in 1946.[35] By 1947 the parity ratio was 115 per cent, its highest point since 1918, and the farmers' share of the retail price of food was well above its inter-war level.[36] The pre-war concern with surpluses re-emerged by 1948 following a run of good harvests. Against this background the 1948 Agricultural Act reduced certain price supports, allowed greater flexibility and revised the parity ratio. In the following year Charles F. Brannan, the new Secretary of Agriculture, proposed reform aimed at lowering food prices and the cost of agricultural programmes. The existing high price supports would be maintained for staple commodities, but they would apply only to the first $25,700 worth of each farmer's output, thereby reducing the programmes' total cost at the expense of large operators. The price-support system was to be extended to perishable commodities without any output controls; any gap between the prevailing market price and the support price would be met by a direct payment to the farmer. The Brannan plan drew fierce opposition from the AFBF which rejected both the idea of limits on payments to large producers and the extension of price supports. Moreover the parity ratio and the real value of net farm income declined in 1949 as the economy moved into recession. The resulting farm protests generated sufficient pressure to ensure that Congress extended the guaranteed price supports for a further two years. In the event this assurance remained in force to 1956. Although the 1948 and 1949 Agricultural Act allowed for reductions in price-support levels, the option was never exercised. These events were an early indication of the barriers to reforming farm programmes.

High price supports and the bias in favour of major commercial operators continued. Korean War demand revived farm incomes, but the problem of surpluses reappeared after the war as exports declined and the domestic economy went into recession. In addition there was the underlying force of accelerating productivity growth.

The return of a Republican administration brought a more *laissez-faire* philosophy, enunciated by Ezra Taft Benson, Secretary of Agriculture between 1953 and 1961, into the debate over farm policy. Benson believed that government support undermined initiative and self-reliance and he advocated the swift removal of price supports in order to create 'freedom to farm'.[37] In Benson's view improved efficiency was the best route to higher incomes while better marketing was the solution to surpluses. There was an intense debate over policy in which Benson's desire for dramatic change was countered by the unwillingness of the various commodity interests to risk the probable price falls involved in making a break for freedom. The AFBF was willing, however, to support legislation in 1954 introducing flexible price supports at between 75 per cent and 90 per cent of parity from 1956. The 1954 Act placed $2.5 billion of stocks outside the price-support scheme to be disposed of through a combination of aid, donations and a school lunch programme. Farm exports were encouraged as a useful transitional device until the operation of a freer agricultural market, which Benson anticipated would solve the problem of surpluses. The principal expression of this aspect was the Agricultural Trade Development and Assistance Act (Public Law or PL 480) of 1954: shipments under this legislation accounted for between one-quarter and one-third of US farm exports from 1954 to 1961.[38] PL 480 allowed sales of surplus produce via commercial companies in exchange for foreign currency; barter, subsidised sales and donations for relief purposes were also permitted. The mix of aims created tensions over the operation of PL 480 between agricultural, trade and foreign affairs interests; there was also a contradiction between the Act's role in dumping surpluses and Benson's advocacy of using normal commercial channels. Despite his initial optimism, the problem of surpluses led Benson to follow the New Deal precedent of offering payments in return for acreage reductions. His Soil Bank scheme in 1956 had taken deposits equivalent to 12 per cent of total cropland by 1960 when it closed and its final contracts continued to 1972.[39] Overall direct federal payments to farmers increased from $229 million in 1955 to $1,089 million three years later; the total cost of farm programmes was $4.6 billion during 1958–59.[40] An expansion in the supply of public and private credit and in the resources devoted to research augmented the forces of technology, exposing the contradictions between Benson's faith in efficiency to raise incomes and his belief that surpluses would be temporary.

A new Democratic Administration in 1961 brought a change of emphasis. It accepted high price supports, but in return aimed to tighten production controls in the hope of limiting surpluses. Since efforts to reduce output via reductions in the area of cultivated land had been undermined by higher yields on smaller acreages, quotas on physical output were proposed.[41] The AFBF and most commodity groups resisted stricter limits on production and the Administration lacked the political will to force through major price reductions as a stick to bring about compliance with production controls. Support prices were lowered in the 1965 Food and Agriculture Act which directed subsidies to farmers who reduced output, but farm organisations lobbied successfully to moderate the limits on production. The existing armoury of surplus disposal schemes was augmented by a Food Stamp programme, modelled on a New Deal measure; after a trial programme, Food Stamps were made permanent in 1964.[42] In the 1964 Congressional elections the number of urban Democratic representatives increased, which symbolised a broader shift, with rural influence diminishing and the beginnings of a more assertive phase of environmental and consumer activism. The latter was marked by concerns about the use of pesticides and food quality as well as attacks on USDA as too uncritical of the practices of farmers and the food industry. Such developments signalled a more defensive tone in farm policies, but of more immediate significance was a new 'boom and bust' cycle unlike any since the 1930s.

Exports had risen steadily to the mid-1960s and then stabilised; throughout they provided a key outlet for the principal surplus commodities. In 1972 and 1973 Russian grain purchases increased sharply following a poor harvest, triggering a general upsurge in world demand, particularly for grains and rice. Farmers and distributors received windfall profits on their current stocks and the value of US agricultural exports rose by 184 per cent between 1971 and 1974. As a proportion of farm receipts, export values rose from 14 per cent in 1970 to 29 per cent in 1980. The resulting farm prosperity was remarkable: real net farm income doubled between 1971 and 1974.[43] For the first time in the post-war period farm families enjoyed a higher disposable income than non-farm families.[44] The CCC was able to run down its surpluses and USDA relaxed production quotas as the Nixon administration sought to ride the wave of prosperity towards a more market-based farm policy. After initially repaying debts in a cautious fashion, farmers accepted the market and policy incentives for expansion. Grain producers ploughed up vast tracts of grassland and extended irrigation in the Plains states; by 1975 the harvested acreage was 42 million acres greater than three years before. The quantities of agricultural chemicals applied escalated. With real interest rates low, farmers borrowed to purchase land and equipment, raising levels of indebtedness. The export boom continued through the 1970s with agricultural prices running ahead of the average rate of inflation, and the only checks were higher energy costs and the effects of drought across parts of the Great Plains.[45]

The spectacular boom broke in an equally dramatic fashion after President Carter placed an embargo on grain exports to Russia following the invasion of Afghanistan. This dent to the optimism about exports was compounded by faltering domestic demand so that the problem of stocks reappeared. There were further problems due to the rising value of the dollar, which made exports less competitive, and higher real interest rates which raised the cost of earlier borrowings. In real terms net farm income slumped by 46 per cent in 1980; half of the loss was regained in the following year, but real incomes slipped from $34.1 billion in 1981 to $16.3 billion in 1983. Farmers reduced their purchases of machinery and other supplies, spreading the contraction into the agribusiness sector. A further downward twist was provided by a fall of one-third in average land values between 1981 and 1986; in Iowa the value of land fell by 63 per cent. By 1984 one-quarter of US farmers were reported to be in severe financial difficulties, despite an expansion of lending by the Federal Land Banks and the FHA. This devaluation of assets aggravated the farmers' debt burden and, in turn, weakened rural banks and other lenders since land had served as collateral on loans. From only one in 1981, the number of failures among rural banks increased to 68 in 1985, which represented one-third of all bank failures during the year.[46] The scale of the financial crisis was such that the federal farm credit system experienced losses between 1985 and 1987 which forced a reorganisation and required additional federal guarantees of the system's solvency.

As the farm crisis worsened, mounting stocks drove moves toward freer markets off course. The Reagan administration assumed office as the 1970s boom broke. The farm programmes offered a tempting target for a government which advocated reductions in federal expenditure and regulation, but the immediate crisis created demands for federal assistance. An emergency Payment-In-Kind programme was introduced in an attempt to reduce surpluses: farmers who removed land from the production of grain, cotton, or rice received grain from federal stocks. In order to ensure maximum participation, there was no limit on individual payments and by 1983 around one-third of grain acreage was enrolled at a cost of some $9.7 billion.[47] In grain areas drought helped to reduce output, but added to existing hardship. The old strategy of promoting exports continued to be central with a relaxation of export credits and in the terms of PL 480, though trade barriers overseas posed an obstacle to this tactic. The implementation of soil-conservation practices was made more rigorous in response to the 1983 drought and the ecological impact on the marginal lands which had been ploughed up during the 1970s. This measure was in a long tradition of utilising conservation as a device to aid acreage and output reductions.

Despite the extensions of federal intervention, farm policies were reformed in the 1980s, although each sector fared rather differently. In the tobacco programme CCC loans were replaced by a system based on growers' co-operatives and production became concentrated in fewer hands as the way of allotting production quotas was altered.[48] In dairying efforts to reduce subsidies were stymied by the producers' effective lobbying, but the old co-operative-based form of regulation fragmented as new producing regions came to the fore. Despite new payments for output reductions, surpluses of dairy products rose.[49] The hope of the 1950s that short-term export growth offered a route to stability and higher incomes in a market system reappeared in the 1985 Farm Bill's proposals for freer markets. The commodity groups again emphasised the immediate crisis conditions and managed to restrict the extent of reform during the passage of the 1985 Food Security Act so that high target prices remained. The bias towards major commercial operators persisted so that proposals to direct greater support to smaller and family farms were dropped from the final legislation. Nonetheless support levels were lowered through changes in the formulas used to calculate parity and support payments.

Overview

Few aspects of American society have been transformed more completely since World War II than farming. The driving force has been a sustained process of mechanical and scientific innovation resulting in large farms operating highly capital-intensive businesses. Agricultural productivity recorded spectacular advances compared to its earlier record or to the post-war performance of other sectors. A counterpart of these trends was the 'shake-out' of tenants, labourers and smaller farmers: the number of people on farms had fallen by 20 million by 1990. The seeds of this trans-formation were sown before the war in the form of the destructive impact of the Depression on staple-crop farmers, earlier mechanisation and the research and development work by firms, colleges and USDA. By 1945 there was a considerable stock of new or lightly-used mechanical and chem-ical technologies which were adopted swiftly. Despite earlier roots, post-war developments were distinctive in their pace and impact, especially in the South, where the old labour-intensive cotton culture vanished. The con-tinuing 'pull' of alternative employment ensured that higher wartime farm wages were more than a temporary phenomenon and the emphasis on maximum production plus the ready availability of credit increased farmers' willingness to mechanise. The greater use of purchased inputs contributed to productivity growth, but exposed farmers to a treadmill of rising capital costs and to the risk of a 'cost–price' squeeze. Smaller farmers were falling by the wayside from the 1950s and thereafter middling farmers were under pressure; the 'boom and bust' of the 1970s and 1980s under-mined even substantial farmers in a way reminiscent of the period between 1910 and 1933.

Against this background of structural transformation, farm policy tacked between the effects of short-term crises and the contending demands of the various interested parties. The four- or five-yearly farm bill usually featured a similar array of proposals for expanding exports whilst reducing expenditure and surpluses by making price supports more flexible. Democratic administrations emphasised production controls while Republican ones generally favoured a greater role for market forces. Farmers and their organisations generally preferred weak production controls, but were often reluctant to abandon at least minimum price supports; they acted opportunistically so that policy-making generated considerable heat as the different interests clashed. The influence of commodity groups in the legislative process tended to avert major price reductions or strict production controls so that policy largely centred on questions of rather more or rather less subsidy for a given commodity. In general programmes continued to favour large commercial operators rather than smaller producers. Indeed, farm organisations were highly effective in portraying their problems in terms of the threat to family farms, in order to draw on a convenient and well-respected symbol which was sufficiently vague to blur the direction of policy and fundamental changes in the character of family farms. After 1964 rural interests were less powerful in Congress and the consumer movement brought a more critical note to the debates. There were reforms, such as the banning of DDT, and conservation practices have made an important contribution to environmental improvement. Production controls, however, remain a key concern and the 'plough-ups' of the 1970s indicate the potential fragility of conservation policies.

Overall New Deal farm programmes still provided the basis of the regulatory system through price supports, production controls and federal farm credit agencies. Since the late 1940s exports were a major outlet through normal commercial channels and via government measures such as Marshall Aid, PL 480 from 1954 and other export subsidies. Another element of continuity was the emphasis within USDA and Congress on promoting efficiency as the route to higher incomes. This approach was facilitated by the research and development and promotional work of agricultural chemicals and machinery companies as well as the extension service and agricultural colleges. The efficiency aspect has the associated, but paradoxical, effect of expanding the volume of surpluses. With the criteria of efficiency and the desire of maximising participation in production control, federal policy-makers continued to direct subsidies at large commercial farmers who benefited most from the cheaper credit and reduced risks brought by federal programmes. As a result the federal government has presided over a major rural depopulation, driven by technological changes and the nature of farm policy. While not managing this decline in any systematic fashion, federal programmes cushioned it to a certain extent and in the absence of price supports farm prices would have been lower; estimates of the probable fall range between 15 and 50 per cent according to the commodity.[50] Such a fall would have reduced all farm incomes and presumably accelerated rural depopulation in the 1940s and 1950s. Conversely the high domestic prices involved some loss of exports and encouraged import competition for certain foodstuffs by the 1970s, although the domestic and overseas trade restrictions relating to agriculture made it difficult to evaluate the consequences of reduced prices. Increased or more sustained protectionism might well have offset any price falls. The price support system imposed higher costs on consumers. Equally the 'boom and bust' cycle of the 1970s and 1980s indicated the instabilities inherent in world markets and climate plus the potential for wide swings in farmers' expectations. The swings of demand and price cast the stabilising role of farm policy before 1970 in a rather more positive light. Although federal measures did not prevent the crisis of the early 1980s – indeed, they contributed both to the earlier over-expansion and to bursting the bubble – it seems likely that such episodes would be more frequent in an open market, with substantial acreages shifting in and out of production according to market signals and the vagaries of climate. These elements remained liable to produce fluctuations in agricultural incomes and past experience suggests a continuing trend towards concentration and declining employment in agriculture, but the advent of new biotechnology may provide a further twist to the productivity spiral.

Notes

1 Thomas K. McCraw, *America Versus Japan* (Boston, MA, 1986), p. 155.
2 US Bureau of the Census, jointly with the Department of Agriculture, Current Population Reports, series P-27, No. 61, *Rural and Rural Farm Population: 1987* (Washington, DC, 1988), p. 2.
3 US Bureau of the Census, *Historical Statistics of the United States,* Part 1, p. 457, series K1–2.
4 Daniel Nelson, *Farm and Factory: Workers in the Midwest, 1880–1990* (Bloomington, IN, 1995), pp. 140–1.
5 Carlos A. Schwantes, 'Wage Earners and Wealth Makers' in Clyde A. Milner *et al.* (eds), *The Oxford History of the American West* (New York, 1994), pp. 441–2.
6 James H. Street, *The New Revolution in the Cotton Economy: Mechanization and Its Consequences* (Chapel Hill, NC, 1957), p. 229.
7 US Bureau of the Census, *Historical Statistics of the United States,* Part 1, p. 489, series K353.
8 Gilbert C. Fite, *American Farmers: The New Minority* (Bloomington, IN, 1981), pp. 85–6.
9 Wayne D. Rasmussen, 'A Postscript; Twenty-five Years of Change in Farm Productivity', *Agricultural History,* 49(1), 1975, pp. 84–6; Nathan Rosenberg, *Technology and American Economic Growth* (New York, 1972), pp. 130–41.
10 James G. Maddox, 'Impacts of Non-Commodity Programs on the Structure of Agriculture' in Iowa State University Center for Agricultural and Economic Development, *Food Goals, Future Structural Changes, and Agricultural Policy: A National Basebook* (Ames, IA, 1969), pp. 102–3.
11 Willard W. Cochrane, *The Development of American Agriculture: A Historical Analysis* (Minneapolis, MN, 1979), p. 127.
12 US Bureau of the Census, *Historical Statistics of the United States,* Part 1, p. 469, series K184, K187–8.
13 Gilbert C. Fite, *Cotton Fields No More: Southern Agriculture, 1865–1980* (Lexington, IL, 1984), p. 184.
14 Dennis Nodin Valdes, 'Machine Politics in California Agriculture, 1945–1990s', *Pacific Historical Review,* 63(2), 1994, p. 209.
15 Street, *The New Revolution in the Cotton Economy,* p. 167.
16 Fite, *Cotton Fields No More,* p. 184; Richard H. Day, 'The Economics of Technological Change and the Demise of the Share-cropper', *American Economic Review,* 57(3), 1967, pp. 427–49.
17 US Bureau of the Census, *Historical Statistics of the United States,* Part 2, p. 465, series K128–9.

18 Street, *The New Revolution in the Cotton Economy*, p. 167; Charles R. Sayre, 'Cotton Mechanization since World War II', *Agricultural History*, 53(1), 1979, pp. 105–24.

19 US Bureau of the Census, *Historical Statistics of the United States,* Part 2, p. 469, series K193.

20 John L. Shover, *First Majority-Last Minority: The Transforming of Rural Life in America* (De Kalb, IL 1976), pp. 167–8; Mary C. Ahearn *et al.*, 'The Production Cost-Size Relationship: Measurement Issues and Estimates for Major Crops' in Arne Hallam (ed.), *Size, Structure, and the Changing Face of American Agriculture* (Boulder, CO, 1993), pp. 107–49.

21 Philip M. Raup, 'Corporate Farming in the United States', *Journal of Economic History*, 33(1), 1973, pp. 274–90; Shover, *First Majority-Last Minority*, pp. 165–6.

22 Edward Higbee, *Farms and Farmers in an Urban Age* (New York, 1963), pp. 16–17.

23 Joseph N. Belden *et al.*, *Dirt Rich, Dirt Poor: America's Food and Farm Crisis* (New York, 1986), p. 57.

24 Schwantes, 'Wage Earners and Wealth Makers', p. 457.

25 Valerie Grim, 'The Impact of Mechanized Farming on Black Farm Families in the Rural South: A Study of Farm Life in the Brooks Farm Community, 1940–1970', *Agricultural History*, 68(2), 1994, pp. 169–84.

26 Sarah Elbert, 'Amber Waves of Gain: Women's Work in New York Farm Families' in Carol Gronemann and Mary Beth Norton (eds), *'To Toil The Livelong Day': America's Women At Work, 1780–1980* (Ithaca, NY, 1987), pp. 250–68; Thomas A. Lyson and William W. Falk (eds), *Forgotten Places: Uneven Development in Rural America* (Lawrence, KS, 1993).

27 US Bureau of the Census, jointly with the Department of Agriculture, Current Population Reports, Series P-27, No. 61, *Rural and Rural Farm Population: 1987*, p. 3.

28 Pete Daniel, *Breaking The Land: The Transformation of Cotton, Tobacco, and Rice Cultures since 1880* (Chicago, 1985), chapters 11–13.

29 Loren Schweninger, 'A Vanishing Breed: Black Farm Owners in the South, 1651–1982', *Agricultural History*, 63(3), 1989, pp. 41–60.

30 James C. Cobb, '"Somebody Done Nailed Us On The Cross": Federal Farm Policy and Welfare Policies and the Civil Rights Movement in the Mississippi Delta', *Journal of American History*, 77(3), 1990, p. 922.

31 Valdes, 'Machine Politics in California Agriculture'.

32 Willard W. Cochrane and Mary E. Ryan, *American Farm Policy, 1948–1973* (Minneapolis, MN, 1976), pp. 366–7.

33 James T. Patterson, 'Poverty and Welfare in America, 1945–60' in Robert H. Bremner and Gary W. Reichard (eds), *Reshaping America: Society and Institutions, 1945–1960*, (Columbus, OH, 1982), p. 196; US Bureau of the Census, jointly with the Department of Agriculture, Current Population Reports, Series P-27, No. 59, *Rural and Rural Farm Population of the United States: 1984* (Washington, DC, 1988), p. 7.

34 H. Wayne Morse and Timothy E. Josling, *Agricultural Policy Reform: Politics and Process in the EC and the USA* (New York, 1990), pp. 131–4.

35 Fite, *American Farmers*, pp. 90–1.

36 US Bureau of the Census, *Historical Statistics of the United States*, Part 1, p. 489, series K353, K357.

37 Edward L. Schapsmeier and Frederick H. Schapsmeier, 'Eisenhower and Ezra Taft Benson: Farm Policy in the 1950s', *Agricultural History*, 44(4), 1970, pp. 369–78.

38 Trudy Huskamp Peterson, *Agricultural Exports, Farm Income, and the Eisenhower Administration* (Lincoln, NB, 1979), p. 99.
39 Hugh Ulrich, *Losing Ground: Agricultural Policy and the Decline of the American Farm* (Chicago, 1989), p. 106.
40 US Bureau of the Census, *Historical Statistics of the United States,* Part 1, p. 487, series K326; Fite, *American Farmers*, p. 144.
41 James N. Giglio, 'New Frontier Agricultural Policy: The Commodity Side, 1961–1963', *Agricultural History*, 61(3), 1987, pp. 53–70.
42 Norwood Allen Kerr, 'Drafted into the War on Poverty: USDA Food and Nutrition Programmes, 1961–1969', *Agricultural History*, 64(2), 1990, pp. 154–66.
43 *Economic Report of the President: 1994*, pp. 379, 383.
44 Fite, *American Farmers*, p. 144.
45 *Ibid.*, pp. 211–14.
46 William A. Galston, *A Tough Row To Hoe: The 1985 Farm Bill and Beyond* (Lanham, NY, 1985), p. 51; Neil E. Harl, *The Farm Debt Crisis of the 1980s* (Ames, IA, 1990).
47 Morse and Josling, *Agricultural Policy Reform*, pp. 149–51; Belden *et al.*, *Dirt Rich, Dirt Poor*, pp. 44–5.
48 Daniel, *Breaking the Land*, p. 269.
49 Brigitte Young, 'The Dairy Industry: From Yeomanry to the Institutionalization of Multilateral Governance' in John L. Campbell *et al.* (eds), *Governance and the American Economy* (Cambridge, 1991), pp. 236–58.
50 Walter W. Wilcox, 'Major Price and Income Consequences From Policies Over The Past Thirty-Five Years' in Iowa State University Center for Agricultural and Economic Development, *Food Goals, Future Structural Changes, and Agricultural Policy*, pp. 78–84; Cochrane, *The Development of American Agriculture*, p. 127; Sally Clarke, 'Innovation in U.S. Agriculture: A Role for New Deal Regulation', *Business and Economic History*, 21, 1992, pp. 46–55.

7

Mastery to uncertainty: corporate America, 1945–90

The business corporation has occupied a central place in US society as a source of economic dynamism and social and political influence. The most distinctive image is that of 'big business', the large, vertically-integrated firm deploying complex and capital-intensive technologies. The origins of this type of firm are considered, along with tendencies since 1945 to more diversified and conglomerate forms of business organisation. Greater evidence of the diversity of business is available through a discussion of regulated industries, the defence sector, and the numerous small enterprises which exist within the US business system; this chapter considers their competitive strategies. Finally the problems encountered by US business since 1970 and their responses are examined as the earlier sense of corporate and technological leadership gave way to uncertainty and less sense of direction.

In the long economic boom from 1949 to 1968 output, profits and productivity increased and business prospered. The numbers of single-owner firms, partnerships and corporations increased and the business sector remained highly diverse. However, the durability, growth and profitability of the leading companies contributed to a diverse literature emphasising their power and influence. Averitt identified a 'core' of large corporations dominating the economy.[1] Alfred Chandler's analysis of leading corporations portrayed a managerial capitalism in which the selection of an appropriate corporate organisation enabled firms to expand in scale and to administer their affairs across ever greater distances.[2] The post-war growth of US multinational business lent credence to this view and American production methods and management practices were admired and copied internationally. Literature in economics and management explored the scope for managers to seek goals other than profit-maximisation, but took comfortable profit margins for granted. In 1967 J. K. Galbraith's vision of the large corporation was based on its ability to plan and to exercise control over its environment. This planning was conducted by managers who possessed autonomy through the use of retained earnings and easy access to capital markets.[3] Galbraith, Vance Packard and other critics of US business emphasised the power of large-scale organisations to manipulate consumers via advertising in order to maintain sales, a view echoed by Ralph Nader and the consumer movement of the 1960s.[4] Anti-trust prosecutors suspected large firms of holding their position through anti-competitive methods. Whether positive or negative in tone, all of these portrayals of US business in the 1950s and 1960s were predicated on its dominant position and economic mastery.

Conditions altered dramatically from 1970: four recessions in twelve years produced excess capacity, especially in durable goods industries such as cars and steel, and productivity growth slowed. The impact of recessions was aggravated by more extensive and effective foreign competition as overseas firms, suffering from their own domestic recessions, entered the large American market more aggressively. Manufactured imports were equivalent to only 14 per cent of US domestic production in 1969: a decade later imports were equal to 38 per cent of home production, rising to 45 per cent by 1986. Import penetration was greatest for shoes, clothing, cars, machine-tools and steel, but also had a major impact in the consumer electronics sector. With the greater presence of overseas firms and in the context of changes in consumer demand in the 1970s, there was an increased probability that overseas rather than domestic producers would possess the most efficient operation, greater financial resources or superior products. The 1970s and 1980s ushered in a new era of 'global' competition which undercut earlier American business practices and challenged the post-war emphasis on large, vertically-integrated corporations.[5] The debate about the sources of the recent problems of US business echoes that over Britain's economic performance since the late nineteenth century. As in the British case, there is the challenge of accounting for the capability of business to achieve growth and profitability in one era, but to perform far less well subsequently. These issues are taken up in Chapter 11: this chapter considers the business system itself.

The business system before 1945

The nature of the post-war business system and the dominance of large corporations was a product of earlier influences. Merger waves in the 1890s and 1920s had created large-scale firms in many industries and the US Supreme Court's various interpretations of anti-trust law had accepted a pattern of oligopolistic competition among several big companies rather than monopoly.[6] New products and manufacturing methods were a potential threat which leading firms sought to counter through patents and investments in research and development. Alfred Chandler has argued that the longer-term position of industry leaders depended upon undertaking, and sustaining, a three-pronged investment in large-scale production, distribution and management systems.[7] In industries where such investments provided economies of scale, big business held an advantage in terms of efficiency and established a virtuous and profitable cycle which enabled pioneering firms or first movers to gain a considerable lead over smaller rivals. Moreover the strategy created substantial barriers to entry for any potential rivals by raising the costs and complexity of competing. This was especially significant where brand-names and corporate reputations could be promoted and maintained through advertising. This sequence of events then favoured large firms and industrial concentration. Nonetheless there was diversity. Chandler's grand strategy applied to more capital-intensive manufacturing industries, but elsewhere smaller business remained well to the fore. Even among Chandler's managerial corporations, the degrees of vertical integration and methods of competition varied. The meat-packers invested in production, distribution and management, but also used a pool to regulate prices and competition in the first two decades of the twentieth century until faced by an anti-trust suit. US Steel's domination of its industry was aided by its influence over raw-material supplies and prices, not simple productivity, and its market share was gradually eroded due to the firm's decision to seek steady prices and profits.[8]

During the 1920s business was accorded considerable respect, but the 1930s exposed limits to industry's ability to sustain prosperity and undermined its social standing. Corporate America was on the defensive throughout the 1930s: profits were poor, excess capacity deterred new investment and the expansion of unions challenged managerial supremacy on the shop floor. Generally business was hostile to the New Deal, with only a brief and limited interest in seeking stability through business–government co-operation under the National Recovery Administration (NRA) codes. The ineffectiveness and demise of the NRA and the New Deal's closer alliance with labour unions, plus its welfare policies, emphasised the estrangement between government and business. Corporate liberal supporters of New Deal policies were very much in the minority in the business community.[9] Following the 1937–38 recession New Deal industrial policy, except in coal and oil, switched to a renewed anti-trust campaign in the belief that 'administered prices' in monopolistic industries were the explanation for low levels of new investment and persistently high unemployment.

Against this background World War II had a profound effect. Certain New Deal tendencies were accentuated as the federal government took control over materials, production and prices and the place of labour unions was consolidated. Nonetheless the war years rehabilitated business from its associations with the Depression and business–government relations were more co-operative, with many wartime agencies staffed by '$-a-year' executives seconded to government service. Output and employment expanded rapidly under the stimulus of military demand and, where industry lacked capacity or was unwilling to invest, the government financed defence plants which were then operated by the private sector. Federal sponsorship of research and development work on a range of new technologies was an important stimulus to the electronics, communications and chemicals industries. The resurgence was dominated by the leading firms since the majority of government contracts went to the 100 largest corporations, reflecting the emphasis on mass production of tanks, aircraft, steel and munitions. Despite specific federal assistance, smaller manufacturers received far less government business and were dependent on obtaining sub-contracts. The revival of the fortunes and reputation of business was confirmed in the immediate post-war years. Despite the uncertainties of reconversion and post-war inflation, the economy embarked on a consumer boom rather than the feared return to depression, and 'pent-up' consumer demand provided the incentive for business to exploit the new technologies from the 1930s and war period. By the 1950s the capacity of business to 'deliver the goods' had restored profits and the confidence of business, and the public, in its economic role. In the sphere of labour relations, corporate America acted to confine the role of unions.

Industrial structure, corporate strategy and company organisation

The largest 100 manufacturing corporations' share of assets had fallen below the level of the 1930s by 1945, but rebounded strongly to 1960, then levelled off and increased again in the 1970s and 1980s.[10] An alternative measure is the share of added value in each manufacturing industry accounted for by the four largest producers; by this criterion the rise in concentration between 1947 and 1972 was more modest. Greater concentration remained evident if non-industrial firms were added: the largest 200 US companies accounted for 30 per cent of output by value added in 1947, but by 1970 their share was 42 per cent. A further indication of greater stability among the leading companies was lower turnover in the list of the 100 largest companies between 1935 and 1977 than had been the case earlier in the century.

The established strategies of large-scale investments in production, distribution and management were applied more widely in manufacturing after 1945. The business methods and managerial hierarchies pioneered by DuPont and General Motors were adopted more widely during the 1950s and became a staple of business-school teaching as the professionalisation of management proceeded apace. The professionalisation of management implied a certain similarity in the outlook and actions of managers and at IBM, for instance, there were rigid dress-codes. Such features and the complexity of the bureaucratic systems led to Whyte's idea of 'Organisation Man'. Overseas operations furnished an additional source of profits for leading corporations which strengthened their position *vis-à-vis* their smaller domestic rivals. The major firms' profitability supplied internal funds for expansion and they had better access than smaller businesses to capital markets.

Chandler's interpretation of the rise of big business emphasised its superior efficiency and assumed a basic similarity in terms of corporate organisation. In practice, as Chandler's case-studies acknowledged, leading firms varied in their precise structure and strategy. In part this reflected variations in the precise advantages of size and in part differences in how firms chose to exploit them. Porter identified certain generic strategies, principally cost leadership and product differentiation, and the balance of strategy varied between these poles in different firms and industries.[11] In principle economies of scale favoured minimising costs in order to maintain market leadership, and this influence was apparent in the declining position of smaller firms in US manufacturing for two decades after 1954. But non-price competition had its attractions.[12] With incomes rising, firms had more scope to exploit advertising and features other than price. In consumer goods sectors, such as food or automobiles, firms went further in developing forms of product differentiation and branding as means of maintaining sales and profits. Car-makers endeavoured to balance economies of scale through the use of standard components, with the element of marketing advantages from supplying a variety of higher-priced vehicles and regular model changes. To some extent economies of scale could be reflected in higher profits rather than minimal costs and, where market shares were fairly stable, leading firms moderated price competition or reached temporary, sometimes local, price-fixing agreements. Large firms were present in the service and financial sectors and they too exploited economies of scale in financial resources, reputation and bargaining power with suppliers. The further expansion of supermarkets in regional and national chains was a striking example of the scope for big business in wholesaling and distribution. By 1991 supermarkets accounted for 9 per cent of retail outlets, but had 71 per cent of total sales.

Developments of new technologies, such as plastics and electronics, encouraged smaller enterprises, but often large business had established itself in these areas during the 1930s and 1940s, as in the case of the chemicals and synthetic materials firms. At the same time new materials did cut into the sales of rival or substitute products. The metal trades had to adjust to new materials, as did the cotton and woollen textile manufacturers. In the case of the steel industry a slow pace of technological change, antagonistic industrial relations and the passing-on of wage rises into higher prices signalled a decline in competitiveness during the 1950s and 1960s which was reflected in the increased level of steel imports. Other companies coped with technological change more effectively. IBM used its powerful position in mechanical data-processing to finance the development of its computer business, building technical systems as a barrier to entry for rival firms.[13] In the pharmaceuticals industry, leading firms combined intensive research and development and patent protection with vigorous marketing in a fashion which maintained high profits, but deterred new entrants.[14] In some cases federal policies for disposing of defence plants created new competitors, but these new ventures either struggled, as with Kaizer–Fraser in automobiles, or were accommodated by the industry leader, as in aluminium. In electronics, new ventures and smaller companies had greater scope, but there tended to be a shake-out of firms following a product life-cycle pattern of initially rapid growth and then growing concentration.

Diversification and conglomerates

Diversification was another strategy which sustained the position of large corporations against the threat of declining profits due to industrial maturity. Major companies developed their research and development activities as a route to new products from the 1920s.[15] For instance, oil and rubber companies extended their chemicals businesses into synthetic materials. In response to the Depression many leading firms widened their product ranges to compensate for weaknesses in their primary business. Wartime restrictions on civilian sales and the availability of government contracts in defence-related lines forced further moves into new areas, and private-sector activity received a powerful added impetus from the federal government's wartime financing of research and development. Overall manufacturers sustained a high rate of new product introduction during the 1930s and 1940s, with a growing tendency to add products in new areas of activity.[16] The earlier investments in the search for innovations and the continuation of a high rate of federal support after 1945 generated new products and substitutes for existing goods, particularly in the more high-technology industries. Consequently this incentive to diversification was most evident in the chemicals, electrical machinery, petroleum and rubber industries as well as in food manufacturing. The revival of consumer demand provided the incentive to bring new products into full-scale production. Fligstein identified a movement away from emphasis on a single industry into production in closely-related areas between 1939 and 1959.[17]

The economic advantages of diversification were most pronounced where firms could attain economies of scope, that is the capacity to use existing resources, expertise or facilities in producing and marketing a related product.[18] In 1939 22 per cent of the 100 largest firms had interests in activities closely related to their primary business, but forty years later the proportion was almost 50 per cent.[19] Diversification also provided a means of investing profits from one sector into new areas. Tobacco firms expanded into pet foods, foods and distribution as cigarette sales peaked in the late 1950s and defence contractors frequently sought to increase their civilian business to counter fluctuations in military expenditure. In this way

Table 7.1 *Types of merger of large US manufacturing and minerals companies based on assets acquired, 1948–79 (%)*

Type of merger	1948–55	1956–63	1964–71	1972–79
Horizontal	39.0	18.7	12.0	14.9
Vertical	12.7	20.0	6.6	8.3
Product extension	36.1	36.9	38.9	28.2
Market extension	2.1	6.7	7.7	3.0
Pure conglomerate	10.1	17.7	34.8	45.5

Note: Product extension is a move to a similar product for sale via existing outlets; market extension is a move to sell an existing product in a new geographic region.
Source: Scherer and Ross, *Industrial Market Structure and Economic Performance*, p. 157.[22]

diversification reduced the threat of declining profitability in maturing industries. Diversification was an attractive option because the M-form or decentralised management structure offered managers a mechanism for controlling diverse business activities within a single corporation; it provided an organisational structure that made diversification appear more practicable and likely to be profitable.[20]

The most pronounced form of diversification was the conglomerate firm, a company whose activities encompassed a wide range of unrelated fields. In 1948 only 2 per cent of the largest 100 firms had operations in unrelated industries, but the proportion was 27.3 per cent by 1979. Conglomerate mergers accounted for only 10 per cent of all mergers between 1948 and 1955, but represented over one-third of merger activity from 1964 to 1971.[21]

The new conglomerate movement can be illustrated by considering its leading practitioners. Litton Industries acquired 115 other firms in the 1960s; LTV, an electronics company, made thirty-two acquisitions which included meat-packing, food, pharmaceuticals and iron and steel businesses. Gulf and Western undertook sixty-seven acquisitions covering films, sugar, zinc, cigars, fertilisers, paper, publishing, insurance and real estate. Other leading conglomerate firms were ITT (International Telephone and Telegraph Corporation), Beatrice and Thompson–Ramo–Wooldridge (TRW). The conglomerate movement gained momentum from intense merger activity during the 1950s and 1960s due to a combination of favourable influences. There was scope to finance purchases through rising share values and by restructuring acquired firms. In mature, slower-growing industries, if a firm's assets exceeded its share valuations entrepreneurs could split up the businesses or raise the earnings per share ratio by absorbing a business into a firm with a higher share valuation.[23] The other prominent strand in conglomerate activity was mergers involving businesses in the expansive electronics sector, where there was a high rate of new company formations and the financial markets' optimism supplied ready capital and lucrative share dealings. Ironically competition policy also promoted the use of a conglomerate strategy for growth. The 1950 Celler–Kefauver Act declared horizontal mergers, that is those among firms in the same line of business, to be illegal if they could be seen as reducing competition. Once this policy had been confirmed by the US Supreme Court following a series of anti-trust prosecutions, firms had a powerful incentive to exploit the conglomerate form, since it was difficult to portray the acquisition of firms in different industries as anti-competitive.[24]

The diversity of business

Despite the prominence of large corporations, the US business system retained considerable diversity. There were different business cultures within the major corporations and regional locations, managerial backgrounds and market conditions varied between industries. Even within firms, divisions, such as marketing, engineering or accounting, had rather different objectives and personnel. Diversity was most readily apparent in the case of regulated industries, the defence sector and the numerous small firms and partnerships.

Business and regulation

In certain industries regulatory policies set the parameters of numbers of firms, pricing policy and other aspects of competition. Among the regulated sectors were banking, telecommunications, railroads, trucking, radio and television, natural gas and airlines. The pattern of regulation reflected the belief that such industries were either prone to 'natural monopolies' which obviated competition or that they were marked by a particular type of 'public interest' which justified intervention. Policy was driven by the impact of economic or political crises in particular industries and as a result the New Deal established a considerable legacy of regulation.[25] Control of regulation rested with federal agencies such as the Federal Communications Commission, the Civil Aeronautics Board or the Interstate Commerce Commission. As well as federal influence, there were elements of state and local control and regulatory policies were open to interpretation by the courts. During the 1950s and 1960s regulation maintained stable industrial structures and regulated industries were marked by incremental changes in technology and restrictions on entry. The Civil Aeronautics Board allocated airline routes and, thus, controlled entry, and airlines primarily competed through increasing capacity and maximising the number of non-stop flights. Railroads regulation maintained an extensive network, but traffic was lost to trucks with the regulatory regime restricting railroads' scope to respond. Competition occurred primarily through quality of service rather than price, with the main achievement being the creation of national networks in telecommunications, air travel and trucking.

The highly-regulated banking system was characterised by a very fragmented structure both in terms of banks and the regulatory system. Long-held suspicions of large financial institutions had been strengthened during the banking crisis of the early 1930s when state and federal regulations separated commercial and investment banking. Oversight lay with the Federal Reserve System, itself a hybrid of national and regional offices, the Federal Deposit Insurance Corporation and state regulatory agencies as well as federal agencies concerned with particular segments of the financial system. Central direction increased, but the regulatory divisions remained and banking laws restricted interstate and, in many cases, even intrastate branch banking. The result was a diverse mix of some large and many small banks, all primarily catering to local or regional markets and with a low rate of failure. There were 14,126 commercial banks in 1945, still 13,690 in 1970 and nearly 12,000 in 1991. The number of branches increased from 3,723 to 22,508 between 1945 and 1970, but it was a piecemeal and mainly local process. Where interstate branching was allowed, as in California, major banks expanded, and elsewhere they used holding companies as a means of acquiring several banks. But growth was not straightforward, and New York banks faced regulatory and political resistance to their efforts to follow their customers into the suburbs by opening branches or acquiring other banks.[26] Federal restrictions on commercial banks' rates on deposits provided scope for rapid expansion by other, less constrained financial institutions, such as insurance companies, finance companies, pensions trusts and even savings and loan companies. These specialists benefited not only from their ability to pay higher rates, but from a general expansion in public use of finance, notably for pensions and insurance, and demand for more specialist services.

The defence sector

Defence-related business was one distinctive sector. Links between business and the defence establishment existed before World War II, but in 1961 Eisenhower's reference to the economic and political implications of a military–industrial complex highlighted their mushroom growth after 1945.[27] Military contracts cut across several different types of business system. In some cases, such as textiles or food, defence business was merely one element in a broader consumer market and standard mass-production methods. But the highly specialist nature of certain military applications led to some products which were customised or made by small batch methods and had little or no civilian application.[28] In the case of semiconductors and computers, military demand supported research and early production and fundamentally shaped industrial structure and technology.

The development of the electronics and instruments industries in Silicon Valley and Orange County was underpinned by military orders and research funding in the 1950s. Prime contracts were dominated by large corporations, but small firms and new ventures received support, especially for initial research. Networks of sub-contracting sustained a more competitive element within the defence sector and included long-term relationships and contracts between major producers of aircraft, missiles or ships. Contractual ties were accompanied by the flow of personnel between defence industries and the military and other government agencies so that the defence sector has its own business culture. The development of programme management and systems approaches to planning and completing major weapons contracts provided organisational and managerial responses to the complexities of co-ordinating the activities of numerous suppliers with the requirements of their military customers.[29] The tendency of, say, the navy or air force to favour a particular supplier created its own set of links.

The defence business involved elements of competition and uncertainty. Uncertainties were inherent in the fluctuating nature of defence expenditure and the often limited scope for transferring capacity to non-defence business. The aircraft industry faced major problems during the contractions of orders after World War II and the Korean and Vietnam wars, as well as during the late 1980s. Several of the early conglomerates had roots in defence-related activities and the prospect of declining defence expenditure prompted mergers between Grumman and Northrop and between Martin–Marietta and Lockheed in 1994. The defence contractor faced customers with the capacity and incentive to alter product specifications unilaterally so that even 'cost-plus' contracting might yield only moderate returns.[30]

Smaller firms and their strategies

There was a periphery to Averitt's core of large corporations and the average entrepreneur ran a small or medium-sized business. Overall small business lost ground within manufacturing and, to a lesser degree, in its traditional strongholds in the service sector from 1945 to the mid-1970s.[31] Small firms fared best in retailing, construction and services as the growth of consumer demand provided greater opportunities. They relied on personal reputation, contractual ties and access to networks of credit.[32] Despite the growth of chains and supermarkets, independent stores remained important, primarily as specialist food stores, restaurants and bars. Their business strategies included concentrating on high-value goods, offering particular services such as convenience or longer hours or specialising in specific lines as the market expanded. Although service industries contained many large companies, there was an expansion in the number of businesses supplying specialist services such as management consultancies, brokers, accountancy services, secretarial agencies and advertising agencies. Some of these providers of business services expanded into major corporations in their own right, like the J. Walter Thompson advertising agency or the McKinsey consultancy firm. The development of a prestigious corporate image could lead to higher fees, greater access to information and business contacts and advantages in recruiting staff. Even so advertising, legal or consultancy firms often retained partnership forms of organisation and the importance of personal contacts limited the extent of economies of scale. There was a tendency for key personnel to establish new independent firms and the major financial districts were distinguished by clusters of specialist enterprises trading heavily on reputation and trust. The finance, insurance and real-estate sectors had a large number of partnerships throughout the post-war period. The construction business was characterised by a plethora of small firms, emerging new specialisms and sub-contracting.

Small companies were present in manufacturing, especially in less capital-intensive industries, and the development of new technology spawned waves of new businesses in electronics and plastics during the 1950s. Some enterprises, such as Hewlett-Packard or Microsoft, developed into industry leaders, but many others fell by the wayside as product lines matured. For the smaller firm or even the medium-sized company in an industry dominated by large firms, there were various strategies for survival.[33] One approach was to operate as a supplier to a larger manufacturer or a major retailer, thereby obtaining substantial contracts and perhaps support in product development. Other small companies differentiated their product or services in some way in order to attract premium prices. Specialisation in one segment of a market or the flexibility to meet a range of customised orders contributed to the persistence of smaller companies in branches of the metal trades.[34] Government policies offered some support for small business. In 1953 earlier forms of assistance were merged into the Small Business Administration, which provided loans, and there were tax incentives.[35]

Piore and Sabel have argued that the tendency for large corporations to integrate separate stages of production and distribution left the US business system lacking a base of small specialised companies linked by those contractual ties and personal connections which created an industrial district or region.[36] Yet this generalisation is too sweeping. Vertical integration was far from complete and even the leading car-makers relied to varying degrees on buying in parts. Detroit or the steel towns were dominated by major corporations whose orders determined local conditions, but they also supported a mix of smaller, specialist firms with their distinctive business cultures. Other industries contained networks of separate small firms connected by market relationships rather than the vertical integration characteristic of core firms in capital-intensive sectors. At various points the electronics industry and the computer business involved a mix of large companies and smaller specialists and suppliers.[37] The personal computer industry developed out of a loose mix of educated enthusiasts and a hobbyists' culture where systems were based on existing components. Antitrust policies also exerted an influence. For instance, in the film industry the major production and distribution companies divested their cinema chains following a Supreme Court anti-trust decision. The general decline of the integrated studio system resulted in a diverse industry headed by the major companies which financed film-making and dominated wholesale distribution, but operated through contracts with independent film producers and the combined efforts of numerous small specialist suppliers.[38] Hollywood's successful transition into television production was based on a similar clustering of specialist companies with varying degrees of integration and devices to smooth co-operation.[39]

In many sectors small firms tried to attain some of the advantages of scale through co-operative purchasing arrangements such as drug-store chains. Franchising was a significant area of corporate growth from the 1850s and, as Dicke noted, was used extensively between the wars as part of a managerial emphasis on the importance of marketing. It combined elements of large and small or independent business. For large firms marketing was critical to ensure profits and steady production, but direct involvement in retailing was costly, especially following the introduction of anti-chain store legislation in the 1930s. Reliance on completely independent agents carried risks such as loss of business if the agent switched suppliers or damage to a brand-name if agents were of poor quality. A common response was the establishment of franchises where retailers sold a firm's product under specified conditions and received support in terms of advertising and marketing advice. For the franchise-holder the link provided access to outside expertise and certain economies of scale, but retained elements of an independent business. A particular growth area after 1945 was 'business-format' franchising where the supplier provided a brand-image and a system for its delivery, including preparing and selling the item as well as training in accounting and customer relations. Again, the petrol-station chains, car dealerships and Howard Johnson restaurants had pre-war origins, but the later growth of franchising was symbolised by fast-food businesses like McDonald's or by the Coca-Cola bottling operations, as well as real-estate operations.[40] There were certain special cases in the sports business where team franchises were part of league systems and operated within their own regulatory frameworks.

Franchising was facilitated by the post-war expansion of consumer expenditure on services which extended territory favourable to the strategy. The franchiser earned franchise fees, supplied goods and services and could expand rapidly with relatively little capital outlay. The franchise-

holder obtained a less risky route into business compared to the high attrition rate among newly-formed independent companies, although by the
1980s the rising cost of popular franchises was restricting the number of
potential entrants.[41] Franchising offered economies of scale, for example,
in advertising and retained the franchise-holder's personal incentive to
maximise effort. Equally there were risks to the franchise-holder in dependency on a single supplier whose licensing charges could be substantial and
whose effectiveness in sustaining the brand-image was so critical to the
business. Dissatisfaction among car dealers led to federal legislation in 1956
and protection was extended to other franchise-holders in the 1970s as the
practical limits on their autonomy and the dangers from unscrupulous
franchisers received greater attention.[42] Nonetheless it remained a growth
area during the 1980s.

American business since 1970: a new era?

From the early 1970s American companies faced the challenge of responding to greater competition and technological change in more turbulent
markets at a time when their financial standing was weak. There were
several recessions and inflation accelerated under the impetus of the
Organisation of Petroleum Exporting Countries'(OPEC) price hikes in
1972–73 and 1978–79. Profit margins declined and blue-chip companies
such as Ford experienced serious losses. The rate of turnover among the
100 largest US firms rose appreciably in the decade to 1987. The result was
a kaleidoscope of corporate strategies and a concern that fundamental
flaws existed in the US business practices which had appeared so effective
during the post-war boom. Large corporate organisations created in the
1950s and 1960s no longer possessed sufficient competitive advantages to
deter foreign competition or to ignore its impact. From being models of
best practice in management and production, US business was less dynamic
and now looked to learn from other approaches, particularly Japanese business.

The clearest case was the automobile industry. Imports of sub-compact
cars from Europe and Japan rose steadily from the 1950s, often as families'
second cars, but US manufacturers retained their hold on the lucrative
markets for larger vehicles. However, a crisis in US car-making developed
as a result of sudden, unforeseen shifts in the general environment which
allowed overseas producers to expand market share rapidly. New car sales
faltered in the 1970s and excess capacity increased. At the same time the
leap in fuel prices shifted consumer preference towards smaller, more fuel-
efficient cars which Japanese and European makers already supplied in
their domestic markets and were better able to produce than were US
manufacturers used to making larger, more up-market 'gas-guzzlers'. The
investment costs of transferring to new models and production set-ups

were difficult to finance, given weak sales and heavy losses. General Motors, .Ford and Chrysler all experienced financial crises in the late 1970s and only a federal loan saved Chrysler from bankruptcy. In the longer term Japanese car firms could design new vehicles and bring them into production more quickly. Critics pointed to the failure of US car-makers to achieve sustained improvements in efficiency or innovation and concluded that their products and corporate strategies were ill-equipped to meet the changed circumstances.[43] When US firms extended their model range, this undermined economies of scale in the existing system of branch plants, and factories were closed to reduce capacity and to focus production of individual models in fewer plants.[44] The sequence of events had wider ramifications, since the car-makers' problems affected the bloc of producer goods industries and Japanese component suppliers and tyre-makers followed their corporate customers into the US. In the late 1960s US tyre manufacturers had invested in the production of new tyre designs, but held back from the more fundamental re-equipping necessary to make radial tyres. When higher fuel costs led US car-makers to adopt radial tyres rapidly after 1973, European tyre companies exploited their greater expertise in radial tyre manufacture. Domestic tyre producers had to undertake reinvestment just as the greater durability of radials accentuated the recession's impact on sales and profits.[45]

The post-1970 developments signalled a powerful revival of multinational activity by nations, notably Japan and Germany, which had been significant earlier in the century. Japanese multinational interests in the United States had been dominated by trade, banking and other services and the level of these investments rose rapidly in the 1980s.[46] Japanese manufacturing activity in the United States also increased as protectionist rhetoric and the fact of quota agreements threatened imports. Further foreign capital flowed into steel, tyres and electronics as overseas producers exploited their competitive advantages, encouraged by the low value of the US dollar. The challenges from overseas were evident in the US share of total overseas direct investment which declined from 48 per cent in 1973 to 31 per cent in 1988.[47] The effects were most pronounced in manufacturing and the distribution of US multinational investment shifted towards services during the 1970s and 1980s.

Business response to economic problems

The mix of instability, technical change and government policy varied between industries, but the overall effect was a search for managerial strategies to cope with more uncertain times.[48] The search process proceeded haltingly and firms often lacked any sense of direction or experimented with various approaches at different times or in particular parts of their operations. There were attempts to implement established strategies more fully, but also experiments with new approaches and often several strategies were deployed simultaneously. In all sectors the most common response was retrenchment through factory closures and redundancies. The relationship between business and unions became more antagonistic as companies endeavoured to limit wage increases and increasingly renegotiated agreements on working practices. Unions demanded higher wages in response to inflation, but were thrown on to the defensive by the spread of plant closures. The pressure on major firms was intensified by the entry of new firms using new, less capital-intensive technology, located in areas where labour was cheaper and often non-union. Both overseas companies and US firms located new factories in less industrialised districts as a route to a cheaper, younger and less unionised workforce.

The longer term response to competition varied. In consumer goods industries, such as food and tobacco, international competition was less potent, though European firms absorbed some US firms amid a general sequence of mergers and reorganisations. In the food business fluctuating sales had long been met by a mix of heavy promotion of long-running or staple brands with periodic promotion of 'new and improved' versions, plus a high turnover of speculative new products. In the 1980s firms responded to changes in consumer tastes and the increased segmentation of markets with the introduction of lines of 'lite' foods and more diverse ranges of prepared foods.[49] The persistence of established strategies was evident in other consumer goods sectors such as clothing where firms marketed a diverse product range and sought cheaper labour at home and overseas. A divergence of business strategies was apparent in retailing where the conventional supermarkets were losing ground to, on the one hand, even larger superstores with extensive lines and, on the other hand, to warehouse stores which sold fewer lines at lower prices. The influences on the defence sector were rather different from the general economic cycle. In real terms defence expenditure declined from 1968 to 1976 with the American withdrawal from Vietnam accentuating the downward trend. However, the Carter and Reagan administrations presided over an extraordinary defence build-up in which defence spending rose at an annual rate of 5.5 per cent between 1980 and 1985 and reached its highest level in real terms during the post-war period.[50] It was a major stimulus to the ordnance, aerospace, shipbuilding and communications industries. Among publishing and media firms there was a vogue for the creation of large-scale corporations with the aim of exploiting economies of scale.

Chandler detected continuity with earlier corporate strategies as a means by which certain American industrial companies remained internationally competitive.[51] He identified chemicals, pharmaceuticals, electronics and aircraft manufacture as 'high-tech' industries where leading firms continued to invest, improving their capabilities for production, research and distribution. Chandler suggested that in 'stable-tech' industries, such as automobiles, rubber, oil and metals, US companies experienced the full force of increased competition, declining profits and escalating debt which all constrained new investment. Chandler's division between high-tech and stable-tech firms is rather arbitrary and his stable-tech group of industries encountered problems precisely because products and production methods changed after 1973. Some long-established manufacturers abandoned their original, now less profitable, lines of business in response to the immediate financial crisis or following a review of prospects in related sectors. For instance, Goodrich and Uniroyal retreated from tyre production in favour of their chemicals and plastics divisions and in effect both firms pursued economies of scope within a narrower range. By the 1980s management literature advocated moving away from 'mature' industries or focusing on 'core' businesses in contrast to the earlier notions of unlimited managerial capabilities. Economies of scale were still important. Indeed US multinationals, like IBM and ITT, made greater efforts to integrate the previously discrete operations of their overseas subsidiaries into a global business, with the aim of maximising economies of scale.

US firms began to make greater use of coalitions with other firms in the form of technical agreements, joint ventures and marketing arrangements. There was a shift between 1970 and 1982 towards alliances with overseas firms as US business sought to improve its access to technological expertise. US car producers turned to co-operative agreements with overseas manufacturers in order to obtain access to superior engines and production expertise; Toyota and General Motors established a California plant as a joint venture.

In manufacturing there was a distinct shift to less centralised business structures. The recessions of the 1970s undercut the logic of a mass production strategy and made economies of scope and greater flexibility in production more significant.[52] Automobile firms were a leading example of a more general attempt to identify and imitate the sources of Japanese competitive advantage. Japanese 'lean production' systems of manufacturing yielded lower costs, higher productivity and superior products.[53] Japanese work practices and labour relations appeared more flexible and more co-operative than those in the United States.[54] American mass-production methods were perceived as too rigid to accommodate sudden switches in consumer tastes or adapt to volatile markets since US manufacturers took longer to design and market new products. In organisational terms US firms appeared too vertically integrated and their management structures were more hierarchical and complex than their Japanese equivalents. Indeed Piore and Sabel argued that computers, new forms of telecommunications and an accelerated rate of technical change favoured decentralisation away from the large, vertically integrated company towards smaller-scale operations linked by contracts and networks of business relations.[55]

Such analysis provided the basis for a response to the problems of US business after the initial phase of contraction. US firms moved to introduce new working practices, reducing vertical integration and trying to reduce the size and complexity of management structures. The impetus in growth sectors, like computers and electronics, came from the pace of product innovation. IBM, the dominant computing firm, was a large, vertically-integrated corporation with a complex management structure; its business was based on mainframe computers and its established market share posed a major barrier to new entrants. In the 1980s, the development of higher-powered chips and smaller personal computers weakened IBM's position and profits compared to the producers of smaller computers and the software houses, notably Microsoft. Such firms thrived on rapid product innovation and a decentralised structure, that is buying in components rather than making them and operating through networks of small special-ised firms, rather than the IBM model of absorbing most activities in the one business. By the early 1990s IBM's response was to dismiss workers and split its divisions into separate or more autonomous businesses. Saxenian explained the capacity of Silicon Valley to adjust to new technologies by identifying a system of firms linked via co-operative contractual arrange-ments and a common, open work culture.[56] In contrast the problems of the electronics industry in the Boston area in the 1980s were linked, in Saxenian's work, to its emphasis on vertically-integrated firms which were less receptive to new ideas.

It is less clear whether these events signalled a fundamental shift of prior-ities in favour of production. In practice changes were implemented in a fragmented way; even Japanese-owned factories in the United States rarely applied all elements of 'lean production'.[57] Where firms were laying off workers or closing plants, the Japanese model served as an additional ratio-nale for retrenchment rather than a basis for investing in radically different strategies. The established practice of close managerial control over shop-floor operations was intensified rather than reduced as manufacturers endeavoured to increase work effort and reduce wage costs. The introduc-tion of robots and computer-controlled machine-tools followed Japanese practice, but maintained the emphasis on controlling assembly operations closely. As a result changes involved an element of compromise. The impact of schemes for greater worker participation were constrained by taking place in the context of a managerial emphasis on maximising output and reducing employment.[58] Similarly, where firms turned to outside suppliers, the development of co-operation and trust was a long-term project and often the initial emphasis was on price rather than loyalty. Indeed, to the extent that vertical integration in manufacturing had been a solution to a low level of trust and then limited the incentive to promote such co-opera-tion, it was hard to switch to institutional systems based on a high degree of trust.

The restructuring of large enterprises was facilitated by the capital markets and by changes in regulatory policy. Many of the 1960s conglomerates performed poorly in the 1970s and were now perceived as poorly managed or excessively diversified. In the financial and merger boom of the mid-1980s financial entrepreneurs bought out companies in order to dismantle and sell off their different parts as separate businesses.[59] Such operations were facilitated by the availability of 'junk bonds' and other forms of short-term debt which enabled firms or financial operators to purchase companies for comparatively small outlays and then to repay debt through the sale of parts of the business. The conglomerate logic was reversed with arguments in favour of focusing on core businesses in order to maximise production and marketing skills. Even where corporations successfully resisted takeover bids, they often sold off parts of their business in order to counter criticisms of a lack of focus or to reduce debts incurred in the contest. The regulatory regime which had deterred mergers of firms in the same line of business altered, too, as overseas competition in key sectors challenged domestic oligopolies and business and government perceived size as essential to compete in world markets. The move to deregulation and the Reagan administration's emphasis on free markets further weakened the regulatory restraints on mergers.

The late 1970s were marked by a rapid transformation in the scale and scope of regulation which triggered shifts in business strategy in such regulated sectors as banking, trucking, telecommunications and airlines. There were new entrants, a loss of market share for leading firms and greater price competition. Vietor identified several corporate strategies in the airline business after 1978. Existing regional carriers, such as US Air in Pittsburgh, expanded their operations across the country and smaller commuter airlines concentrated on local traffic from small cities. A rather different niche strategy was adopted by some eighteen new entrants between 1979 and 1985, such as People Express, who chose a policy of cheap fares for a basic level of service between a few major cities. For established major carriers, deregulation altered the basis upon which they had made decisions about aircraft, routes, labour and operating costs. Their response was to reduce fares, wages and employment and to seek fundamental changes in working practices in order to compete with the smaller non-union carriers. In the cases of Continental and Braniff, reorganisations after a period of bankruptcy were used to escape from existing labour contracts in favour of lower wages, reduced fringe benefits and fewer rules on working practices. However both companies remained financially weak and their low-cost approach held revenues low.

A more successful strategy was deployed by American Airlines, United and Delta which reduced costs and capacity, and exploited economies of scale in operations and marketing by concentrating on directing traffic in and out of particular hub cities, in place of the previous pattern of direct flights to many destinations. This strategy was sustained by acquisitions of regional carriers, co-operative agreements with commuter airlines, and price competition on selected routes with the low-cost airlines. By the mid-1980s the effects of excess capacity, exacerbated by the 1979–82 recession, were reflected in a swirl of mergers and exits from the industry, leading to a rise in concentration.[60]

In the financial sector the expansion of global capital markets plus deregulation in the United States and overseas stimulated expansion of branch banking and the creation of financial institutions performing a far wider range of functions. The earlier rather stable arrangements were superseded by mergers and an emphasis on the potential of new technology and integrated businesses to generate higher throughput of business and economies of scale. In the banking sector multinational expansion was a common feature for banks in all leading economies with cross-cutting flows of investment. The underlying factors had been present since the late 1950s in the shape of incentives to maximise returns by circumventing or capitalising on varying regulatory regimes plus the effects of improved communications. The post-1970 expansion of the international capital market provided further impetus, but the process assumed an even more spectacular form in the 1980s as deregulation allowed financial institutions greater access to overseas markets and accentuated the movements of capital. As in the case of airlines, there was retrenchment from the mid-1980s as results failed to match expectations, especially when falling energy prices undermined investments in oil and related industries. Commercial and investment banks pruned recently acquired activities such as securities dealing. In the savings and loan sector changes in the regulatory regime stimulated higher-risk lending which culminated in a federal rescue operation in the face of huge losses.

Business responses to the changed conditions included the political sphere. From the mid-1970s corporate concerns over inflation and rising federal spending made little impact on public policy. Even during the more conservative Nixon administration, business exercised little influence, despite a growing desire to restrain wage increases. A flow of legislation introduced new regulatory controls, such as environmental standards, which affected a wide range of industries and, as McQuaid suggested, this type of regulation was less amenable to lobbying by a single industry.[61] In the context of recession, business had every incentive to lower its costs and avert the potential future costs of compliance. Leading executives initiated a campaign to reverse the recent legislation controlling their conduct.[62] In contrast to earlier disparate lobbying efforts by individual firms or trade associations, the new strategy emphasised the common interests of business in checking regulation and aimed to reduce union influence. This more co-operative effort included peak business associations, such as the newly-established Business Roundtable and the United States Chamber of

Commerce, and drew on the influence of local business organisations. This far more effective and assertive business lobby criticised consumer, worker-protection and environmental legislation, sought the extension of deadlines for attaining environmental standards and lobbied more intensively in Congress to block further legislation. However the strategy developed a broader momentum. Drawing on evidence of declining profits and a loss of international competitiveness, business organisations linked their problems to federal intervention and taxation in general. Business leaders demanded more favourable corporate tax policies and, where import penetration was rapid, US industry sought protection from trade barriers. Pressure from business and government resulted in a series of voluntary export agreements restricting imports of steel from Japan during the 1970s and 1980s and imports of automobiles in the early 1980s. One effect was a move towards higher-value models by the Japanese industry which improved their profits and extended the long-term threat from imports further across the car market. On a more localised level, hard-pressed executives frequently sought to avert unwanted takeovers through the passage of protective state laws which raised the costs of acquisition.

By the 1990s the US business system remained characterised by concentration in terms of the leading position of large firms in many industries. However, the earlier perceptions of the large corporations' mastery now appeared as reflections of the calmer economic waters of the 1950s and 1960s. Corporate strategies displayed considerable diversity across the post-war years with variations between sectors, by size of firm, and in the degrees of centralisation in large firms. There was a tendency towards concentration where economies of scale were significant, but the regulatory context, either for specific industries or through general anti-trust policy, established parameters for industry structures and forms of competition. The role of business in the United State's relatively slow growth was twofold. On the one hand, within firms the post-war tendency to emphasise financial controls and targets became detached from concerns with innovation and productivity. On the other hand, the multinational activities of US corporations contributed to growth overseas and foreign competitors proved adept at incorporating US technology and management methods. Both elements were rational managerial responses to post-war prosperity, changes in US consumer demand and expanding overseas markets, but neither equipped American firms to cope with unstable conditions and greater foreign competition.

Notes

1 Robert T. Averitt, *The Dual Economy* (New York, 1968).
2 Alfred D. Chandler, *Strategy and Structure* (Cambridge, MA, 1962).
3 John Kenneth Galbraith, *The New Industrial State* (New York, 1967), chapter 7.
4 Vance Packard, *The Hidden Persuaders* (London, 1957); J. K. Galbraith, *The*

Affluent Society (London, 1957); Galbraith, *The New Industrial State*; C. Wright Mills, *The Power Elite* (Oxford, 1956); William H. Whyte, *The Organisation Man* (London, 1957).

5 Scott Lash and John Urry, *The End of Organized Capitalism* (Madison, WI, 1987).

6 Naomi Lamoreaux, *The Great Merger Movement in American Business, 1895–1904* (Cambridge, 1985).

7 Alfred D. Chandler, *Scale and Scope: The Dynamics of Industrial Capitalism* (Cambridge, MA, 1990).

8 Lamoreaux, *The Great Merger Movement in American Business*, pp. 143–58.

9 Kim McQuaid, *Big Business and Presidential Power: From FDR to Reagan* (New York, 1982), chapter 1.

10 F. M. Scherer and David Ross, *Industrial Market Structure and Economic Performance* (3rd edn, Boston, MA, 1990), pp. 62, 70–1, 84.

11 Michael Porter, *Competitive Strategy: Techniques for Analysing Industries and Competitors* (New York, 1980); Michael Porter, *Competitive Advantage: Creating and Sustaining Superior Performance* (New York, 1985).

12 Chandler, *Scale and Scope*, pp. 605–12.

13 For example see Richard Thomas DeLamarter, *Big Blue: IBM's Use and Abuse of Power* (New York, 1986), pp. 18–20, 30–6; Franklin M. Fisher, James W. McKie and Richard B. Mancke, *IBM and the US Data Processing Industry: An Economic History* (New York, 1983), pp. 19–20, 94–8.

14 Ann Roell Markusen, *Profit Cycles, Oligopoly, and Regional Development* (Cambridge, MA, 1987), pp. 141–50.

15 Jon Didricksen, 'The Development of Diversified and Conglomerate Firms in the US, 1920–1970', *Business History Review*, 46(2), 1972, pp. 202–19.

16 For evidence see the discussion in Neil Fligstein, *The Transformation of Corporate Control* (Cambridge, MA, 1990), pp. 148–60.

17 *Ibid.*, p. 261, table 8.1.

18 Chandler, *Scale and Scope*.

19 Fligstein, *The Transformation of Corporate Control*, p. 261, table 8.1.

20 On the advantages of the M-form see Chandler, *Strategy and Structure*; Alfred D. Chandler, *The Visible Hand: The Managerial Revolution in American Business* (Cambridge., MA, 1977) and Fligstein, *The Transformation of Corporate Control*, pp. 232–8, 275–7.

21 Robert Sobel, *The Age of Giant Corporations: A Microeconomic History of American Business, 1914–1984* (2nd edn, Westport, CT, 1984).

22 For an argument for a greater rise in conglomerate activity see Barry Bluestone and Bennett Harrison, *The Deindustrialization of America: Plant Closings, Community Abandonment, and the Dismantling of Basic Industry* (New York, 1982), pp. 122–9.

23 Robert Sobel, *The Rise and Fall of the Conglomerate Kings* (New York, 1984).

24 Fligstein, *The Transformation of Corporate Control*, chapter 5.

25 Richard H. K. Vietor, *Contrived Competition: Regulation and Deregulation in America* (Cambridge, MA, 1994); Richard H. K. Vietor, 'Contrived Competition: Economic Regulation and Deregulation, 1920s-1980s', *Business History*, 36(4), 1994, pp. 1–32.

26 John Donald Wilson, *The Chase: The Chase Manhattan Bank, N.A., 1945–1985* (Boston, MA, 1986); Harold van B. Cleveland and Thomas F. Huertas, *Citibank, 1812–1970* (London, 1985).

27 Paul A. C. Koistinen, *The Military-Industrial Complex: A Historical Perspective* (New York, 1980).

28 Jay Stowsky, 'From Spin-off to Spin-on: Redefining the Military's Role in

American Technological Development' in Wayne Sandholtz *et al.* (eds), *The Highest Stakes: The Economic Foundations of the Next Security System* (New York, 1992), pp. 114–40; Ann Markusen and Joel Yudken, *Dismantling the Cold War Economy* (New York, 1992).

29 Davis Dyer, 'Necessity as the Mother of Convention: Developing the ICBM, 1954–1958', *Business and Economic History*, 22(1), 1993, pp. 194–209; Glenn E. Bugos, 'Programming the American Aerospace Industry, 1954–1964: The Business Structure of Technical Transactions', *Business and Economic History*, 22(1), 1993, pp. 210–22.

30 Gregory Hooks, 'The Rise of the Pentagon and US State Building: The Defense Program as Industrial Policy', *American Journal of Sociology*, 96(2), 1990, pp. 379–82; Ann Markusen *et al.*, *The Rise of the Gunbelt: The Military Remapping of Industrial America* (New York, 1991).

31 Mansel G. Blackford, *A History of Small Business in America* (New York, 1991); Harold G. Vatter, 'The Position of Small Business in the Structure of American Manufacturing, 1870–1970' in Stuart Bruchey (ed.), *Small Business in American Life* (New York, 1980), pp. 142–68.

32 Thomas C. Cochran, *American Business in the Twentieth Century* (Cambridge, MA, 1972), pp. 185–92.

33 Michael J. Piore and Charles Sabel, *The Second Industrial Divide: Possibilities for Prosperity* (New York, 1984), pp. 27–9.

34 James H. Soltow, 'Origins of Small Business and the Relationships between Large and Small Firms: Metal Fabricating and Machinery Making in New England, 1890–1957' in Bruchey (ed.), *Small Business in American Life*, pp. 192–211; John N. Ingham, *Making Iron and Steel: Independent Mills in Pittsburgh, 1820–1920* (Columbus, OH, 1991).

35 Cochran, *American Business in the Twentieth Century*, pp. 189–90.

36 Piore and Sabel, *The Second Industrial Divide*.

37 Richard N. Langlois, 'External Economies and Economic Progress: The Case of the Microcomputer Industry', *Business History Review*, 1992, pp. 1–52; Richard N. Langlois, 'Creating External Capabilities: Innovation and Vertical Disintegration in the Microcomputer Industry', *Business and Economic History*, 19, 1990, pp. 93–102.

38 M. Storper and S. Christopher, 'Flexible Specialization and Regional Agglomerations: The Case of the U.S. Motion Picture Industry', *Annals of the Association of American Geography*, 77, 1987, pp. 104–17; Richard Maltby and Kate Bowles, 'Hollywood: The Economics of Utopia' in Jeremy Mitchell and Richard Maidment (eds), *The United States in the Twentieth Century: Culture* (Milton Keynes, 1994) pp. 117–19.

39 Michael J. Enright, 'Organisation and Coordination in Geographically Concentrated Industries' in Naomi R. Lamoreaux and Daniel M. G. Raff (eds), *Coordination and Information: Historical Perspectives on the Organization of Enterprise* (Chicago, 1995), pp. 103–42.

40 On franchising see Thomas S. Dicke, *Franchising in America: The Development of a Business Method, 1840–1980* (Chapel Hill, NC, 1992) and John B. Rae, *The American Automobile Industry: A History* (Boston, MA, 1984), pp. 131–3.

41 Harvey Levenstein, *Paradox of Plenty: A Social History of Eating in Modern America* (Oxford, 1993), pp. 231–2.

42 Rae, *The American Automobile Industry*, pp. 131–3.

43 David Halberstam, *The Reckoning* (New York, 1986).

44 James M. Rubinstein, *The Changing US Auto Industry: A Geographical Analysis* (New York, 1992), chapter 6.

45 Michael J. French, *The US Tire Industry: A History* (Boston, MA, 1990), chapters 9–10.
46 Mira Wilkins, 'Japanese Multinationals in the United States: Continuity and Change, 1879–1990', *Business History Review*, 64(4), 1990, pp. 585–629.
47 John H. Dunning, *Multinational Enterprises and the Global Economy* (Wokingham, 1993), p. 17.
48 For a discussion of perspectives on changes in forms of governance see John L. Campbell *et al.* (eds), *Governance of the American Economy* (Cambridge, 1991), chapters 1 and 11.
49 Levenstein, *Paradox of Plenty*, chapters 13–16.
50 D. K. Henry and R. P. Oliver, 'The Defense Build-Up, 1977–85: Effects on Production and Employment', *Monthly Labor Review*, 110(8), 1987, pp. 3–11.
51 Alfred D. Chandler, Jr, 'The Competitive Performance of US Industrial Enterprises since the Second World War', *Business History Review*, 68, 1994, pp. 1–72. For an earlier, similar discussion see Didricksen, 'The Development of Diversified and Conglomerate Firms in the US, 1920–1970'.
52 Piore and Sabel, *The Second Industrial Divide*, pp. 27–9.
53 Michael Borrus and John Zysman, 'Industrial Competitiveness and American National Security' in Sandholtz *et al.* (eds), *The Highest Stakes*, pp. 20–3.
54 For criticisms of American management and its labour relations see William Lazonick, 'Creating and Extracting Value: Corporate Investment Behavior and American Economic Performance' in Michael A. Bernstein and David E. Adler (eds), *Understanding American Economic Decline* (Cambridge, 1994), pp. 79–113.
55 Piore and Sabel, *The Second Industrial Divide*.
56 AnnaLee Saxenian, *Regional Advantage: Culture and Competition in Silicon Valley and Route 128* (Cambridge, MA, 1994).
57 Martin Kenny and Richard Florida, *Beyond Mass Production: The Japanese System and its Transfer to the United States* (Oxford, 1993); Tetsuo Abo (ed.), *Hybrid Factory: The Japanese Production System in the United States* (New York, 1994).
58 Mike Parker, 'Industrial Relations Myth and Shop-floor Reality: The Team Concept in the Auto Industry' in Howell John Harris and Nelson Lichtenstein (eds), *Industrial Democracy in America: The Ambiguous Promise* (Cambridge, 1993), pp. 249–74; Ruth Milkman, 'Labor and Management in Uncertain Times: Renegotiating the Social Contract' in Alan Wolfe (ed.) *America At Century's End* (Berkely, CA, 1992), pp. 131–51.
59 Allen Kaufman and Ernest J. Englander, 'Kohlberg Kravis Roberts & Co. and the Challenge to Managerial Capitalism', *Business and Economic History*, 21, 1992, pp. 97–108; Gerald F. Davis *et al.*, 'The Decline and Fall of the Conglomerate Firm in the 1980s: The Deinstitutionalization Of An Organizational Form', *American Sociological Review*, 59, 1994, pp. 547–70.
60 William M. Leary, *Encyclopedia of American History and Biography: The Airline Industry* (New York, 1992).
61 McQuaid, *Big Business and Presidential Power*, p. 287.
62 This account is based on David Vogel, *Fluctuating Fortunes: The Political Power of Business in America* (New York, 1989), chapters 5–8.

8

African-Americans and the civil rights movement

The question of racial inequalities, particularly the African-American struggle for civil rights, has been the driving-force for much of the social and political history of the United States. This chapter considers the civil rights movement's pre-1945 origins and the areas of continuity and departure with the campaigns between 1945 and 1965, including reactions to the protests. Important local campaigns in the South are discussed along with their relationship to national organisations and trends. With the achievement of legislative goals in 1964 and 1965, the civil rights struggle assumed rather different forms. The extent to which African-Americans have improved their economic and social standing since 1945 is discussed in the final part of the chapter, which assesses the influence of class and race.

Among the fundamental transformations in post-war America were the mechanisation of southern agriculture and the region's urban and industrial development. These developments had particular impact on African-Americans who, as Chapter 1 indicated, changed from a largely rural, southern population to predominantly urban-dwellers with far less of a regional concentration. Prevailing pluralist political theories of the 1950s and 1960s assumed that rural migrants and immigrants would follow a path of gradual assimilation in terms of employment and culture akin to that taken by immigrants in the late nineteenth and early twentieth centuries. For most migrants there was at least the hope of upward social mobility for their children. Against this optimistic vision, there was the force of racism and discrimination which had the capacity to affect the operation of market forces by influencing access to education and employment and the degree of social assimilation. Since African-Americans were long-term residents rather than recent immigrants, they already had established positions in society, but equally these were circumscribed in ways which were also firmly rooted. Even here some observers were optimistic; Gunnar Myrdal's examination of race relations in the United States in 1944 argued that white Americans would feel compelled to reduce inequalities in order to live up to the basic values of an American creed.

In the early 1900s public deference by rural blacks to the racial etiquette of Jim Crow was maintained by economic dependence, a lack of political influence through the ballot box and the risk of violent repression. Under such circumstances there was a presumption in favour of the status quo, though the African-American struggle for equality had a long tradition. By the 1920s African-American political philosophies spanned a range from the self-improvement associated with Booker T. Washington to the more assertive pursuit of integration via constitutional rights by the National Association for the Advancement of Colored People (NAACP) and Marcus Garvey's black nationalism, which emphasised self-reliance and separatism. The collapse of the cotton economy and wartime migration fundamentally altered the economic and social position of black Americans in the 1930s and 1940s. Urbanisation and migration increased the resources for protest and political influence at local and national levels. Urban blacks were less constrained than their rural counterparts and their indigenous institutions, such as schools and churches, were larger and better financed. As a result collective behaviour was more likely. A specific civil rights era, associated with non-violent, direct-action campaigns based in the black community, was evident between 1954 and 1965. Certain land-mark events delineated this era, notably the Brown decision (1954), the Montgomery bus boycott (1955–56), the schools crisis in Little Rock (1957), student sit-ins in Greensboro (1960), the Freedom Rides (1961) and demonstrations in Birmingham (1963) and Selma (1965). All were located in the South, conferring a regional identity to this phase of the civil rights struggle. The formal culmination of the protest campaigns was the enact-ment of the Civil Rights Act (1964) and Voting Rights Act (1965). Thereafter the civil rights movement was more diffuse, and riots produced new images which fuelled a conservative white reaction under a 'law and order' banner. This chapter examines the impact of the changes which affected black Americans and the sources and nature of the post-war civil rights campaigns. It considers the overarching issue of the extent to which the changing economic and social standing of African-Americans consti-tuted an advance or improvement after 1945.

Pre-war developments

At the turn of the century there were roughly 9 million African-Americans of whom 90 per cent lived in the South; only 20 per cent of the total black population lived in urban areas. The average black Southerner worked in agriculture as a tenant, sharecropper or labourer, primarily in cotton-growing. Some black farmers acquired sizeable holdings, but most had low incomes and sharecroppers frequently moved at the end of their annual tenancies in search of better terms or treatment. Rural blacks were a scattered, rather isolated population who lacked power and status com-pared to white landlords and merchants. As small farmers, tenants and sharecroppers at the bottom of the agricultural ladder, African-Americans were hard hit by the Depression and lacked the economic or social power to shape public policies, so that New Deal farm policy aggravated their problems.[1]

Migration within the South and to the northern cities provided an outlet for rural black labour and an escape from southern segregation. The pace of migration accelerated during the 1910s as European immigration was curtailed by war and in the inter-war years the pull of northern jobs was given added impetus by the mounting problems in the cotton economy. There was a more diverse mix of occupations among urban blacks, including skilled trades, and a middle class of entrepreneurs and professionals; domestic service was the mainstay of female employment. From the 1890s to the 1920s local and state laws, usually labelled the Jim Crow laws or black codes, were introduced across the South, restricting black voting and enforcing social segregation between the races. During the 1930s persistent unemployment depressed black incomes, resources and prospects, leaving work-relief schemes as a crucial source of support. With limited exceptions, even federal agencies, such as the Tennessee Valley Authority (TVA) and the CCC, perpetuated discrimination in relief payments as well as social segregation.

The 1940s, especially the war years, offered further significant change. The rural exodus continued, with 1.5 million blacks moving north during the 1940s which yielded higher incomes and greater potential influence at the polls.[2] Recruitment of blacks into the military and war industries proceeded slowly until labour leader A. Philip Randolph threatened a March on Washington in 1941 to demand an end to discrimination in government and defence employment. The march was cancelled after President Roosevelt's introduced Executive Order 8802 in June 1941, establishing the President's Committee on Fair Employment Practices (FEPC). Although underfunded and with weak enforcement powers, the Committee's investigations documented racial discrimination in employment. Of more immediate significance, rising demand for labour increased black employment by 1942, including entry into a wider range of occupations. Among African-American women the concentration in agriculture and domestic service diminished.

Despite the evident inequalities, migration and employment changes had significant effects on the civil rights movement during the 1930s. African-American voting strength increased in northern cities and swung towards the Democratic Party. Eleanor Roosevelt offered public sympathy for equality and African-Americans received some recognition, in the form of lower-level political appointments, within the New Deal administration. However southern white politicians were a powerful counter to any liberal tendencies and President Roosevelt avoided alienating their support. The chief legacies of the 1930s then were a toehold in federal and union circles and NAACP local activism, plus its campaign in the courts against segregation, especially the southern educational system, with its separate and limited provision for African-Americans.

During the 1940s opinion polls indicated a more assertive attitude among blacks. NAACP membership increased from 50,000 in 1940 to 450,000 in 1946 and the organisation's branches engaged in boycotts and picketing over jobs and housing. The NAACP's protracted legal campaign reaped a substantial reward with the US Supreme Court decision striking down the all-white primary (1944), which had confined the selection of Democratic candidates, the crucial political choice in the solidly Democratic South, to whites. The general anti-fascist propaganda provided additional scope for the assertion of domestic rights, as did linkages between the circumstances of American blacks and anti-colonial movements across the world.[3] The black press called for the 'Double V' of victory at home over discrimination as well as overseas.[4] The extent of pre-1945 gains should not be exaggerated. Relationships changed least in rural areas and in the cities residential segregation increased during the 1940s.[5] White workers frequently walked out over upgrading of black workers and resisted the movement of African-Americans into predominantly white neighbourhoods. There was recurring racial violence including major race riots in Chicago, Detroit, New York, Mobile and Beaumont, Texas, during 1943.

The character of the civil rights struggle, 1945–60

By 1944 many black professionals placed considerable faith in the prospects of progress through federal and labour institutions in a continuation of the later New Deal tendencies.[6] There were some advantages from the changing international scene. As the US government endeavoured to gain support from Third World nations, domestic inequalities were a potential embarrassment. Moreover, decolonisation created newly-independent African nations, which were a symbol of black autonomy.[7] President Truman's administration oversaw integration in the armed forces and in 1947 the report of the President's Committee on Civil Rights provided additional support for demands for equality. Support was forthcoming from the New Deal's liberal–labour coalition and many black activists gained organisational experience through union activities or federal agencies. However, the degree of external support diminished markedly as a result of the impact of post-war anti-Communism on labour unions, liberalism and interracial groups. The more conservative Congress refused to extend the FEPC into peacetime and rejected anti-poll tax and anti-lynching bills. The rhetoric of a resurgent anti-Communism was directed against the NAACP, which was assailed as Communist and 'un-American'. In response the NAACP distanced itself from more radical groups and,

Fairclough suggested, its efforts were directed away from economic issues and emphasised voter registration and legal challenges.[8] The employers' anti-union drive and the rising tide of anti-Communism placed the labour movement on the defensive.[9] Post-war union-organising drives in the South were ineffectual and the Congress of Industrial Organisations (CIO) reacted to the Cold War hysteria by excluding several unions with Communist associations which had been strong advocates of racial equality. The 1930s connections to labour unions and the political Left were not completely destroyed since many black activists drew on their earlier political and organising experiences, but there was a greater reliance on all-black institutions. In 1944 Leslie Pinckney Hill advocated a combination of local black leadership and mass action rooted in religious commitment. The most detailed tactical proposals were presented by Randolph in the form of the demands of the 1941 March on Washington Movement. He suggested a mix of negotiation, pressure, mass marches, picketing, boycotts, union co-operation and public relations efforts. Randolph referred to 'non-violent direct action' as a means of desegregating public facilities using volunteers possessing the 'self-control and the requisite moral and spiritual resources' necessary to accept any injury as the price of combating evil. Also prescient, and rooted in inter-war rivalries, was Randolph's rejection of political alliances with Communists on the grounds that 'It is silly and suicidal for Negroes to add to the handicap of being *Black*, another handicap of being *Red*.'[10] Randolph's resumé delineated tactics from boycotts to litigation which featured in the post-war campaign.

Writing in 1954, Henry Bullock suggested that post-war campaigns reflected the impact of urban life in stimulating a more positive self-image and a sense of collective identity among African-Americans. Bullock argued that urban blacks experienced less pressure to maintain deference than those in rural areas where isolation and economic dependency were greater.[11] Describing the cities as a 'breeding ground for discontent', Bullock pointed to a corps of black leaders drawn from the professions and rooted in the ghettos.[12] Segregation nurtured a small, rather ill-defined black elite: only 3.3 per cent of black male workers and 6.5 per cent of black women workers were in the Census category of professional and managerial occupations in 1950.[13] From this elite came political leaders and the initial momentum for the civil rights movement.[14] David Lewis suggested that professionals had an interest in improved access to equal higher education facilities, an area of NAACP legal pressure, for their children. Teachers, predominantly female, were major contributors of funds and their grievances over pay discrimination were significant in NAACP campaigns for improved education provision. Entrepreneurs in service industries such as insurance, banks, retailing, undertaking and hairdressing, and professionals, such as dentists, doctors and ministers, were less exposed to economic reprisals from the white community.

In Atlanta and Mississippi to 1955 civil rights leadership was male, but in Montgomery and elsewhere women occupied leading roles in local organisations as well as being prominent among the membership. [15] In small towns protest movements were dependent on a handful of activists.[16] In college towns, such as Tuskegee and Greensboro, staff and students participated in campaigns. Although it cannot be quantified, returning veterans had a presence in post-war campaigns, as in the independent Voters' and Veterans' Association in Mobile or the Citizens' Steering Committee in Montgomery in 1952.[17] Veterans had broader experience and were assertive of their rights, as well as possessing a symbolic value.

The middle class was by no means a unified group nor was its direction accepted wholeheartedly. There were many conservatives as well as considerable differences of opinion over tactics and goals. Indeed in 1957 E. Franklin Frazier portrayed a black middle class preoccupied by its own status which had failed to provide responsible leadership for 'liberation'.[18] Some lower-class blacks resented middle-class attitudes or were critical of the NAACP. Nonetheless, alongside its middle-class leadership, the civil rights movement's impact rested upon the willingness of thousands of ordinary African-Americans to assert themselves. The NAACP's legal challenges depended on the commitment of individual people as litigants, as parents pressing for transfers, or to enter a school. Participation in protest, even seeking to register to vote, risked reprisals such as dismissal, blacklisting, and physical attack on the individual and their family. For some activists, the loss of jobs led to full-time commitment to the civil rights struggle, but others moved away or avoided involvement.

The civil rights struggle in the late 1940s and early 1950s chiefly took the form of voter-registration drives, with Negro Voters' Leagues active in many southern cities. Registration efforts were impeded by southern legislatures and officials who discriminated against black applicants, restricted registration periods and the number of cases processed, periodically removed voters from the lists and used intimidation. Even so the proportion of southern blacks registered to vote increased from 5 per cent in 1944 to 12 per cent in 1947 and 20 per cent in 1954. Gains were concentrated in the cities, with little change in the heavily populated black-belt rural counties; the percentage registered was highest in Texas, Florida and Louisiana and lowest in Mississippi.[19] Improvements in local services were demanded by groups such as the Greater Fifth Ward Citizens' League of Houston, the Atlanta Negro Voters' League, and the Richland County Citizens' Committee.[20] Where groups achieved non-partisan alliances and where African-Americans comprised a potentially critical share of votes, they could achieve practical results. A handful of black politicians were elected to local councils; there were piecemeal improvements to health and recreation provision and in some cities black policemen were hired.[21] There were local campaigns over education. Black parents lobbied for additional resources in public schools and established the United Negro Fund to aid black colleges; Marable concluded that 'greater progress in improving black educational prospects was achieved' from 1943 to 1950 than in the previous three decades.[22] In these terms the 1940s were characterised by rising expectations and greater organisation among blacks, though campaigns probed the fringes of existing racial mores cautiously. The framing of black demands in terms of constitutional rights, anti-fascism, international black struggles and US foreign policy interests, and in religious terms, appealed to established value-systems.

A local struggle in Montgomery, Alabama, in 1955 illustrated how urbanisation, local activists and some of the legacy of the 1930s and 1940s came into play at a local level. When Rosa Parks refused to give up her seat on a bus under segregated seating, her arrest sparked a black boycott of Montgomery buses. Parks had been secretary of the local NAACP from 1943 and organised its youth council. There was a link to the labour politics of the 1930s since Parks had attended the Highlander Folk School, an organisation which trained union organisers in the 1930s and from 1952 promoted citizenship schools and interracial workshops on school desegregation. After her arrest, the idea of a boycott was initiated and publicised by members of the local Women's Political Council which had complained about buses a year earlier as part of its demands for improved local facilities. Parks's legal case was handled by NAACP lawyers. Another key influence was Edgar D. Nixon, head of the local chapter of the Brotherhood of Sleeping Car Porters (BSCP) and a former president of the local and state branches of the NAACP. [23] Nixon provided organisational experience and publicity in the union's paper, benefiting from the connection to A. Philip Randolph, national leader of the BSCP union. Nixon's work as a Pullman porter involved regular travel and the union link was a valuable asset in fund-raising from the wider African-American community.

In order to bring together the efforts of diverse groups, a new organisation, the Montgomery Improvement Association (MIA), was formed to direct the boycott. With an eye to maximising involvement, Nixon and others turned to ministers, rather hesitant participants, to head the MIA and Martin Luther King, a recent arrival in the city, was chosen as president. Among African-American institutions the church had the broadest membership and greatest prestige and, therefore, provided the best prospect for mobilising mass support. Rosa Parks was a stewardess at the St Paul African Methodist Episcopal church.[24] Churches possessed the means to arrange meetings and to circulate publicity and information.[25] The element of religious solidarity helped to maintain motivation and community spirit over the long boycott and provided a language in which to express African-American aspirations.[26] One consequence of events in Montgomery was the formation of the Southern Christian Leadership Conference (SCLC), a regional organisation based on churches and designed to unify local protests, which provided the base for Martin Luther King's subsequent role in the civil rights movement. The various institutional links evident in Montgomery counter perceptions of the civil rights movement as an unstructured release of tensions or the product simply of charismatic leadership, since the character of the Montgomery campaign highlighted the degree of planning and co-ordination based in black institutions.[27] For Morris, Montgomery was characteristic of the local 'movement centers' which possessed the organisational capabilities to mobilise and sustain civil rights campaigns.[28] Events in Montgomery revealed shifts in white attitudes. In the year before the boycott the Montgomery city council was willing to listen to black political demands because black voters were potentially decisive in a political divide between an older upper-class political elite and a growing white lower middle class. However in an election after the Brown decision Clyde Sellers successfully used racism to appeal to lower-class white support. As a result the city authorities resisted the bus boycott.

Into the 1960s

By the early 1960s there were several national civil rights organisations and their roles and relationships defy simple classification. To some extent there was functional differentiation and each group occupied a particular niche of support and emphasised rather different objectives and tactics, which made them complementary in the struggle for civil rights. The SCLC did not create a membership base, in part, to avoid direct competition with the NAACP and was far more a southern regional body than was the NAACP.[29] The NAACP sometimes provided legal assistance to members of other groupings. Frequently organisations engaged in the same work, such as voter-registration drives, or co-operated, particularly in the aftermath of major incidents; for instance in the continuation of the march through Mississippi following the shooting of James Meredith. In 1961 the Southern Regional Council established a Voter Education Project funded by foundations and which involved the Student Non-Violent Coordinating Committee (SNCC), the Congress of Racial Equality (CORE), the SCLC, the NAACP and the Urban League, though they operated in different places. Individuals also moved between national organisations. Ella Baker provided the most remarkable example. An NAACP field secretary from the mid-1930s to 1946, Baker raised funds for the National Urban League Service Fund, played a key role in the foundation of the SCLC, including establishing its Atlanta office and local links, and in 1960 was central to the formation of the SNCC. Equally, Baker's career is symptomatic of tensions within the civil rights movement since her move in 1960 reflected dissatisfaction with the SCLC's strategy.

National organisations competed for funds from individual donors, foundations and, later, federal agencies and tactical, philosophical and personal differences were ever present. Contrasts had a positive function where they supplied leverage, and in bargaining with government or private interests in the 1960s, the NAACP or the SCLC portrayed themselves as moderates whose demands should be met in order to forestall more radical demands.[30] The existence of other political movements, such as black nationalism, and the potential danger of violence and, by the mid-1960s, actual experience of riots, provided similar sources of pressure. Nonetheless rivalries could be distracting. There was internal fragmentation within the national civil rights bodies: Fairclough shows the persistent tensions within the SCLC between those who sought clearer administrative structures and systems and the organisation's effective role as a flexible, unstructured 'movement'.[31] The 1964 March on Washington, one of the defining images of the civil rights movement, was characterised by disagreements, divisions and the absence of certain groups and individuals.[32] Disputes between national organisations were often less pronounced on the ground, where individuals were members of several groups or co-operated in pursuit of common aims or particular campaigns. Frequently new organisations were established locally to provide an umbrella under which existing groups co-operated.[33]

A key aspect of the civil rights movement was the reciprocal relationship between the national and local levels. The NAACP's financial and organisational foundation was its local branches and legal challenges originated in local initiatives. The SCLC and the SNCC developed out of local campaigns and maintained their momentum by co-ordinating disparate localised efforts. At times national organisations promoted the establishment of local groups, as in Mississippi, where the Freedom Rides by outsiders and, later, the SNCC's voter-registration efforts, revived a local civil rights effort which had been repressed during the previous three years.[34] The vital links were grass-roots organisers such as Fannie Lou Hamer in Mississippi and Amelia P. Boynton in Selma who played a key role in sustaining and directing the civil rights movement. Local activists sought to involve national bodies and leaders in order to highlight existing protests and, in turn, the degree of local organisation and strength was a critical factor in the impact of national civil rights bodies. Yet national and local organisations did not always agree on tactics or on when or how to agree to end protests. The SCLC, in particular, was criticised by local groups for abandoning or withdrawing from a campaign, leaving issues unresolved and greater intransigence among whites. For the SCLC long-term commitments were regarded as dangerous, given limited resources, especially where little progress had been achieved. The NAACP and the SNCC advocated more sustained involvement.

Although the Montgomery boycott had succeeded, its wider impact was limited and the power of a mass movement remained to be tested elsewhere. A new phase of the civil rights movement was initiated by a sit-in by four black students at the Woolworth lunch counter in Greensboro, South Carolina in 1961. The Greensboro sit-ins generated similar protests across the South which involved more young blacks and led to the formation of the Student Non-Violent Coordinating Committee (SNCC) in 1960. The SNCC was a younger, student-based organisation, critical of the SCLC and the NAACP as cautious and conservative. The 'sit-in' and Freedom Ride campaigns created powerful images by creating potential confrontations, and this aspect became increasingly central to the civil rights movement. Neil McMillen described the second phase of the civil rights campaign in Mississippi in 1964 as 'guerrilla theater', designed to influence elite and public opinion and thereby federal policy by demonstrating the hazardous nature of voter registration.[35] The SCLC's tactics hinged on its capacity to create such publicity. The importance of police reactions was indicated by the limited effectiveness of a campaign in Albany where police imprisoned demonstrators, but avoided major confrontations. In stark contrast the violent reactions by the police departments and state police in Birmingham in 1963 and in Selma in 1965 resulted in massive publicity.

Like the SCLC though, the SNCC had black leadership and was based in the South. In the 1960s the character and leadership of the movement broadened. In Mississippi the established middle class and churches remained to the fore in towns, but in rural areas the role of outside organ-isers and women increased compared to the 1950s.[36] In 1961 the new phase of protest went further with the revival of the CORE around a series of Freedom Rides to test desegregation of interstate travel in the south. White liberals were still present, especially students and church groups, along with financial assistance from foundations. However, from 1963 black leader-ship assumed complete direction of the national organisations with white staff steadily leaving the CORE and the SNCC. This trend reflected an assertion of the importance of self-reliance and racial identity and it involved a reassessment of the goal and meaning of assimilation.[37]

White responses to the civil rights movement

The nature and impact of the civil rights movement was conditioned by white responses. Political channels were blocked in the South by the barri-ers to voter registration, repression and whites' powerful presumption that existing racial etiquette was sacrosanct. The Democratic Party's southern wing was a powerful obstacle to reform. The principal positive response came from the federal judiciary where constitutional and legal principles and language provided a source of leverage. However, the scale of white resistance was evident following the Brown decision in 1954 where the US Supreme Court ruled that segregation in public education was inherently unequal and unconstitutional. The decision, the first landmark event of the post-war era, rewarded the NAACP's legal strategy, and the promise of integrated education, with its implication of increased resources, raised African-American hopes. Initially boards of education and southern governments appeared prepared to implement the Brown decision, but a lack of positive leadership at federal and state levels left the field to the opponents of desegregation, notably the Citizen's Council movement which grew rapidly between 1954 and 1957. McMillen identified the Citizen's Council leadership as a planter–merchant–lawyer elite from the small towns and the organisation was strongest in 'black-belt' areas where African-Americans constituted a high proportion of the population.[38] The NAACP was subjected to particular attack and was declared illegal in Alabama, Texas and Louisiana. Southern congressional leaders, fearful of white apathy, advocated defiance of the Supreme Court in the Southern Manifesto. The rise of massive resistance suppressed the feeble forces of southern liberalism which in any case counselled caution and gradualism. As resistance gathered, the Supreme Court in 1955 required local school authorities to produce plans for school desegregation to proceed 'with all deliberate speed' under the scrutiny of local federal judges. Deliberation and evasion proved more common than speed, and administrative pro-cedures for pupil placement provided considerable scope for delaying tactics which effectively slowed transfers of black students into previously all-white schools. More dramatically, in Little Rock in 1957 Arkansas's governor used troops to exclude black pupils and President Eisenhower responded by federalising the state national guard and mobilising 1,000 paratroops to ensure access. Governor Faubus then closed all high schools in Little Rock during 1958 and 1959.

In the early 1960s the new wave of protest forced local and national polit-ical responses. There remained plenty of examples of violent repression whether in Birmingham, Mississippi or Selma and very little advocacy of racial equality by southern whites. Nonetheless the Citizen's Council move-ment ebbed, and in many cities white business and political elites tried at least to avert public confrontations or restore what historian William Chafe termed 'civility' through limited concessions. Jacoway and Colburn described southern businessmen as favouring segregation, but choosing reform rather than disorder under the pressure of the civil rights movement and federal courts.[39] Business furnished rather reluctant leadership based on a desire for stability more than a positive commitment to desegregation. Cramer's interviews with eighty white community leaders in five southern cities which had encountered little civil rights pressure found that attracting investment was a general article of faith and created a preference for avoiding school closures or massive disruption.[40] Cramer concluded there had been little or no effort to prepare the ground for desegregation. In Little Rock, Virginia and New Orleans business elites moved belatedly to reopen schools and mobilised middle-class white opinion under a 'law and order' banner, but intransigence persisted in cities such as Memphis and St Augustine. The process also constrained the civil rights movement, as when North Carolina governor Luther Hodges portrayed both the Ku-Klux-Klan and the NAACP as extremists.

The federal government offered an alternative forum to the state level and, thus, a means to challenge southern racial mores in terms of national values, but in an era when the size and influence of the federal government increased substantially, federal policy on civil rights was chronically hesitant. Lawson suggested that Eisenhower, Kennedy and Johnson were most prepared to support extensions of voting rights as a constitutional issue where there might also be party interests.[41] In other spheres the executive hesitated, moving only reluctantly to challenge local jurisdiction over education and law enforcement. Successive administrations were reluctant to appear to contravene states' rights and, therefore, preferred to rely on local and state authorities. The result was a pattern of responding only to sustained pressures, usually where there was an element of public disorder or 'guerrilla theater'. Eisenhower and Congress established precedents for limited intervention and the Kennedy administration appointed more black officials and staff and had a more active Civil Rights Division in the Department of Justice. Yet Kennedy preferred behind-the-scenes lobbying to direct federal action. Like Eisenhower, Kennedy was driven to go further by white resistance. Following police action against demonstrators in Birmingham and the refusal of Alabama Governor Wallace to admit blacks to the state university, Kennedy advocated legislation on employment discrimination and segregation of public facilities. In the event, it was President Lyndon Johnson who finally introduced the major civil rights legislation, the Civil Rights Act (1964) and the Voting Rights Act (1965). Johnson appreciated the civil rights issues more than Kennedy had done, had more faith in legislation as a solution and capitalised on a moment of liberal influence. Arguably, too, the pressures exerted by the civil rights campaigns were greater: the 1965 Act was brought forward in response to the violence in Selma.

A movement in decline?

Passage of the Civil Rights Act and the Voting Rights Act achieved two major objectives. Rapid desegregation of public facilities followed the 1964 Act and voter registration increased after 1965. In the South 60 per cent of blacks were registered by 1970.[42] Although boundary changes and the election of 'at-large' representatives reduced the full effect, the number of black elected officials increased from only 103 in 1964 to 3,503 a decade later and totalled 7,190 in 1989. Most were local posts in small towns, though black mayors were elected in Atlanta, Cleveland and Chicago.

By 1965 the movement had achieved its legislative goals, the black community possessed greater economic and political resources than before and had developed a powerful form of collective behaviour and racial identity. But within a few years the movement was fragmented and by 1970, according to McAdam, 'the movement, as a force capable of generating and sustaining organized insurgency, was moribund, if not dead'.[43] The disintegration of the civil rights movement resulted, in part, from incorporation into normal political channels and, in part, from declining federal responsiveness. There were also internal forces. The previous collective behaviour was the product of a loose coalition with diverse local roots and even the phase of maximum unity between 1960 and 1965 had been marked by growing internal tensions. Moreover the process of struggle itself generated not a single racial identity, but an array of contending visions over assimilation and separatism and the significance of class and race. As before 1964, the civil rights movement remained based on disparate local campaigns over housing, jobs, welfare and schools, but McAdam argued that these groups were smaller and lacked the resources and contacts of earlier indigenous black organisations.[44]

Campaigning in Chicago

There was a distinct regional shift. The focus of the civil rights movement switched to northern cities where earlier tactics proved less effective, as illustrated by events in Chicago. The city's black population increased from 282,244 in 1940 to 509,512 in 1950, 837,656 in 1960 and totalled 1.1 million in 1970. Sustained pressure on existing ghettos led to a pattern of piecemeal expansion, especially in West Chicago. In white working-class areas with high levels of home-ownership, the uneven process of ghetto expansion was perceived as a threat and the University of Chicago deployed conservation of its neighbourhood to limit black in-migration.[45] Urban renewal programmes improved public housing, but highway construction cut through some black neighbourhoods. Overcrowding remained a problem since more houses were demolished than built and new units were rented on a largely segregated basis. The concentration of black voters was sufficient for the city's ruling Democratic Party to seek the support of black ward politicians. Yet Hirsch argued that local activism in the 1940s gave way to a more conservative mood among Chicago blacks as black politicians accepted limited reform.[46] Paradoxically, black representation within the local political system reduced the civil rights movement's capacity to act as a unifying force in the black community.

A sustained local campaign in favour of greater integration was directed against the local school board from the 1940s. Local black groups created an umbrella organisation, the Coordinating Council of Community Organizations (CCCO) in 1962, which organised a one-day school boycott

in the following year and the momentum of the national civil rights movement brought black professional bodies and local churches into the CCCO
in 1963. In 1966 the SCLC launched an 'End Slums' campaign in Chicago
and generated the 'theater' of confrontation through marches into white
neighbourhoods, highlighting housing segregation and real-estate practices.
Although the city announced an open-housing policy, SCLC's campaign
produced few gains and it illustrated several general difficulties. The issues
of schools, housing and employment involved a critique of existing arrangements and policies and implied a wider contest for resources with other
social groups. City authorities reacted defensively and largely maintained
existing policies on schools and public housing; the angry response from
some white neighbourhoods, coupled with riots in some black areas,
encouraged the city government to emphasise 'law and order' rather than
reform. Such perceptions gave added weight to what Anderson and
Pickering identified as a 'civic credo' which assumed that inequalities would
inevitably diminish so that there was a presumption in favour of minimal
intervention. Major Daley's national influence within the Democratic Party
limited the willingness of federal agencies to intervene. The civil rights
campaigners differed over tactics and goals, with divisions between the
SCLC and local groups over the terms for ending marching, and divisions
had arisen within the CCCO between advocates of integration, separatism
and various forms of black power.[47]

The changing character of the civil rights movement

Some writers identify fragmentation within the black community as a
source of weakness after 1964. Certainly the strength of national organisations diminished as internal divisions over tactics and goals widened, a tendency apparent by 1961. The NAACP lost influence while the CORE and
SNCC declined rapidly as did the SCLC following the assassination of
Martin Luther King in 1968. The earlier civil rights struggle relied on developing black self-confidence and assertiveness via indigenous institutions.
The NAACP's broadly integrationist view remained the dominant mood,
but, particularly among activists, other strands became prominent.
Churches remained influential, but their role was more contested. The
'black power' slogan, first propounded by Stokely Carmichael in 1966,
captured the mix of angry dissatisfaction, greater assertiveness and emphasis on black autonomy. The black nationalist movement spoke to similar
ideas and rejected the assimilation which had underpinned the post-war
movement. One symptom was a decline in the extent of white liberal
participation in the civil rights movement. If separatism was always a
minority opinion, there was a broader emphasis on the importance of sustaining a distinct black culture. Perhaps the starkest contrast with earlier
policy was in education, where some African-American parents and edu-

cators began to advocate separate education, in part on the grounds of quality and local control and in part as a means for promoting black culture.

With the achievement of *de jure* desegregation and voting rights, emphasis shifted to economic issues. Economic concerns had never been absent from the civil rights struggle. In 1944 W. E. B. DuBois argued that economic freedom was essential if blacks were to be able to 'cast a free ballot' and the NAACP always demanded greater economic opportunity. Activists, notably in the SNCC, began to address the extent and impact of poverty and the need for economic strategies from the early 1960s. NAACP labour secretary Herbert Hill argued in 1965 that legal and social advances could be undermined by economic conditions.[48] More radical elements espoused class analyses and collectivist, and in some cases revolutionary, ideologies. A small, but highly-publicised expression of this trend, as well as a more aggressive stance, was the Black Panther Party, formed in 1966. Whitney M. Young of the Urban League called for a domestic Marshall Plan as a 'compensatory effort' for blacks. The change of direction was evident in the thinking of Martin Luther King, who increasingly emphasised economic reform as the basis for full equality.

Federal administrations were notably less responsive after 1965. Policies on civil rights issues were diffused among different federal agencies and programmes and in a sense were less visible, but there were changes in perceptions of black politics. On an ideological level radical and collectivist views provoked criticism for being out of line with prevailing tenets of individualism and capitalism. The earlier identification of the civil rights movement with peaceful protest was challenged by new images following the series of major urban riots. C. Vann Woodward estimated there were at least 150 major incidents between 1965 and 1968 including Watts (1965) and Detroit (1967). President Johnson regarded rioting as straightforward ingratitude after the legislation of 1964 and 1965 and this distancing went further as some black political groups participated in anti-Vietnam War protests. More broadly, the riots placed liberal reformers on the defensive against critics who argued that earlier reforms had not prevented unrest. After the assassination of Martin Luther King, there was no authoritative moderate figure for government to deal with; even before then King exerted less influence with activists. The report of the Kerner Commission into the causes of civil disorder highlighted poor housing and economic problems and there was increased expenditure, but the pace of reform was limited. An indication of the changing atmosphere was an anti-riot clause in the 1968 Fair Housing Act.

The Nixon administration continued the 'law and order' approach; the President emphasised co-operation rather than coercion in relations with the South and stated that education rather than integration was the federal government's priority. Greater emphasis was placed on the rhetoric of 'black capitalism' as an individualistic response to economic constraints. In a State of the Union address Nixon argued that 'It is time for those who make massive demands on society to make minimal demands on themselves.' Although part of a general critique of welfare policy, it signalled a more critical approach to black demands. Yet there continued to be significant developments. The courts were still endeavouring to enforce school desegregation nearly twenty years after the Brown case. School boards prevaricated and white parents moved children to private schools or to suburbs where there were no African-Americans. In several cities courts established schemes to bus children outside their neighbourhoods in order to achieve more racially integrated schools. This policy triggered resistance from white working-class parents, particularly in the northern cities. Some black parents feared for their children's safety or resented the loss of local schooling, especially where schools in black neighbourhoods had excellent reputations and offered the autonomy associated with the ideas of 'Black Power'. In 1974 the US Supreme Court found against plans for combining inner-city and suburban schools in Detroit in order to obtain racially integrated schools. The decision marked an acceptance of the *de facto* separation established by residential divisions.[49]

In 1969 the Nixon administration initiated stricter enforcement of the prohibitions on employment discrimination enshrined in the 1964 Civil Rights Act so that employers, especially government and federal contractors, had to actively promote recruitment of minorities and women. Such 'affirmative action' held advantages for African-Americans, but aroused white accusations of favouritism. During the early 1970s rising unemployment and the check to white income growth stimulated attacks on affirmative action, busing, welfare programmes and federal policies in general as unduly favourable to African-Americans, despite the greater impact of recessions on black employment and incomes. In 1974 Allan Bakke sued the University of California Medical School for 'reverse discrimination' through its fixed admissions quotas for racial minorities and in 1978 the US Supreme Court declared racial quotas unconstitutional. In this context blacks suffered from the generally more conservative mood among whites which, in turn, was reflected in less responsive governments.

The economic and social status of African-Americans since 1945

After 1945 African-Americans continued to transfer away from low-wage occupations in the low-wage South to urban areas in higher-wage parts of the United States. Even within the South, there was a shift away from agriculture to cities. These demographic trends, coupled with post-war economic growth, provided scope for economic and social advancement. Describing the city as 'more rational' than rural areas, Bullock emphasised a combination of market relationships and anonymity as influences for changing social norms, though he acknowledged the likelihood of resistance and violence by whites.[50] Ethnicity theory, the dominant sociological approach, portrayed African-Americans as a 'new immigrant' group who would achieve a place within a pluralist democratic system.[51] However, the extent of such improvement depended on continued economic opportunities and how far access to jobs and education were limited by discrimination and racism. It proved a complex process in which there were marked economic and social gains, but the civil rights movement emphasised the powerful barriers.

When African-Americans left the rural South, they obtained higher incomes and better educational provision in southern and northern cities.[52] Access to and funding for education were major elements in the civil rights campaigns. Southern educational expenditure rose during the 1950s in response to, and in part in a bid to counter, black political campaigns. In 1940 the median years of schooling for African-Americans were 5.7 compared to 8.8 for whites. By 1980 the median years of schooling completed by young white and black people were almost equal. The proportion of African-Americans who completed high school increased from 8 per cent in 1940 to 51 per cent in 1980 and the proportions who completed college rose from 1.3 per cent to 8 per cent over the same period.

There were improved opportunities for African-Americans to enter higher skilled work, clerical posts and professions after 1945 as demand for labour and white workers' upward mobility altered hiring practices.[53] As black workers accumulated experience and training, there were greater prospects of higher earnings. The entertainment business provided one avenue for black talent and the popularisation of blues music and its transfer into mainstream rock-and-roll opened new opportunities in the 1950s and 1960s. There was an expansion in the numbers of black athletes in professional sports, too. The successes of individual artists and the Motown record label were evidence of the opportunities. Higher black incomes also produced a burgeoning market which supported specialist publishing companies and consumer-products firms as well as insurance companies. A rising proportion of African-Americans owned their own home after 1945 and average life-expectancy increased.

Average data conceal varying tendencies. Generally younger people gained more in terms of education and income and younger, educated African-American couples achieved income parity with white Americans by the mid-1970s. Income gains were most pronounced for black women: the ratio of black/white average annual earnings for women rose from 50 per cent in 1950 to rough equality by the mid-1970s, although black women worked a greater number of hours. The income gap for men narrowed to the mid-1950s, fell back slightly before closing again from 1963 to 1970, but then widened again. Progress was far less marked than in the case of women: black male earnings averaged 40 to 45 per cent of white male earnings in the 1940s and around 67 per cent in the 1980s. In the Midwest the average income of black men actually lost ground compared to white men after the 1950s, indicating the loss of wartime gains. The narrowing of the income gap occurred across all regions and was most rapid in the South, though the size of the initial gap still left the ratio of black/white incomes lowest in the South. Since average incomes were generally lower in the South than elsewhere, the continued concentration of African-Americans in the region held down earnings compared to the national average.

There were persistent gaps in terms of income: one-third of African-Americans were below the official poverty line in 1969, nearly three times the rate for white Americans. While following national trends, the male rate of unemployment among African-Americans was more than double that for white men in all but six years between 1948 and 1993. Unemployment for black women was over 150 per cent of that for white women in all but three years in the same period.

The greater diversity of employment and the narrowing of income gaps were particularly marked during the economic boom of the 1960s, which testified to the influence of market forces, including southern economic development. Markets are unlikely to produce equality, especially where groups occupy very different starting points and racial discrimination had created a considerable legacy of educational disadvantage. Educational and employment gains were offset by the continued advances for white Americans into higher education and white-collar occupations and the lower average age of the black population held down relative earnings. There was a paradoxical widening of income differentials where African-Americans clustered on the lower rungs of skilled or professional occupations, with highly-skewed salary scales.[54] Other evidence indicated that the operation of market forces was shaped by white attitudes and discrimination. For employers, lower black wages were a potential cost saving, but against this was the force of convention and racial assumptions. The resistance of white workers and union locals, particularly in small firms, skilled trades and construction, limited the entry of African-Americans. Segregated job allocations and promotion structures persisted, which hindered access to training and better-paid work.[55] Such evidence was consistent with segmented job markets in which race was a factor. In 1947 the Brooklyn Dodgers brought the first black player, Jackie Robinson, into major-league baseball. Professional sports gradually opened up to African-Americans, though even by the 1990s relatively few blacks had been able to enter managerial posts in sport. In the wider entertainment business black artists became more prominent and the civil rights movement's influence slowly resulted in greater participation and less stereotyped images of African-Americans in films and on television.

The distribution of income within the black population was more unequal than for the population as a whole throughout the post-war

Table 8.1 *Median income of black and Hispanic families and unrelated individuals as a percentage of white median family income in the US, 1947–91*

Year	Black families	Unrelated individuals	Hispanic families
1947	51	72	
1948	53	75	
1949	51	73	
1950	54	74	
1951	53	78	
1952	57	69	
1953	56	79	
1954	56	69	
1955	55	69	
1956	53	78	
1957	54	68	
1958	51	69	
1959	52	67	
1960	55	61	
1961	53	62	
1962	53	67	
1963	53	68	
1964	56	69	
1965	55	74	
1966	60	63	
1967	62	74	
1968	63	69	
1969	63	70	
1970	64	69	
1971	60		
1972	59		71
1973	58		69
1974	60		71
1975	62		67
1976	59		66
1977	57		68
1978	59		68
1979	56		69
1980	58		67
1981	56		70
1982	55		66
1983	56		66
1984	56		68
1985	58		65
1986	57		65
1987	57		63
1988	57		64
1989	56		65
1990	58		63
1991	57		63

Sources: US Bureau of the Census, *Historical Statistics of the United States, Colonial Times to 1970, Bicentennial Edition*, Part 1 (Washington, DC, 1975), p. 297, series G203–4; US Bureau of the Census, *Statistical Abstract of the United States: 1993* (113th edn, Washington, DC, 1993), p. 462, table 721.

Table 8.2 *Income distribution of non-white families and unrelated individuals in the US, 1950–90 (%)*

	1950	1955	1960	1965	1970	1975	1981	1985	1990
Lowest fifth	3.5	4.0	3.7	4.7	4.5	4.7	4.0	3.6	3.3
Second fifth	10.2	10.3	9.7	10.8	10.6	10.1	9.4	9.1	8.6
Third fifth	17.6	17.8	16.5	16.6	16.8	16.7	16.0	15.7	15.6
Fourth fifth	25.2	25.5	25.2	24.7	24.8	25.1	25.5	25.1	25.3
Highest fifth	43.6	42.4	44.9	43.2	43.4	43.3	45.1	46.4	47.3
Top five %	16.6	14.3	16.2	15.1	15.4	15.4	16.0	17.1	17.3

Sources: US Bureau of the Census, *Historical Statistics of the United States*, Part 1, pp. 292–3, series G1–138; US Bureau of the Census, *Statistical Abstract of the United States: 1977* (98th edn, Washington, DC, 1977), p. 443; US Bureau of the Census, *Statistical Abstract of the United States: 1982–3* (103rd edn, Washington, DC, 1983), p. 435; US Bureau of the Census, *Statistical Abstract of the United States: 1987* (107th edn, Washington, DC, 1987), p. 437; US Bureau of the Census, *Statistical Abstract of the United States: 1992* (112th edn, Washington, DC, 1992), p. 450.

period. The share of the top 20 per cent of non-white families, largely though not exclusively African-Americans, increased significantly from the mid-1970s compared to the lowest 40 per cent. This implies wider class divisions, but the relative shares in 1990 were closer to those of 1950 and in line with the general tendency for inequalities to widen over the last two decades.

The southern economy experienced significant industrial and urban development during the 1940s and 1950s which offered an alternative to the rigidity of rural society. For liberals economic development offered the broader prospect of reform of the southern caste system. Generally the issue was given a political focus as liberals and labour unions contemplated extending the New Deal coalition into the South. Industrialisation was expected to be a solvent of traditional societies, replacing status with contractual relationships as the basis of society.[56] William H. Nicholls anticipated that industrialisation would produce a new white middle class inimical to agrarian southern culture, including segregation.[57] Nonetheless the South's political system and limited urban growth preserved the influence of rural society. Since southern economic development occurred in a patchy fashion, rural society and racist attitudes retained a powerful hold. In any case urban and industrial development between the 1880s and 1920s had been accompanied by the widespread imposition of segregationist 'Jim Crow' laws.[58] Segregation proceeded most rapidly in faster-growing southern cities such as Birmingham, Atlanta and Charlotte and residential segregation increased in the South during the 1950s.[59] Southern industry was based on access to resources or to cheap, less unionised labour and, to that extent, was compatible with the region's low-wage economy. The southern textile industry, based in smaller towns, recruited white women and children, but rarely employed black labour.[60] Even where there was new inward investment in capital-intensive industries from the 1930s or commercial expansion after 1945, incoming managements generally conformed to prevailing employment and wage patterns.[61] The limits of social change were clear in Birmingham, Alabama where coalmining and iron and steel manufacture had developed from the 1880s. Black workers constituted around half of coalminers and two-thirds of iron and steel workers in 1910, but patterns of racial job reservation were consolidated during the 1930s and 1940s: blacks were restricted to less skilled work and there were separate white and black promotion ladders.[62] By the 1950s the city's steelworks and mines were shedding labour and an ageing white workforce tried to block competition from black labour.[63] Birmingham's 'Big Mule' industrialists made little effort to attract new investment.[64] There was rigid social division: only the bus station was desegregated by 1963 and there were few blacks on the voting register. Working-class white voters supported state efforts to limit black suffrage after 1945 and an interracial committee of black and white business leaders achieved little between 1951 and 1956. Across the South economic development and existing racial etiquette proved relatively compatible as far as white attitudes were concerned, and change required a further political challenge from an expanded civil rights movement. If anything, there was some hardening of southern white attitudes during the 1950s in reaction to the demands for change. Even in the 1960s the southern elite preferred compromises based on minimal concessions. The collapse of public forms of segregation was accompanied by continued racial divisions in housing which tended to preserve separation. Southern economic development and civil rights campaigns did open new opportunities during the 1970s and early 1980s. In Atlanta political strength improved access to jobs and services and black politicians tapped federal and foundation funding effectively. There was a reversal of the out-migration of blacks from the South as growth slackened in the midwestern industrial cities. Yet even in places and periods when blue-collar employment was expanding, as in the dynamic cities of the Sunbelt after 1960, African-Americans remained over-represented in low-wage occupations and in particular neighbourhoods.[65] Elected black officials achieved advances in employment and the provision of services, but embraced the general ethos of development via low taxes which limited the scope for large-scale assistance.

Overall, then, the economic status of African-Americans combined substantial advance with continued and marked inequalities. A controversial analysis of these conditions emphasises structural factors in the post-war economy which lessened opportunities. In 1978 William Julius Wilson argued that problems encountered by African-Americans were a result of their concentration in a working class which was progressively disadvantaged by broader economic changes.[66] Although he acknowledged the impact of earlier discrimination, Wilson concluded that class was becoming a more important force than race in determining life chances. He argued that there was a general decline in demand for less skilled labour. In manufacturing productivity growth reduced labour requirements, thereby diminishing the prospects for black migrants and producing high rates of unemployment. These tendencies fell most heavily on young people as the 'baby-boom' generation competed for jobs and were, therefore, especially serious for the black population where fertility was higher. The expansion of the service sector offered some compensation, but contained a divide between low-wage, menial and casual work and more lucrative careers in white-collar and professional occupations, accessible only with education beyond high school. With the reinforcing effects of more regressive taxation in the 1980s, income inequalities widened for all groups and these tendencies were particularly acute for African-Americans, given their concentration in low-income jobs and unemployment.[67]

Wilson highlighted the concentration of poor blacks in the inner cities.[68] For Auletta or Glasgow this process produced an 'underclass' who were disconnected from economic and social institutions, liable to be involved in crime and to experience family break-up. [69] Wilson also argued that welfare dependency and involvement in criminal activities developed as ways of coping with unemployment and low incomes.[70] In conservative interpretations the underclass are regarded as culturally distinct from the rest of the population.[71] There are major problems over whether the concept of an underclass is appropriate and the nature of the causal relationships. Even the extent of detachment from wider society might be misleading: unemployment rates rose among inner-city black men, but so did the proportions of men and women in part-time work, which indicated contact with the labour market, albeit the low-paid end. Overall Wilson called for universal public policies to assist working-class neighbourhoods. His analysis offered an explanation for the patchwork of economic gains coupled with persistent disadvantage which characterised African-Americans' experience after 1945. The focus on demand for labour highlighted the critical importance of changing labour market conditions, particularly in the key industrial cities of the Midwest. Productivity growth slowed the recruitment of unskilled and semi-skilled workers in the 1950s and 1960s, thereby limiting opportunities in occupations where black men were heavily concentrated. After 1970 the contraction of midwestern heavy industry and the associated urban problems further undercut black male employment prospects. Black women fared better in relation to white female earnings, but generally had modest incomes, so the rise in the number of female-headed families tended to depress average black family incomes. The ratio of black/white median family incomes in the Midwest fell from 73 in 1970 to 51 in 1988 and there was a smaller fall in the Northeast too.

If Wilson's emphasis on structural changes in employment is linked to the black demographic pattern of a more youthful population, it offered some explanation for the persistence of economic disadvantage. However Wilson's account too easily dismissed the long-term consequences of earlier disadvantage and the force of racial discrimination. The most critical responses to Wilson's analysis have concerned his claim that class superseded race as the key influence. Alphonso Pinkney's assertion that 'race is still the critical variable for black people' was representative of the principal counter-argument.[72] For Pinkney, discrimination cut across class differences among African-Americans and shaped the operation of markets and public policy. The children of earlier European immigrants made educational gains at a faster rate than blacks and had preferential access to the unionised areas of heavy industry. Thernstrom's study of ethnic groups in Boston highlighted discrimination as a persistent barrier to black entry to semi-skilled and skilled work compared to immigrant groups possessing less schooling.[73] This contrast in job opportunities provides a clue to the persistently high rates of black unemployment well before the contraction of the northern cities' industrial base. One test of the significance of race is to examine the fortunes of white rural migrants, such as those from Appalachia, whose skills and education were comparable to those possessed by black migrants. The Appalachian whites were able to move between neighbourhoods more easily and their children were more upwardly mobile than those of black migrants. In any case physical concentrations are not an inherent barrier to employment, indeed black workers characteristically travelled out to work. Of primary importance was the impact of discrimination in determining access to the job market. White Appalachians resembled blacks as rural migrants lacking education and experience of urban life and confronted the same post-war industrial economy. However the Appalachians gained access to semi-skilled work and, thus, training more easily than did African-Americans.[74]

Writing in the late 1940s Robert Weaver argued that blacks were trapped in urban ghettos and, unlike earlier immigrants, were unable to move out due to restrictive housing covenants and other forms of discrimination.[75] Although the Supreme Court ruled that restrictive covenants were not enforceable in 1948, such practices persisted along with informal barriers and intimidation of new black residents. Since 1940 the extent of racial residential segregation has declined slightly in the major cities, but remains high.[76] The label 'chocolate city and vanilla suburbs' was coined as white Americans surged out to the suburbs and left blacks concentrated in metropolitan areas which lacked the resources to overcome economic and social problems. There has, particularly since 1970, been black movement to the suburbs, but this involves a smaller proportion of blacks than whites and residential segregation by race is evident in the suburbs too. According to Wilson the situation was exacerbated by black advancement when an educated black middle class profited from opportunities, especially in government employment, opened up by the civil rights movement and anti-discrimination laws. This picture attracted two opposing responses, though both stressed forms of continuity. Some accounts emphasised the existence of class divisions among blacks throughout the post-war period so that recent residential changes merely accentuated established tensions.[77] The other response argued that whatever class differences exist, these are secondary compared to the force of racial stereotyping and discrimination which are applied to all African-Americans regardless of income. Massey, for instance, concluded that residential segregation between middle class and working class was less pronounced among blacks than whites.[78] The concentration of African-Americans in inner-city areas was more pronounced and more persistent than that for any white ethnic groups or later Hispanic and Asian immigrants. Residential segregation in 1980 existed across the range of incomes, too, implying that race rather than class was the key variable.[79] Discrimination existed in the public and private housing sectors rather than being a simple reflection of income levels.[80] The residential divide by race had profound effects, particularly in limiting African-Americans' choice of housing, which tended to raise their housing costs, limiting social contacts and impeding the desegregation of schools.

Wilson concluded that poor education was a barrier to upward mobility for working-class African-Americans. The advances in average time in school or proportions completing college have been impressive, but have not always kept pace with the advancing level of credentials required for higher-paid jobs. Educational attainment levels have not matched the rate of increase in attendance and debate has continued about whether black children receive sufficient or comparable educational resources, given the frequent divide between black pupils in public schools and white pupils in private education. Higher levels of education lowered average unemployment rates. Nonetheless there was a striking rise in the ratio of black to white unemployment among college graduates which indicated limits on the gains from qualifications. College-educated blacks and whites had equal chances of being unemployed in 1970, but by 1987 the rates were 5.3 per cent for African-Americans and 2.3 per cent for whites.

Summary

Race relations, particularly the place of African-Americans, has been one of the central features in American society since 1945. During the first two post-war decades the otherwise conservative mood was broken by the continued challenge of the black struggle for equal rights. The economic changes associated with black urban migration supplied greater resources for the black community, including the long-running struggle for equality. Demands for constitutional rights were given added force by the moral tone of wartime anti-fascism, decolonisation and the United State's new world role in defence of democratic values. Ultimately, as Morris and others have argued, the impact of the civil rights movement depended on the cumulative impact of a series of local campaigns. The resources for these struggles were strengthened by economic changes associated with urbanisation, but a relatively small number of committed leaders had crucial roles. Industrialisation or economic development did not have the dramatic effects on white attitudes that some liberals predicted and southern white opposition remained obdurate and at times extremely violent; liberal voices were few and cautious. The main leverage came through legal victories in a handful of federal courts. In the early 1960s, however, the civil rights campaign drew in a broader cross-section of the black population, and created sufficient disruption to lead local white elites to make concessions in order to end open conflicts. It also persuaded the federal authorities, principally President Johnson, that national legislation was required. The results were decisive advances in terms of black voting and the dismantling of segregation in the South. However the force of economic disadvantages and racist attitudes were less easily addressed, especially in the North. Moreover the civil rights movement itself fragmented. Like other effective social movements this was in part a measure of success as black activists were absorbed into the political mainstream and exerted greater influence, primarily at a local level, but at the same time faced less favourable economic circumstances and more hostility over any forms of government assistance. The fragmentation also reflected divergent views about the proper aims and tactics for the civil rights struggle as the ideal of integration was increasingly questioned, and the complex issues of economic conditions and cultural values led to a contending array of priorities and policies.

Assessments of the civil rights movement often hinge on a combination of economic improvements which aided protest and at the same time the gap between hopes and inequalities. There were undoubtedly improvements in the economic and social status of African-Americans after 1945, especially in the ability to vote and the fall of legal segregation. Educational provision and results improved, there was a broadening in the range of jobs held and some progress up the occupational ladder. These advances were largely a product of migration and periods of economic expansion, but opportunities were also opened up by the campaigning of the civil rights movement. Nonetheless inequalities persisted, particularly above average rates of unemployment, concentration in less well-paid work, and marked residential segregation. In part these were interlinked elements and, as Wilson has argued, African-Americans were particularly affected by the contraction of industrial employment and the dichotomy between the professional end of the service sector and its less lucrative jobs. Only government employment supplied a solid niche for black workers and this support was also less reliable during the 1970s and 1980s. As in US society as a whole, the class divisions among African-Americans widened. Yet market forces provide only a partial explanation. Throughout the post-war period the civil rights movement exposed forms of racial discrimination whether in housing, employment, education, law enforcement or general attitudes. The parameters of discrimination shifted substantially, but it has remained a major influence.

Notes

1 L. J. Alston and J. P. Ferrie, 'Resisting the Welfare State: Southern Opposition to the Farm Security Administration', *Research in Economic History*, supplement 4, 1985, pp. 83–120.
2 Manning Marable, *Race, Reform and Rebellion: The Second Reconstruction in Black America, 1945–1982* (London, 1984), p. 9.
3 See the contributions in Rayford W. Logan (ed.), *What The Negro Wants* (Chapel Hill, NC, 1944) and Pete Daniel, 'Going Among Strangers: Southern Reactions to World War II', *Journal of American History*, 77(3), 1990, p. 893.
4 Lee Finkle, 'The Conservative Aims of Black Militant Rhetoric: Black Protest during World War II', *Journal of American History*, 60, 1973, pp. 692–713.
5 Neil A. Wynn, *The Afro-American and the Second World War* (London, 1976), p. 65.
6 Logan (ed.), *What The Negro Wants*.
7 August Meier and John H. Bracey, 'The NAACP as a Reform Movement, 1909–1965: To Reach the Conscience of America', *Journal of Southern History*, 59(1), 1993, p. 22.
8 Adam Fairclough, 'Historians and the Civil Rights Movement', *Journal of American Studies*, 24(3), 1990, p. 390.
9 Marable, *Race, Reform and Rebellion*, chapter 2.
10 Logan (ed.), *What The Negro Wants*, p. 148.
11 For a similar argument see Aldon D. Morris, *The Origins of the Civil Rights Movement: Black Communities Organizing* (New York, 1984), pp. 78–81 and Doug McAdam, *Political Process and the Development of Black Insurgency, 1930–1970* (Chicago, 1982), pp. 99–112.
12 Harvard Sitkoff, *The Struggle For Black Equality, 1954–1980* (New York, 1981), p. 15.
13 Frank Levy, *Dollars and Dreams: The Changing American Income Distribution* (New York, 1987), p. 134, 148. Morris estimates that black professionals constituted 3 per cent of the black community in a typical southern city: Morris, *The Origins of the Civil Rights Movement*, p. 3.
14 August Meier and Elliot Rudwick, *From Plantation to Ghetto* (London, 1970).
15 Meier and Bracey, 'The NAACP as a Reform Movement', p. 19.
16 David R. Colburn, *Racial Change and Community Crisis: St Augustine, Florida, 1877–1980* (New York, 1985).
17 Steven F. Lawson, *Black Ballots: Voting Rights in the South, 1944–1969* (New York, 1976), p. 94. J. Mills Thornton, 'Challenge and Response in the Montgomery Bus Boycott', *The Alabama Review*, 33, 1980, pp. 163–235, reprinted in Sarah Woolfolk Wiggins(comp.), *From Civil War to Civil Rights: Alabama, 1860–1960* (Tuscaloosa, AL, 1987), p. 471.
18 E. Franklin Frazier, *Black Bourgeoisie* (Glencoe, IL, 1957).
19 David R. Goldfield, *Black, White and Southern: Race Relations and Southern*

Culture 1940 to the Present (Baton Rouge, LA, 1990), p. 45; Lawson, *Black Ballots*, pp. 128–30 for 1944 and 1954 data.

20 Henry Allen Bullock in Rupert B. Vance and Nicholas J. Demerath (eds), *The Urban South* (Chapel Hill, NC, 1954), p. 227. Alton Hornsby, Jr, 'A City That Was Too Busy To Hate' in Elizabeth Jacoway and David R. Colburn (eds), *Southern Businessmen and Desegregation* (Baton Rouge, LA, 1982), p. 124.

21 Lawson, *Black Ballots*, pp. 128–9.

22 Marable, *Race, Reform and Rebellion*, p. 16.

23 For a profile of Nixon see Milton Viorst, *Fire in the Streets: America in the 1960s* (New York, 1979).

24 Morris, *The Origins of the Civil Rights Movement*, pp. 51–2.

25 On the church role see Adam Fairclough, *To Redeem the Soul of America: The Southern Christian Leadership Conference and Martin Luther King, Jr.* (Athens, GA, 1987), pp. 16–18.

26 Michael Omi and Howard Winant, *Racial Formation in the United States: From the 1960s to the 1980s* (New York, 1986), pp. 92–5; Morris, *The Origins of the Civil Rights Movement*, pp. 4–10.

27 Morris, *The Origins of the Civil Rights Movement*, pp. 275–8.

28 *Ibid.*, pp. 74–5, 194.

29 Fairclough, *To Redeem The Soul of America*, pp. 32–3.

30 Nancy Weiss, 'Creative Tensions in the Leadership of the Civil Rights Movement' in Charles W. Eagles and David L. Lewis (eds), *The Civil Rights Movement in America* (Jackson, MS, 1986), pp. 39–64.

31 Fairclough, *To Redeem the Soul of America*.

32 Sitkoff, *The Struggle For Black Equality*, pp. 164–6.

33 Neil R. McMillen, 'Black Enfranchisement in Mississippi: Federal Enforcement and Black Protest in the 1960s', *Journal of Southern History*, 43(3), 1977, p. 360.

34 John Dittmer, 'The Politics of the Mississippi Movement, 1954–1964' in Eagles and Lewis (eds), *The Civil Rights Movement in America*, pp. 65–93.

35 McMillen, 'Black Enfranchisement in Mississippi', pp. 364–6.

36 John Dittmer, 'The Politics of the Mississippi Movement, 1954–1964', pp. 65–93.

37 Meier and Rudwick, *From Plantation to Ghetto*, p. 252.

38 Neil R. McMillen, *The Citizen's Council: Organised Resistance to the Second Reconstruction* (Urbana, IL, 1971).

39 Jacoway and Colburn (eds), *Southern Businessmen and Desegregation*.

40 M. Richard Cramer, 'School Desegregation and New Industry: The Southern Community Leaders' Viewpoint', *Social Forces*, 1963, pp. 384–9.

41 Lawson, *Black Ballots*.

42 Goldfield, *Black, White and Southern*, p. 176.

43 McAdam, *Political Process and the Development of Black Insurgency*, p. 182; William Chafe in 'The End of One Struggle, The Beginning of Another' in Eagles and Lewis (eds), *The Civil Rights Movement in America*, pp. 127–56.

44 McAdam, *Political Process and the Development of Black Insurgency*, pp. 184–5.

45 Arnold Hirsch, *Making the Second Ghetto:Race and Housing in Chicago* (Cambridge, 1983).

46 *Ibid.*

47 Alan B. Anderson and George W. Pickering, *Confronting the Color Line: The Broken Promise of the Civil Rights Movement in Chicago* (Athens, GA, 1986), pp. 308–9.

48 Herbert Hill, 'Racial Equality in Employment: Patterns of Discrimination',

The Annals of the American Academy of Political and Social Science, 357, 1965, p. 47.

49 James T. Patterson, *Grand Expectations: The United States, 1946–1974* (Oxford, 1996), pp. 730–5.

50 Henry Allen Bullock, 'Urbanism and Race Relations' in Vance and Demerath (eds) *The Urban South*, pp. 207–29.

51 On ethnicity theory see Omi and Winant, *Racial Formation in the United States*, pp. 14–24.

52 James P. Smith and Finis R. Welch, 'Black/White Male Earnings and Employment, 1960–70' in F. Thomas Juster (ed.), *The Distribution of Economic Well-Being* (Cambridge, MA, 1977), pp. 00–00.

53 Gerald D. Jaynes, 'The Labor Market Status of Black Americans: 1939–1985', *Journal of Economic Perspectives*, 4(4), 1990, pp. 9–24.

54 Stephan Thernstrom, *The Other Bostonians: Poverty and Progress in the American Metropolis, 1880–1970* (Cambridge, MA, 1973), p. 207; Diane Nilsen Westcolt, 'Blacks in the 1970s: Did They Scale The Job Ladder?', *Monthly Labor Review*, 105(2), 1982, pp. 29–38.

55 Robert J. Norrell, 'Caste in Steel: Jim Crow Careers in Birmingham, Alabama', *Journal of American History*, 73, 1986–87, pp. 669–94.

56 Herbert Blumer, 'Industrialisation and Race Relations' in Guy Hunter (ed.), *Industrialisation and Race Relations: A Symposium* (London, 1965), pp. 220–53; Talcott Parsons and Kenneth Clark (eds), *The Negro American* (Boston, MA, 1967), pp. 739–42.

57 William H. Nicholls, 'Southern Tradition and Regional Economic Progress', *Southern Economic Journal*, 26(3), 1960, cited in Stanley B. Greenberg, *Race and State in Capitalist Development: Comparative Perspectives* (New Haven, CT, 1980), p. 211.

58 C. Vann Woodward, *The Strange Career of Jim Crow* (Oxford, 1966).

59 John W. Cell, *The Highest Stage of White Supremacy: The Origins of Segregation in South Africa and the American South* (Cambridge, 1982), p. 134.

60 James C. Cobb, *Industrialization and Southern Society, 1877–1984* (Lexington, KY, 1984), p. 84.

61 Greenberg, *Race and State in Capitalist Development*, pp. 228–32.

62 Norrell, 'Caste in Steel'; Greenberg, *Race and State in Capitalist Development*, pp. 216–17, 220–8.

63 Norrell, 'Caste in Steel', p. 694.

64 James C. Cobb, 'Beyond Planters and Industrialists: A New Perspective on the New South', *Journal of Southern History*, 54(1), 1988, p. 65.

65 Robert D. Bullard (ed.), *In Search of the New South: The Black Urban Experience in the 1970s and 1980s* (Tuscaloosa, AL, 1991); Kenneth L. Kusmer, 'African Americans in the City since World War II: From the Industrial to the Post-Industrial Era', *Journal of Urban History*, 21(4), 1995, pp. 458–504.

66 William Julius Wilson, *The Declining Significance of Race: Blacks and Changing American Institutions* (Chicago, 1978); Loic J. D. Wacquant and William Julius Wilson, 'The Cost of Racial and Class Exclusion in the Inner City', *The Annals of the American Academy of Political and Social Science*, 501, 1989, pp. 8–25.

67 Jaynes, 'The Labor Market Status of Black Americans'.

68 For an earlier discussion of this possibility see St Clair Drake, 'The Social and Economic Status of the Negro in the United States' in Parsons and Clark (eds), *The Negro American*, pp. 3–46.

69 Douglas Glasgow, *The Black Underclass: Poverty, Unemployment and Entrapment of Ghetto Youth* (New York, 1981); Ken Auletta, *The Underclass* (New York, 1982).
70 William Julius Wilson, *The Truly Disadvantaged: The Inner City, The Underclass, and Public Policy* (Chicago, 1987).
71 Lawrence Mead, *Beyond Entitlement: The Social Obligations of Citizenship* (New York, 1986).
72 Alphonso Pinkney, *The Myth of Black Progress* (Cambridge, 1984).
73 Thernstrom, *The Other Bostonians*, chapter 8.
74 Jacqueline Jones, 'Southern Diaspora: Origins of the Northern 'Underclass' in Michael B. Katz (ed.), *The Underclass Debate: Views From History* (Princeton, NJ, 1993), pp. 46–52.
75 Robert Weaver, *The Negro Ghetto* (New York, 1948).
76 Farley and Allen, *The Color Line and the Quality of Life in America*.
77 Pinkney, *The Myth of Black Progress*; Robin D. G. Kelley 'The Black Poor and the Politics of Opposition in a New South City, 1929–1970' in Katz (ed.), *The Underclass Debate*, pp. 293–333.
78 Douglas S. Massey and Nancy A. Denton, *American Apartheid: Segregation and the Making of the Underclass* (Cambridge, MA, 1993).
79 Farley and Allen, *The Color Line and the Quality of Life in America,*, pp. 142–50; Massey and Denton, *American Apartheid*.
80 Kenneth T. Jackson, *Crabgrass Frontier: The Suburbanization of the United States* (New York, 1985), chapters 11 and 13.

9

US incomes and consumption since 1945

The previous chapter addressed some of the important questions of inequalities and the theme is taken further in a consideration of trends in income and consumption. Measures of income distribution are outlined and there is then a discussion of poverty and of the evidence on women's earnings. The United States' place as the consumer society and the advances in average standards of living are assessed in a review of consumption and the debates over its implications.

In Rostow's stage model of economic development, post-1945 America was the first economy to enter an 'age of high mass consumption' based on widespread purchasing of durable goods and services.[1] Significant inequalities of wealth and differences in consumer habits persisted, but the nature and effects of a consumer society have been a major theme in the economic and social history of post-1945 America. The post-war period was associated, too, with increased social mobility compared to the restricted opportunities of the 1930s. If class and mobility are addressed primarily in terms of the workplace, the resumption of economic growth and the availability of a larger number of white-collar and technical jobs provided opportunities for upward social mobility after 1945. Men were more likely to enter different occupations from their fathers, and women were more likely to hold paid employment than their mothers and moved further into parts of the white-collar workforce. A widening of access to education, especially college education, facilitated such advances, with school enrolments rising, and the proportions who completed high school or graduated from college rose, offering further prospects of mobility for the children of working-class parents. There was an initial stimulus from the federal support to veterans, primarily men, entering college under the GI Bill of Rights and then higher levels of state and local support for education to accommodate the 'baby boom'. If status is taken as a key dimension of class, rising real incomes and the resurgence of consumption indicated an affluence in which the acquisition of a house, car and other goods was achieved or appeared within reach for a greater proportion of the working class. The appearance of 'affluent workers' suggested a blurring of class differences.

Trends in income and its distribution

Between 1947 and 1979 average family income in constant dollars doubled. The median income of white families increased from $10,388 to $20,502 between 1950 and 1979, and the median income of black families increased from $5,636 to $12,380, so that the rate of increase was more rapid for African-American families. These trends reflected the contraction of certain low-income occupations, notably farming, and the associated decline in regional income differentials, coupled with rural to urban migration and sustained economic growth. From 1970 the periodic recessions and slower economic growth checked the advance.

The fragmented nature of pre-1940 data on income and its distribution hindered evaluation of long-run trends. For Kolko or Kravis inequalities altered little between 1910 and the 1960s.[2] Kuznets and Goldsmith, however, detected declining inequalities between 1920 and 1950.[3] Lindert and Williamson argued that income distribution was more unequal than Kolko or Kravis had assumed for the early 1900s and became less evenly distributed during the 1920s. During the 1920s income distribution had become rather more unequal, initially as unskilled and labouring employment were reduced by mechanisation, and then under the influence of reductions in income tax, favouring the wealthy, who also benefited from the rising stock market. By 1929 the top fifth of the population held 54 per cent of family income while the lowest 40 per cent held 12.5 per cent. Estimates of income distribution in the 1930s indicated some reduction in inequalities due, in large measure, to falls in investment income accruing to the wealthy compared to the 1920s. The main gains accrued to middle-income people who were less affected by unemployment. In 1941 the top fifth accounted for 49 per cent of family income and the lowest 40 per cent had around 14 per cent. A further fall in inequalities occurred with the return of full employment during the war, and this time the effects reached the poor through the impact of migrations, economic development in the South and West and improvements in unskilled earnings in the 1940s. From Lindert and Williamson's work, it appears then that inequalities were at a relatively low point by 1945. After 1945 inequalities in family incomes narrowed before 1957, but widened thereafter due to the uneven impact of recessions and unemployment on families, and the effects of changes in the composition of families as the rising proportion of female-headed families, a group characterised by low incomes, depressed the level of median family incomes. The differential between skilled and unskilled wages altered little after 1950, but white-collar and professional occupations made some gains in income. Slower productivity growth, higher unemployment, the contraction of industrial jobs and the divergence of earnings between different segments of the service sector all promoted greater inequality in the 1970s and 1980s. Public policy exercised considerable influence since the expansion of transfer payments to the poor and elderly reduced inequalities by counter-ing the impact of unemployment and retirement. The rise in the real value of Social Security payments in the 1970s was a major gain for the elderly. In conjunction with low levels of unemployment in the 1960s, public pro-grammes accounted for the rise in the proportion of income accruing to the lowest quintile to 1970. Conversely, as the expansion of welfare was checked from the mid-1970s, federal policies were less of a counterbalance to the tendency for the ageing of the population to add to inequality.

Poverty in the United States

The general growth of incomes provided a remarkable rise in standards of living for all Americans. In absolute terms, that is in relation to people in other nations, Americans were extremely wealthy and consumed a vast array of goods and services. Even the poorest districts or states possessed high per-capita incomes and displayed high levels of ownership of cars, televisions and other products.[4] A different approach is to assess relative poverty, that is the variations in incomes and standards of living within the United States. Such measures are based on the idea that people compared themselves primarily to others in the same society, or perhaps that any inequalities indicated justifiable aspirations or one measure of economic performance. A fundamental problem with relative poverty is that it depends on establishing some level of income below which people's consumption is assumed to establish them as poor. However, this level alters as incomes rise, and at the same time the basket of goods and services which people expect to buy changes. Definitions of poverty vary from ideas of minimum subsistence to the more extensive range of goods required for an adequate or comfortable life-style. The different definitions have yielded wide differences in the proportion of the population defined as poor, and concepts such as minimum subsistence have incorporated an increasing array of products, some of which the poor of a generation or even a decade earlier might have regarded as luxuries. Different agencies and different states operated their own measures of subsistence or poverty. The Social Security Administration devised an official measure of poverty in the early 1960s which was based on money incomes with varying levels, according to family size, and regular reassessments of income levels and the basket of basic goods and services. The series does not include non-cash income such as food stamps, public housing or health benefits and such items can add significantly to people's effective purchasing power. The official measure has provided an index of the number and proportions of the population and different racial groups classified as poor, though again this represents relative poverty, not absolute poverty (Table 9.1). Changes in the methods of calculation in 1987 make the statistics for the later years not comparable to the earlier data.

Table 9.1 *Proportion of the US population below poverty level, 1959–91*

Year	Number (millions)				% of population			
	All	White	Black	Hispanic	All	White	Black	Hispanic
1959	39.5	28.5	9.9	–	22.4	18.1	55.1	–
1960	39.9	28.3	–	–	22.2	17.8	–	–
1966	28.5	20.8	8.9	–	14.7	12.2	41.8	–
1969	24.1	16.7	7.1	–	12.1	9.5	32.2	–
1970	25.4	17.5	7.5	–	12.6	9.9	33.5	–
1975	25.9	17.8	7.5	3.0	12.3	9.7	31.3	26.9
1978	24.5	16.3	7.6	2.6	11.4	8.7	30.6	21.6
1979	26.1	17.2	8.1	2.9	11.7	9.0	31.0	21.8
1980	29.3	19.7	8.6	3.5	13.0	10.2	32.5	25.7
1981	31.8	21.6	9.2	3.7	14.0	11.1	34.2	26.5
1982	34.4	23.5	9.7	4.3	15.0	12.0	35.6	29.9
1983	35.3	24.0	9.9	4.6	15.2	12.1	35.7	28.0
1987	32.2	21.2	9.5	5.4	13.4	10.4	32.4	28.0
1989	31.5	20.8	9.3	5.4	12.8	10.0	30.7	26.2
1990	33.6	22.3	9.8	6.0	13.5	10.7	31.9	28.1
1991	35.7	23.7	10.2	6.3	14.2	11.3	32.7	28.7

Sources: US Bureau of the Census, *Statistical Abstract of the United States: 1993* (113th edn, Washington, DC, 1993), p. 469, table 735.

On this basis nearly 40 million people, some 22 per cent of the population, were classified as poor in 1960, reflecting the impact of the 1957–58 and 1960–61 recessions. Even so the incidence of poverty had declined since 1949 on the basis of Stern's rather different measures of poverty for 1949 and 1959.[5] During the 1950s increased employment, notably of women, and extensions in the coverage of federal welfare programmes were the main sources of a decline in poverty which was most marked among white Americans. Changes occurred in categorical assistance where eligibility for Aid to Dependent Children was widened to include their families, although many states continued to limit access in practice.[6] There remained a sizeable population of the 'working poor' in part-time or low-paid jobs where volatile earnings were countered by the reliance on several members of the household working. The people who made up the largest numbers of the poor in 1959 were drawn from social groups who had predominated among the poor since the nineteenth century, namely the elderly and female-headed families, the unemployed and people from rural areas. Rates of poverty were highest among racial minorities.[7] In regional terms southern incomes were low and there were concentrations of poverty in the Appalachians, the old southern Cotton Belt and the cutover region of the upper Great Lakes.

In 1964 a report by the Council of Economic Advisers again identified rural residence, age, race, level of education and female-headed households as the major factors associated with low income. As discussed in Chapter 2, Johnson's Great Society programmes launched a raft of measures designed to solve the problems of poverty by improving education and training. Over the long boom of the 1960s, both the absolute number and the proportion of the population below the poverty line declined by some 40 per cent, with sustained growth in employment and higher real wages drawing many of the working poor out of the lowest income levels. Southern economic growth provided a stimulus to a low-wage region, and further extensions of federal transfer payments contributed additional support to the poor. The effects of the Great Society remain difficult to disentangle amid the broader economic and demographic trends. There was an extension of the federal role in welfare provision, particularly its financial support, but charities and philanthropy remained active parts of the welfare system, as did private insurance. Given economic expansion from 1961 to 1969, the strategy of improving human capital had reasonable prospects of success.[8] Transfer payments offset the tendencies towards greater inequality created by an ageing population, and access to medical services was widened for lower-income groups.[9] The Great Society's contribution is understated by the data in Table 9.1 since it does not measure the gains in non-cash income, which were a major part of the various schemes such as Medicaid and food stamps.

A sharp rise in poverty might have been anticipated after 1970 as the economy weakened, but the initial rise was modest. There were still countervailing influences as southern development benefited a low-income region, farm incomes received a temporary stimulus and the greater eligibility and higher payments under Social Security assisted the elderly. In 1980 the Veterans' Administration accounted for less than 5 per cent of all welfare spending, but its budget of $21 million included support for 172 hospitals and over one million people in education and training. The real impact of recessions on the overall poverty rate came with a rise from 25 million and 11.4 per cent of the population to 35 million and 15.2 per cent between 1978 and 1983 after which, despite a limited fall, the poverty level remained on a plateau significantly above that for the 1970s. The number of working poor, those with full-time or part-time jobs, increased from 6.2 million in 1973 to 9.1 million by 1985 and consisted chiefly of white males living in rural areas.[10] By the 1980s there had been a major decline in the extent of poverty among the elderly who constituted 40 per cent of the poor in 1959, but only 16 per cent in 1974. The scale of rural poverty also declined. The largest number of the poor remained white Americans and there was a noticeable rise in the proportion of poor whites in the early 1980s. While the elderly as a group fared rather better, single-parent and especially female-headed families made up a growing proportion of the poor. In 1992 46 per cent of single mothers were below the poverty line and for black single-parent families the proportion was 65 per cent.

Gender

Considerable continuity is evident in women's low wages and their greater tendency to engage in part-time work. The ratio of female to male earnings was stable from the 1950s to the 1970s and narrowed during the 1980s.[11] To some extent comparisons of average earnings blur variations between different groups of women. Middle-class women who gained entry to the professions benefited from their education, and in the service sector incomes diverged between higher-paid, more stable work and the mass of lower-paid, often part-time work. Human-capital theory suggested that the gap between male and female earnings reflects women's lower educational qualifications, lower skills or more limited or fragmented work experience compared to male workers. There are indications that education played an important role: improvements in qualifications and in time in paid work since the 1970s were accompanied by increases in relative earnings for women. Women were more likely to have fragmented working lives, which reduced their accumulated work experience and access to the seniority and internal company labour markets which brought higher earnings. Yet studies which applied human-capital theory generally conclude that a considerable portion of the gap between male and female earnings remained unexplained.[12] This implies the existence of broader forms of discrimination which produce gender-based definitions of skill which disadvantage women workers. The passage of equal-opportunity legislation did not ensure equal treatment since the concentration of women workers in certain largely female occupations limited scope for comparisons with male earnings. Where women and men worked in an industry, employers and unions frequently agreed to limited reforms which preserved gender segregation in employment and wage-rates.[13] The elements of affirmative action increased women's access to some jobs, but did not bring men into sectors dominated by female workers. Campaigns to raise rates of pay for women had some effect, but the divide between male- and female-dominated occupations constrained the impact of equal pay laws on low-wage female jobs. For employers, especially in labour-intensive industries, female labour was functional as a means of limiting costs. Thus employers continued to classify women as liable to leave full-time employment to have children or as temporary workers whose pay constituted a secondary element within an overall family income. This perception became less valid as the number of female-headed households increased, but remained a potent influence because it reflected prevailing gender assumptions and corresponded to the experiences of many women.

The role for public policy in raising female earnings was limited. There was greater public debate following the revival of feminist politics after two decades of quiescence. The contemporary civil rights movement stimulated a general climate of assertiveness and, as in other areas, public policy was a little more active. In 1963 the report of the President's Commission on the Status of Women documented discrimination in employment, education and legal status, but did not recommend legislation; in the same year the Equal Pay Act offered largely rhetorical support for a long-debated principle.[14] Betty Friedan's 1963 book, *The Feminine Mystique*, highlighted the economic, social and psychological constraints of domesticity and had a major impact on attitudes among the cohort of 'baby-boom' mothers who began to re-enter the workforce. The Civil Rights Act of 1964 included a prohibition against discrimination on grounds of gender, though effective enforcement of the legislation was delayed until 1972. In 1967 an Executive Order barred sex discrimination in employment by federal contractors. The women's movement's subsequent development brought advances through legal challenges to discrimination in access to jobs and to inequalities in pay, especially using litigation and the Equal Employment Opportunity Commission (EEOC), and in the number of women entering local and national politics. As with the civil rights movement, the revival of feminist political campaigns produced resentment and resistance, which is symbolised by the failure to achieve ratification of the Equal Rights Amendment.

The consumer society

Aspects of post-war behaviour were anticipated in the spread of nationally-advertised branded goods from the 1870s, in the central role of housing and new electrical products in the economic expansion of the 1920s and in the spread of national retailers.[15] In the 1930s, spending on housing and durable goods was depressed and even economic recovery in the 1940s was initially accompanied by some restrictions on civilian consumption. The post-war 'age of high mass consumption' began with the revival of spending on durable goods from the depressed levels of the 1930s and continued with the widening of middle-class purchasing, especially of recreational goods and services; the proportion of families owning two or more cars doubled during the 1950s. Lower-income families continued to spend a higher proportion of their budgets on food, housing and power and remained more susceptible to unemployment, so their post-war prosperity was channelled initially into improved diets and accommodation. Consumer durables could be purchased second-hand or through reliance on instalment credit, though low and unstable incomes forced a reliance on expensive types of debt.[16] Nonetheless there was a tendency for items which had been luxuries at one point to be regarded as standard later, so that consumption embraced a wider array of products. Radio completed its penetration of virtually all households in the 1950s while televisions were acquired more rapidly than vacuum cleaners and washing machines in working-class households. More extensive working-class consumption of cars, electrical appliances and services occurred during the 1960s when low levels of unemployment and greater reductions in the prices of durable goods broadened the market.[17] Throughout the post-war period local studies of blue-collar workers identified television viewing, home decorating, gardening and motoring as their principal leisure activities.[18]

With construction costs declining and house-builders developing new tracts of land, the real cost of house purchases declined and as it became cheaper to buy than to rent, the percentage of Americans owning their own home rose from 40 per cent in 1940 to 60 per cent twenty years later. The rising number of separate households, increased demand for appliances, and new building, plus the continued expansion of rural electrification, increased the proportion of households connected from 76 per cent in 1946 to 90 per cent in 1952.[19] Given this larger market of potential customers, another component of demand for durables was the substitution of electrical versions for existing appliances such as gas cookers. At the same time the shift away from heating with coal to using gas and oil created demand for new equipment. Expenditure on major durable goods, such as radios, telephones, vacuum cleaners and washing machines, was particularly noticeable.[20] The most striking new feature was the rapid diffusion of television. A novelty with only 6,000 sets produced in 1946, television was in two-thirds of US households within a decade and in 90 per cent of households in 1960. The largest rise in consumer spending since 1945 occurred for the buying and running of cars and the car was the classic form of conspicuous consumption. New car sales increased from 2.1 million in 1946 to 7.9 million in 1955, a level not exceeded for a decade. In the immediate post-war years car purchases were predominantly on a cash basis, but as demand stabilised, buying on credit became the standard practice. With car registrations increasing from 28 million in 1946 to 40 million in 1950 and 62 million in 1960, plus a rise in average annual mileage, automobile-related services, such as petrol stations, were revitalised, and motoring contributed to higher spending on recreation and travel, with motels and the new drive-in cinemas among the beneficiaries. Since 1945 Americans have spent a smaller proportion of their incomes on food and alcoholic drink while purchasing more pre-packaged and frozen foods, meat and milk.[21] A number of broad influences lay behind the general trends. The higher proportion of women in employment increased family purchasing power and provided an incentive to substitute prepared foods for home cooking. Growing white-collar employment made employment and incomes more stable, while reduced working hours and increased holidays allowed more time for leisure activities.

After a sluggish phase in the late 1950s consumer spending revived, with more extensive working-class purchasing of cars, electrical appliances and services as lower prices of durables broadened the market.[22] The other strands of 1960s consumption were new versions of established goods and the appearance of new products. Dishwashers, waste-disposal units and air conditioning, which had been luxury items in 1960, were more widely available by the end of the decade, but the expansion of home-ownership slowed in the 1960s. After 1970 the check to real income growth and the trend to greater inequality produced particularly volatile conditions. The prosperity of wealthier consumers stimulated the growth of demand for expensive goods and services. At the same time the cycle of new products which spread into mass purchasing appeared to accelerate, particularly for electrical products such as video recorders, microwave ovens, home computers and compact discs.

During the 1950s and 1960s there were distinct elements of a national popular culture based on urban living, wider availability of consumer products, more extensive advertising and the impact of television. Marchand points to a decline in regional variations in foods and house-styles in favour of a California-culture of suburbs of ranch-style bungalows, car-ownership and more informality in dress and manners.[23] The extent and influence of such developments have been contested. Berger concluded that these developments contributed to a suburban myth of equality which satisfied both proponents of a new classless consumer society and critics of suburban uniformity.[24] Lebergott argued forcefully that mass consumption should not be denigrated as a form of cultural decline from high to popular culture, since it is difficult to define essential purchases beyond a very basic level, and that consumers obtained satisfaction from a variety of goods and services.[25] Pronounced inequalities in levels and distribution of income and the extensive ranges of products, styles and prices emphasised that access to goods and services was neither straightforward nor uniform. Low incomes limited access to consumer products or to particular types of housing and the considerable differentiation among products maintained status differences. Before new car sales peaked, the proliferation of ever more ornate models indicated an emphasis on wealthier customers and colour television, introduced in 1961, was in one-quarter of middle-income households compared to between half and three-quarters of wealthy households by 1970. Commercial interests placed considerable emphasis on niche marketing and product differentiation so that not all cars or jeans were presented as identical.

Basic economic conditions, such as the level of real incomes, set parameters within which consumption occurred, but there are contrasting interpretations of the sources and effects of consumerism. Ewen argued that consumption was a product of commercial interests, as businesses used advertising to create desires for non-essential goods and produce perpetually restless and dissatisfied consumers for whom products either fail to live up to their image, are displaced by a new vogue or lose their novelty.[26] Ewen regarded the suburbs as an escape from industrial or work routines, but based on a consumer culture which contained its own elements of standardisation and conformity.[27] Against the ideas of suburban uniformity, Whyte's study of middle-class suburbs noted elements of diversity in terms of income, age and ethnicity as well as positive features such as the capacity to generate companionship. Later studies place even greater emphasis on such characteristics, highlighting the diverse character of new working-class estates, ethnic suburbanites and growth around small towns or associated with particular types of employment. Berger and Gans suggested that suburban living involved less of a break with the travelling to work, similar types of home, social values and class and ethnic divisions evident in older neighbourhoods.[28]

For business, the central lesson of the inter-war period had been the importance of sales rather than production. As a result there was a greater emphasis, except in the initial post-war restocking, on the role of marketing through a mix of strategies.[29] Advertisers stressed their role in educating the public as consumers. There were inherent limits to the effectiveness of such corporate policies since they attempted to adjust to fundamental instabilities. As a product achieved mass sales so demand tended to become saturated and new models were required to generate further sales. This product-cycle logic was reflected in the regular updating of existing products as, for example, with the introduction of colour television. During the 1970s and 1980s economic instabilities created uncertainty about employment, incomes and wealth and the prospects for upward social mobility. The subdivisions within society were more evident as income inequalities widened. The appearance and diffusion of new consumer durables such as video recorders, compact discs, camcorders, home computers and microwaves indicated the continued potency of consumption, but there were signs that the pace at which new products were introduced was accelerating.[30]

Even Ewen acknowledged elements of ambiguity which limited the degree of control over consumption exercised by business, which never fully regulated consumer behaviour. Other analyses assigned even greater weight to the role and perceptions of consumers, regarding them not passive recipients of the advertisers' messages, but as being able to assess products in a clear, pragmatic fashion. From this perspective consumption served as a fundamental source of self-expression and identity on a par with or exceeding the importance of occupation.[31] For advertisers, producers and distributors, there was an uncertain mix of trying to mould and respond to consumers' preferences. Throughout the post-war period business placed greater emphasis on niche marketing and absorbed elements of counter-cultures into its advertising, placing greater stress, for instance, on environmental themes during the 1980s and 1990s.

There are different visions of the cultural consequences of mass consumption. For Ewen advertising and consumption constituted a powerful cultural force which diverted attention away from class conflicts. Increased home-ownership and consumption represented higher living standards and a sense among working-class people of having 'arrived', in terms of a comfortable life-style which they associated with middle-class status. Daniel Bell took a rather different approach. He regarded the new scale of consumption as the continuation of the dissolution of established cultural values and institutions such as the family and the work ethic, and the establishment of a less structured, more hedonistic society based on a variety of life-styles.[32] From this perspective corporate efforts to increase sales carried the danger of undermining efficiency by centring people's attention on consumption rather than work as their primary expression of identity. Bell's analysis emphasised tensions involved in consumption, but left many issues open. The idea of traditional values or institutions appears suspect, given that the consumer society took shape from the 1870s, and in any case 1950s consumerism coexisted with an assertion of the family as a basic agency whose functions included consumption. The threat to the work ethic fits uneasily against modest falls since 1945 in average hours worked, the expansion of female employment and the potential stimulus to work from desires for consumer goods and services. The post-war economic boom offered confirmation for individualistic routes to advancement, but consumption was far from the only cultural influence. The Cold War provided the basis for reassertions of nationalism and consensus, though certainly consumption and standards of living were cited as evidence of the vigour of American society. Unions and the growth of federal and corporate welfare offered differing collective forms of support and the marked rise in church attendance suggested that there were other sources of values.

As the post-war boom supplied a cornucopia of products and services, people appeared content to acquire rather than complain in the 1950s, though a handful of politicians, largely at state level, federal officials and campaigners maintained some pressure on manufacturers and advertisers. The affluent worker had a more solid presence by the 1960s and yet the civil rights movement, feminism and the anti-war campaign supplied varied critiques of society which included more radical class-based analyses. The Cold War constraints had lessened and there was a distinct generational change as the children of post-war affluence reacted against the elements of conformity. Despite its individualistic character, consumption could carry radical messages in an effective fashion due to its centrality in daily life and because the idea of consumer rights had a resonance in terms of American ideals of individualism. The civil rights movement's demands for equal treatment on buses, in restaurants and in other public facilities demonstrated such tactics. Post-war affluence brought a growth in tourism and outdoor recreation which had mixed effects. It led to further development and damage to the environment, but Hays has argued that at the same time a new view emerged which saw the environment as an amenity to be valued and preserved for itself rather than being treated as a resource to be exploited.[33] This attitude was strongest among younger and more educated people from the 1960s and the environmental movement expanded rapidly in the early 1970s. Equally unexpected was the revival of a general consumer movement during the 1960s and early 1970s after half a century of quiescence.[34] A new generation of young lawyers, notably Ralph Nader, publicised potential hazards in products in the 1960s and triggered a mushroom-like growth of consumer activism. The campaigns tapped a sizeable, if rather diffuse, wellspring of suspicion of business and advertising as well as a lack of confidence in regulators.[35] Political entrepreneurs in a less centralised Congress seized on the publicity value of conducting hearings and promoting legislation across a wide range of issues such as health, safety and advertising standards.[36] The consumer movement contributed to a new sense of the social responsibilities of business. The mainstream of the critique of consumerism emphasised a 'fair deal' rather than dramatic change, though there were more radical elements. A fragmented business community proved ill-equipped to counter this new lobbying. The sense of economic crisis and a new degree of mobilisation by corporate America after 1970 asserted a narrower vision of the proper province of consumer influence as being via the invisible hand of the market. If this represented an expression of elite interests, there was a conservative reaction, too, from middle-class property-owners demanding lower taxes, especially on property, and less federal government, as well as seeking to protect their suburbs against encroachment by developers or crime.

Notes

1 W. W. Rostow, *Stages of Economic Growth: A Non-communist Manifesto* (Cambridge, 1960).

2 Gabriel Kolko, *Wealth and Power in America: An Analysis of Social Class and Income Distribution* (London, 1962); Irving B. Kravis, *The Structure of Income: Some Quantitative Essays* (Philadelphia, PA, 1962).

3 Simon Kuznets, *Shares of Upper Income Groups in Income and Savings* (New York, 1953); Raymond W. Goldsmith, *The National Wealth of the United States in the Postwar Period* (Princeton, NJ, 1962).

4 James T. Patterson, *America's Struggle Against Poverty, 1900–1985* (London, 1986), pp. 78–82.

5 Mark J. Stern, 'Poverty and Family Composition' in Michael B. Katz (ed.), *The Underclass Debate: Views From History* (Princeton, NJ, 1993), pp. 220–42.

6 Robert H. Bremner, 'Families, Children, and the State' and James T. Patterson, 'Poverty and Welfare in America, 1945–1960' in Robert H. Bremner and Gary W. Reichard (eds), *Reshaping America: Society and Institutions, 1945–1960* (Columbus, OH, 1982), pp. 21–4, 200–1.

7 Michael Harrington, *The Other America: Poverty in the United States* (New York, 1962).

8 For positive views on the Great Society see the chapters by Paul Ylvisaker and by Sar Levitan and Clifford Johnson in Marshall Kaplan and Peggy L. Cuciti (eds), *The Great Society and Its Legacy: Twenty Years of US Social Policy*

(Durham, NC, 1986); John E. Schwarz, *America's Hidden Success: A Reassessment of Public Policy from Kennedy to Reagan* (London, 1983).

9 Alan S. Blinder, 'The Level and Distribution of Economic Well-Being' in Martin Feldstein (ed.), *The American Economy in Transition* (Chicago, 1980), pp. 446–8, 458–9.

10 Sar A. Levitan and Isaac Shapiro, *Working But Poor: America's Contradiction* (Baltimore, MD, 1987).

11 Claudia Goldin, *Understanding the Gender Gap* (New York, 1990); see also Suzanne M. Bianchi and Daphne Spain, *American Women in Transition* (New York, 1986), pp. 170–1.

12 Bianchi and Spain, *American Women in Transition*, pp. 190–3.

13 Denis Deslippe, '"We Had An Awful Time With Our Women": Iowa's United Packinghouse Workers of America', *Journal of Women's History*, 5(1), 1993, pp. 10–32.

14 Goldin, *Understanding the Gender Gap*, p. 200.

15 Martha L. Olney, *Buy Now, Pay Later: Advertising, Credit, and Consumer Durables in the 1920s* (Chapel Hill, NC, 1991), chapter 2.

16 David Caplovitz, *The Poor Pay More: Consumer Practices of Low Income Families* (London, 1963).

17 Olney, *Buy Now, Pay Later*, p. 33, table 2.5.

18 David Halle, *America's Working Man: Work, Home and Politics among Blue-Collar Property Owners* (Chicago, 1984).

19 Sue Bowden and Avner Offer, 'Household Appliances and the Use of Time: The United States and Britain since the 1920s', *Economic History Review*, 62(4), 1994, pp. 735–48.

20 Olney, *Buy Now, Pay Later*, pp. 28–9.

21 Blinder, 'The Level and Distribution of Economic Well-Being'; Stanley Lebergott, *Pursuing Happiness: American Consumers in the Twentieth Century* (Princeton, NJ, 1993).

22 Olney, *Buy Now, Pay Late*, p. 33, table 2.5.

23 Roland Marchand, 'US Popular Culture, 1945–60' in Bremner and Reichard (eds), *Reshaping America*.

24 Bennett M. Berger, 'The Myth of Suburbia' in John Kramer (ed.), *North American Suburbs: Politics, Diversity, and Change* (Berkeley, CA, 1972), pp. 5–18; Scott Donaldson, *The Suburban Myth* (New York, 1969).

25 Lebergott, *People of Plenty*.

26 Stuart Ewen, *Captains of Consciousness: Advertising and the Social Roots of the Consumer Culture* (New York, 1976).

27 Stuart Ewen, *All Consuming Images: The Politics of Style in Contemporary Culture* (New York, 1988), p. 245.

28 Herbert J. Gans, *The Levittowners: Ways of Life and Politics in a New Suburban Community* (London, 1967); Bennett M. Berger, *Working-Class Suburb: A Study of Auto Workers in Suburbia* (Berkeley, CA, 1960) and 'The Myth of Suburbia' and Herbert J. Gans, 'Urbanism and Suburbanism as Ways of Life: A Re-evaluation of Definitions' in Kramer (ed.), *North American Suburbs*, pp. 5–18, 31–51.

29 Neil Fligstein, *The Transformation of Corporate Control* (Cambridge, MA, 1990).

30 Maureen Boyle Gray, 'Consumer Spending on Durables and Services in the 1980s', *Monthly Labor Review*, 115(5), 1992, pp. 18–26.

31 Herbert F. Moorhouse, *Driving Ambitions: An Analysis of the American Hot Rod Enthusiasm* (Manchester, 1990).

32 Daniel Bell, *The Cultural Contradictions of Capitalism* (London, 1976).

33 Samuel P. Hays, *Beauty, Health, and Permanence: Environmental Politics in the United States, 1955–1985* (Cambridge, 1987), chapter 1.
34 Ellis W. Hawley, *The New Deal and the Problem of Monopoly: A Study in Economic Ambivalence* (Princeton, NJ, 1966), pp. 75–90, 198–204.
35 Robert N. Meyer, *The Consumer Movement: Guardians of the Marketplace* (Boston, MA, 1989).
36 David Vogel, *Fluctuating Fortunes: The Political Power of Business in America* (New York, 1989).

10

The United States in the world economy

In 1945 the United States occupied a particularly powerful position in the world economy and in international affairs which were reflected in great influence over policy-making. This initial role in trade and finance and the readjustments of the 1950s and 1960s are considered before an account of the growth of US multinational firms. The signs of a less dominant economic position and performance in the 1970s and 1980s are then analysed to suggest ways in which the United States standing in the world economy has altered over the last half-century.

Before 1914 the United States' role in the international economy was as an exporter of agricultural and industrial products. It was a high-income economy which combined exports of food and raw materials with technological leadership in machinery and engineering. Earlier capital inflows left the United States a net debtor nation, but this position was changing as US overseas lending increased, and the impact of World War I accelerated this process. By the end of the war the United States was a net creditor nation. During the 1920s US loans were an important element in European financial reconstruction and the US dollar joined the pound sterling and the French franc as a key reserve currency in the Gold Exchange Standard. By the end of the 1920s the United States was the world's leading exporter and the second largest importer, though its foreign trade sector was comparatively small in relation to the US economy as a whole. Unlike Britain, the US economy was almost completely self-sufficient, which hindered the repayment of dollar debts by other countries. The decline in US lending from 1928, initially as capital flowed to Wall Street and then as the slump took hold, and the collapse of US imports were hammer blows to the world economy. Despite its greater importance, the United States was reluctant to assume political or economic leadership, remained outside the League of Nations and restricted flows of gold under the Exchange System. Links to the world economy diminished. The Hawley–Smoot Tariff Bill in 1930 escalated the general scramble into protectionism which further depressed trade, and a subsequent rise of pro-free-trade sentiment achieved little amid the general autarchy of the 1930s. Immigration, which had declined in the 1920s, fell precipitately during the 1930s due to earlier immigration restrictions and the high level of unemployment. There was an influx of foreign capital seeking refuge in the United States from political and social instabilities elsewhere.

The United States and post-war economic policy-making

By the late 1940s conditions had changed significantly. The wartime expansion of the US industrial base, coupled with devastation in Europe and Japan, placed the US economy in an extraordinarily powerful position. US industrial production was 45 per cent of world output in 1948 and its national income and productivity, especially in manufacturing, far outstripped other economies.[1] The productivity gap had been widening ever since 1900, particularly between 1940 and 1945, and US technology and management appeared as models for other economies in their pursuit of modernisation. Exports of industrial and consumer goods and agricultural commodities were buoyant immediately after the war as other countries embarked on reconstruction. Although shortages of dollar reserves led other governments to restrict the availability of dollar exchange, the United States accounted for one-third of world exports of manufactures in 1950. The revival of immigration to the United States renewed another link to the wider world. More generally, in contrast to inter-war uncertainties, the United States assumed a key role in international policy-making. During wartime discussions about reconstruction, US and British policy-makers were anxious to avoid a return to pre-war conditions of protectionism, financial paralysis and unemployment. The Bretton Woods agreement in 1944 established the International Monetary Fund (IMF) and the World Bank as foundation-stones for a multilateral payments system. However, US hopes for a speedy transition to a functioning international currency and financial system were dashed by economic weaknesses and caution elsewhere. Rather, a more stable environment was achieved through a piecemeal process of adjustment, including European devaluations in 1949 and the dismantling of some tariff restrictions.

While the IMF and the World Bank symbolised the ideal of reconstructing the world financial system, their limited resources and the financial pressures on most economies inhibited the immediate operation of the Bretton Woods system. Of far greater importance was the $11.5 billion of Marshall Aid between 1948 and 1951 which financed imports of machinery, equipment and food which were otherwise limited by a shortage of dollars in both reserves and earnings from trade. Concern that economic collapse would contribute to the spread of Communist influence persuaded the Truman administration to supply Marshall Aid to support European reconstruction efforts, and it provided resources and a political sense of direction. The process was sustained by devaluations in Europe and Japan and tariff reductions, as well as by the continuing flow of government lending and private investment from the United States.

The thrust of US trade policy was an attack on trade discrimination in a rejection of the bilateral agreements and autarchy of the 1930s and an attack on British imperial preferences. This approach combined advocacy of freer trade as a route to economic growth, with the pursuit of US interests in gaining wider access to export markets. Ambitious plans for an International Trade Organisation foundered, as many countries feared the effects of multilateral trading on their fragile economies in the short run and on their longer-term ambitions for industrialisation. From 1947 the General Agreement on Tariffs and Trade (GATT) provided the framework for post-war commercial policy. GATT operated through a series of detailed and lengthy negotiating rounds, eight in all by 1992, in which countries agreed to reductions in, and the removal of, tariffs. Later tariff rounds yielded fewer gains than those in the 1940s since countries had earlier given up their least valued duties. Certain sectors, notably agriculture and textiles, received protection against cheap imports, economies were permitted to restrict trade in the event of balance-of-payments problems and throughout the post-war period many developing economies maintained protectionism as a means of import-substituting industrialisation. Moreover removal of tariffs left considerable scope for non-tariff barriers such as quotas. In the United States there was always a vocal protectionist lobby of special interests drawn from agriculture and industries faced with import competition such as clothing, footwear and steel. Nonetheless GATT contributed to a revival of trade, particularly in manufactures, during the 1950s and 1960s, which supported post-war growth.

Overall post-war US policy was far more active and interventionist in the international economy than had been the case between the wars. This contrast reflected a desire to avoid a return of previous economic problems, but there was the additional motivation of Cold War rivalry. It provided a strategic motivation for the more activist role as well as a rationale for promoting reconstruction in Europe and Japan, and an emphasis on co-operation through international agencies whether in the distribution of Marshall Aid, the IMF, the North Atlantic Treaty Organization (NATO) or trade policy. It ensured that the Soviet Union, Eastern Europe and China remained outside the liberalised trading system and that protectionist pressures encountered powerful strategic arguments for opening US markets to Japanese goods in the 1950s. Wartime military expansion and possession of the new atomic weaponry were further dimensions to the United States' international role and the Cold War consolidated the powerful military element in the United States' greater world role. A major proportion of US aid took the form of military grants and assistance. The military share increased from one-quarter of US aid between 1946 and 1952 to nearly half

Table 10.1 *World growth rates in real Gross Domestic Product per capita compared with the US 1913–89*

Country	1913–50	1950–73	1973–89
France	1.1	4.0	1.8
Germany	0.7	4.9	2.1
Italy	0.8	5.0	2.6
Japan	0.9	8.0	3.1
UK	0.8	2.5	1.8
USA	1.6	2.2	1.6

Source: Angus Maddison, *Dynamic Forces in Capitalist Development: A Long-Run Comparative View* (Oxford, 1991), p. 49, table 3.1.

from 1953 to 1961 and still accounted for about one-third of aid in the 1960s. During the first post-war decade the emphasis was on reconstruction of industrial economies in Western Europe and 69 per cent of US aid went to developed economies. Thereafter aid expenditure was directed almost entirely at developing economies, which became the centre of the Cold War contests in military terms and in the advocacy of capitalist and communist routes to economic development.

Readjustments and new developments in the 1950 and 1960s

During the 1950s and 1960s there were two rather different aspects to the United States' position in the international economy. On the one hand, there was a decline in its dominance in an inevitable readjustment from the exceptional circumstances in 1945 and, on the other hand, US ties to other economies were strengthened. The readjustments were clear. As industrial capacity was restored in Europe and Japan, the United States' share of world industrial production declined, though it was still 40 per cent in the early 1960s. The pace of reconstruction and the impact of the general economic boom were apparent in the rates of growth in the leading industrial economies (Table 10.1).

As the exceptional post-war export boom abated the United States' share of all manufactured exports fell sharply to 18 per cent.[2] In essence trade patterns based on comparative advantage were restored, with the United States importing more labour-intensive consumer products while retaining substantial trade surpluses in machinery, transportation equipment, chemicals and agricultural produce, as well as military products.[3] While the composition of trade altered, there was remarkably little change in the overall significance of trade to the economy. Trade had been depressed during the 1930s, with exports averaging 3 per cent and imports between 2 and 3 per cent of Gross National Product (GNP). Once the immediate export boom of the late 1940s abated, exports settled at around 4 per cent and imports around 3 per cent of GNP to the late 1960s. As a result the trade sector was more important than in the 1930s, but still smaller in relation to the domestic economy than it had been in the 1920s.

While trade recovered some lost ground, the real strengthening of US links to the international economy after 1945 occurred in the currency and capital markets. The US dollar's role was clearly established as the key reserve currency. The surplus on trade in goods and services allowed the United States to sustain massive outflows of private capital and government grants during the 1950s and 1960s. Total overseas investments increased from $36.9 billion in 1945 to $85.6 billion in 1960 and $166.9 billion by 1970. Overseas investments offered higher rates of return, and there was a specific incentive for investors to place funds overseas in the form of the Federal Reserve Board's ceiling on interest rates on deposits in US banks. A central feature of the first two post-war decades was US corporate investment, extending the multinational presence rapidly, especially in manufacturing: private direct investment expanded from $8.4 billion to $78.2 billion between 1945 and 1970. It was a process encouraged by government and by corporate strategies as firms responded to the growth of markets overseas, exploited competitive advantages, and endeavoured to circumvent remaining trade barriers. One consequence was that an increasing proportion of trade was conducted between units of multinational firms. US financial institutions also became more involved in international operations. The US balance of payments was boosted by profits, dividends and interest on foreign investments which also promoted exports of US goods to supply overseas plants and personnel.

Multinational enterprise

The factors which led to the growth of large domestic firms also promoted a major expansion of overseas investment by US business after 1945. US direct investment overseas increased from the 1890s, initially in resource-based activities such as mining, oil and agriculture, but investment in manufacturing expanded rapidly between the wars as firms sought to build on earlier exports and defend their sales against protectionist policies.[4] The Depression of the 1930s had mixed effects as some foreign operations withdrew from unprofitable or unpredictable markets and other firms extended their multinational presence. World War II checked overseas investment, though the wartime developments in transport and communications and the experience of supplying the military abroad arguably encouraged future interests.[5] At the end of the war US multinational investment began a phase of rapid growth with manufacturing firms aggressively taking the lead. The value of US direct foreign investment increased from $11.79 billion in 1950 to $78.18 billion twenty years later with growth averaging between 9 and 10 per cent in each five-year period.[6] Only Britain and some smaller European nations extended their multinational activities in the immediate post-war years and previous important investors, such as Germany, France and Japan, had lost earlier interests or concentrated on domestic investments. As a result the US accounted for almost half of total accumulated foreign direct investment by 1960.[7] Manufacturing's share, already the largest component of US overseas investment between the wars, rose from 32 per cent to 41 per cent between 1950 and 1970.

The surge of US multinational activity prompted fears in some quarters of American 'invasion', an anxiety most evident in France.[8] There was also a growth of interest in explaining the timing and character, particularly of manufacturing investments, as well as overseas concerns about its impact on host economies.[9] An extensive literature in economics and management provided interpretations of the motives for, and direction of, overseas investment and emphasised the diverse range of influences and conditions involved. Indeed the writings of such leading students of multinationals as John Dunning or Mira Wilkins offered 'eclectic' theories based precisely upon the complexity of forces rather than a single or simple model.[10] Dunning's eclectic paradigm provided a convenient summary of three main aspects of multinational activity: ownership advantages, internalisation incentives and location factors. Ownership advantages referred to any form of competitive advantage which a firm possessed compared to its competitors and the emphasis was on the domestic roots of overseas investments. A firm's advantage might lie in its product, manufacturing technology, management, financial resources or some less tangible element. A variant of this approach was Vernon's product-cycle theory which argued that new products were generated in high-income markets where consumer wants could be identified, but as the product became standardised, there was an increased likelihood of multinational investment.[11] Certainly US business possessed a substantial lead in terms of productivity and technology in 1945, particularly in mass-production industries such as the automobile, machinery and chemicals industries. Access to foreign markets and the capacity to oversee subsidiaries were improved by advances in international communications, though such developments favoured exports as well as direct investment. The decision to produce overseas rather than to export can be explained in terms of market imperfections which threatened or deterred reliance on exports. These imperfections included the idea that direct investment allowed greater control and better knowledge of the overseas market compared to using an agent.

Locational influences referred to the geographical distribution of multinational investments and encompassed a wide range of influences from protectionism to the availability of natural resources, labour costs, transport costs, levels of demand and cultural factors. In the immediate postwar years Canada and Latin America were the main destinations for US investments, but Europe was the growth area in the 1950s as US manufacturers exploited their competitive advantages in expanding consumer markets. In the 1960s developing countries attracted rather more investment and in certain cases such markets offered an opportunity to extend the life of technologies which had been superseded in the United States.[12] The timing and direction of some multinational investments were driven by particular concerns. Resource-based sectors such as oil, mining and agricultural businesses sought new sources of supply and more intense phases of overseas investment were stimulated by the greater assertiveness of host countries in the 1960s and soaring energy prices in the 1970s. Some multinational investments were made to escape new environmental regulations and in other cases the impetus came from a desire to reduce labour costs. The traditionally footloose textile industry shifted overseas, primarily to Southeast Asia, from the 1950s and a similar trend was evident two decades later for electronics assembly plants. Despite the general reduction in trade restrictions, overseas investments were encouraged by elements of protectionism which handicapped exports. Corporate rivalries, including threats from overseas producers, also triggered overseas direct investment also, even into small markets where economies of scale could not be realised, if a firm preferred to avoid being completely excluded. In the financial sector US banks had little international presence in the 1940s or 1950s, though a few firms followed corporate clients overseas. However, the expansion of overseas dollar holdings offered US banks a partial escape from the constraining effects of domestic regulatory limitations on branching and interest rates. These incentives, coupled with improvements in communications and information flows, were reflected in a rapid expansion of multinational banking in general and of large US banks in particular.

US multinational activity assumed a variety of forms from direct investments and co-operative ventures to licensing arrangements, but US firms displayed a preference for full ownership, with overseas operations being responsible to an international division. In part this reflected the extent of the initial technological lead, but a contributory factor was anti-trust policy which deterred international cartels and mergers.[13] Overseas operations tended to be run as separate units and Dunning has suggested that their primary role was to channel US technology overseas.[14] Since the aggregate value of US overseas direct investment remained fairly stable, the outflow seems unlikely to reflect the saturation of domestic markets.

On the government side the new world role in military and diplomatic affairs ensured a flow of expenditure, loans and aid to other countries amounting to $51.5 million between 1946 and 1955 and $49.7 from 1956 to 1965. In real terms and as a share of US national income, however, US aid declined from its reconstruction peak in 1949.[15] With much aid taking the form of surplus foodstuffs or being tied to the purchase of US goods, there was a further stimulus to trade. Overall the dollar shortage of the 1940s was transformed into expanding overseas holdings of dollars, which contributed to the general expansion of trade and economic activity.

If the 1950s involved readjustments after the impact of war, the 1960s marked the achievement of much of the Bretton Woods and GATT framework. Sustained economic growth, in which trade played a significant role, gave a basic stability to the international economy and there were considerable reductions in tariff levels. Even so the ideals of a liberalised trade system and multilateral payments system were never completely realised: trade was freer, but not totally so, and exchange controls were widespread. Inevitably the world economy was always in a state of flux. Recovery and industrialisation in Western Europe and Japan and slower growth in the United States and Britain altered trade patterns and strains developed in the international trade and financial systems, especially in the roles of the dollar and sterling. The growth of US imports outpaced exports. The surplus on merchandise trade peaked at $6.8 billion in 1964, fluctuated thereafter and fell sharply in 1968 and 1969 to $607 million, with the earlier trade surplus in automotive products giving way to deficits. As the trade surplus diminished, the United States was less able to support the outflows of private capital and government expenditure. Moreover those outflows had created a pool of dollars abroad, potentially convertible into gold, which represented a potential imbalance in the system if doubts developed over the value of the dollar or the ability to exchange dollars for gold. US dollar reserves fell by half between 1950 and 1968, but, rather like bank lending, dollar liabilities could continue to exceed US gold reserves providing other economies were willing to accumulate dollars for international transactions and as part of their own reserves. But in these conditions the state of confidence in the dollar was critical. The US government made some attempts to limit capital flows and central banks endeavoured to reduce the pressures to convert dollars to gold during the 1960s. However, the devaluation of sterling in 1967 focused attention on the dollar and the increase in the rate of inflation added further instability. The other side of the coin were trade surpluses of Germany and Japan which brought pressures for higher exchange rates for the mark and yen.

The uncertainties apparent during the 1960s developed suddenly into a crisis at the start of the new decade. From a net surplus of $2.1 billion in 1970, the merchandise trade balance turned to deficits of $2.7 billion in 1971 and $7 billion in 1972.[16] Private investors lost confidence in the dollar and converted their holdings to gold or other currencies in anticipation of a devaluation. With the US administration unwilling to restrain its economy and neither West Germany nor Japan prepared to increase their exchange rates appreciably, there was a brief stalemate. The dramatic end of the Bretton Woods system was signalled in August 1971 when President Nixon ended the convertibility of the dollar to gold and abandoned its fixed exchange rates, effectively devaluing the US dollar by 8 per cent. Later in the year the Smithsonian Agreement formalised wider revaluations of currencies and exchange rates were more volatile after 1971, despite varying degrees of management by central banks. The more flexible system eased the adjustment of exchange rates through the turbulent economic conditions of the OPEC oil-price hikes and divergent rates of domestic inflation during the 1970s. The US dollar, though no longer convertible to gold, remained the key international currency. The liberal world-trade system was subject to greater protectionism, primarily via non-tariff barriers such as quotas, after 1971 as economies endeavoured to protect industries from foreign competition.

US economic performance since 1970

All economies experienced lower rates of growth in output and productivity after 1970, but, as in the two previous decades, the US economy's performance ranked below average. Extremely volatile economic conditions created a less stable world economy with mixed results for the United States' international position. The trade sector assumed increased significance as the value of traded goods increased during the 1970s and 1980s in relation to US national income, although it remained small compared to other economies. The rising export values were dwarfed by a surge of imports. Higher oil prices drove up the value of petroleum imports from $2.9 billion in 1970 to $26.6 billion in 1974 and $60.4 billion by 1979. In the 1980s falling oil prices contributed to a marked decline in the cost of petroleum imports. By contrast there was a sustained rise from the late 1960s in the level of imports of automobiles, machinery and capital goods. Imports of textiles and electrical products increased from the newly-industrialising economies of Southeast Asia. The overall effect was to shift the distribution of trade more towards the Pacific Rim. It also brought to a close the era of US trade surpluses. From 1971 the devaluation of the dollar offset some of the pressure from imports, but in the early 1980s a regime of high interest rates, designed to reduce inflation in the early 1980s, raised the value of the dollar which, by making imports cheaper, contributed to the mounting trade deficits. A fall in agricultural commodity prices from 1979 further reduced US export earnings. There were deficits on merchandise trade in 1971, 1972 and 1974 and then continuously from 1976 to 1993. The largest deficit on merchandise trade was with Japan and the rise of manufactured imports implied a loss of competitive advantage in several sectors. The current account was in deficit in 1971, 1972, 1977 to 1979 and then in each year from 1982 to 1993, though the size of the deficits narrowed from 1985, in part due to a new fall in the dollar's value.

Some of the earlier tendencies persisted. US direct investment overseas continued to rise as multinational firms sustained their development of global businesses through the 1970s and 1980s. There was a major growth in bank lending to less developed economies such as Brazil and Mexico in the 1970s, a phase of low real interest rates. However in the early 1980s the combination of recessions, falling commodity prices, and higher real interest rates produced a 'debt crisis' as balance-of-payments problems prevented less developed economies maintaining debt repayments and commercial banks curtailed lending. Government funds still went abroad too: there was a net outflow of $147 million in grants and credits between 1976 and 1990 of which one-third took the form of military assistance. However, US capital was less dominant than before. The oil-exporting economies emerged as major sources of capital from the 1970s, augmenting the flow of dollars overseas and fuelling more volatile international movements of capital. US multinationals encountered more and larger foreign rivals. Overseas investment in the United States had grown at around 6 per cent per annum during the 1950s and 1960s, but rose at double this rate in the 1970s, led by Canada and Europe, with later increases in Japanese investment. The value of overseas direct investment in the United States increased from $172 billion in 1984 to $2,281 billion in 1992. During the 1980s relaxations of controls on capital movements and on overseas banking accelerated the growth of multinational financial corporations and the interconnections between financial markets. With an inflow of foreign capital across all sectors, though most rapidly in manufacturing, borrowing from overseas was vital to finance the widening US budget deficit and the United States had again become a net debtor nation.

By 1990 the United States' position in the world economy had clearly altered. It still possessed considerable strengths as the major industrial producer, accounting for 23 per cent of world output, and surpassed all other economies in terms of total national income. US productivity exceeded the Organization for Economic Cooperation and Development (OECD) average, though the lead in productivity per hour worked was much less.[17] US technological superiority remained intact in manufacturing as a whole and was greatest in chemicals and aerospace. Despite the collapse of the idealised Bretton Woods financial system, the dollar was the key international currency and over the previous thirty years US financial institutions had developed very substantially larger and more extensive overseas networks. The US re-established its role as a destination for large numbers of immigrants. In strategic terms the ending of the Cold War and the fragmentation of the Soviet Union and Eastern Europe left the United States as the pre-eminent military power.

There were equally signs that the United States' international standing had altered considerably since 1945. The lead in total national income had narrowed and a few economies had moved ahead in per-capita income. The balance-of-payments deficits and inflows of overseas capital left the economy more vulnerable to speculation and changes in overseas perceptions of its prospects. The rise of other industrial nations in Europe and Southeast Asia signalled a shift of economic power so that the United States competed and negotiated with stronger, more assertive rivals. The penetration of imports indicated a certain weakening of industrial and technological leadership and the relatively slow growth rates posed the threat of being overtaken in terms of productivity or even income. Just as US banks now operated more overseas, other nations' multinational banks and direct and indirect investments in the United States had expanded rapidly since 1970, so that multinational investment was more diverse in its origins than had been the case during the 1950s and 1960s. Indeed the resurgence of German and Japanese investments and the expansion of multinational involvement in services and public utilities represented a return to pre-1914 conditions.

The notion of a liberalised system of free trade suffered particular damage after 1970. Throughout the world economy slower growth produced a strengthening of existing protectionist measures and the addition of new restrictions. The United States adopted a more combative approach to trade negotiations, placed direct pressure on other nations to limit exports and engagement in more bilateral dealings was evident in the 1980s. Non-tariff controls on trade mounted in an *ad-hoc* response to pressures from domestic industries with, for instance, new restrictions on imports of agricultural commodities and pressures leading to 'voluntary' export restraints on imports of cars, televisions, machine-tools and some steels.[18] In its dealings with Japan and Korea, US policy began to demand 'fair trade', criticised cheap imports and highlighted constraints on exports to Japan. In Europe, US efforts were directed at opening markets for its farm produce and responding to weaknesses in its manufacturing trade by challenging overseas restrictions on films and other service industries. The post-war development of regional trade blocs had increased the bargaining power and widened the free-trade areas of particular groups of countries, and the United States began to seek similar benefits. A regional trade agreement in the Caribbean was reached in 1980 and in 1994 the United States entered the North American Free Trade Agreement with Mexico and Canada. It was an attempt to reap benefits from a mix of cheaper labour and a larger market for which the US itself no longer appeared sufficient, but also signalled a further departure from the ideal of a liberal world-trade system.

Notes

1 Philip Armstrong *et al.*, *Capitalism Since 1945* (Oxford, 1994 edn), p. 151.
2 William H. Branson, 'Trends in United States International Trade and Investment since World War II' in Martin Feldstein (ed.), *The American Economy in Transition* (Chicago, 1980), pp. 192, 196.
3 *Ibid*, p. 207.
4 Mira Wilkins, *The Emergence of Multinational Enterprise: American Business Abroad from 1914 to 1970* (Cambridge, MA, 1974).
5 For instance, Coca-Cola bottling and distribution was extended widely during

the war: see Richard Tedlow, *New and Improved: The Story of Mass Marketing in America* (Oxford, 1990).

6 Branson, 'Trends in United States International Trade and Investment since World War II', p. 238.

7 Wilkins, *The Emergence of Multinational Enterprise*, pp. 329–30; John H. Dunning, *Multinational Enterprises and the Global Economy* (Wokingham, 1993), p. 117, table 5.1.

8 J. J. Servan-Schreiber, *The American Challenge* (New York, 1968).

9 Raymond Vernon, *Sovereignty at Bay: The Multinational Spread of US Enterprises* (New York, 1971).

10 Wilkins, *The Emergence of Multinational Enterprise*; Dunning, *Multinational Enterprises and the Global Economy*.

11 Raymond Vernon, 'The Product Cycle Hypothesis in a New International Environment', *Oxford Bulletin of Economics and Statistics*, 41, 1979, pp. 255–67.

12 Peter J. West, *Foreign Investment and Technology Transfer: The Tire Industry in Latin America* (Greenwich, CT, 1984).

13 Dunning, *Multinational Enterprises and the Global Economy*, p. 126.

14 John H. Dunning, 'Explaining Patterns of International Production: In Defence of the Eclectic Theory', *Oxford Bulletin of Economics and Statistics*, 41(4), 1979, p. 270.

15 Anne O. Krueger, *Economic Policies At Cross-Purposes: The United States and Developing Countries* (Washington, DC, 1993), pp. 37–8.

16 Robert A. Gordon, *Economic Instability and Growth: The American Record* (New York, 1974), p. 180.

17 OECD, *OECD Economic Surveys: United States, 1993* (Paris, 1993), pp. 52–3.

18 Krueger, *Economic Policies At Cross-Purposes*, p. 128.

11

US productivity growth since 1945

At several points in the previous discussions, the performance of the US economy and, especially its record of productivity growth, has appeared or been implicit, notably in assessing overall growth, corporate strategies and the country's international position. In this final chapter US productivity is discussed and the main explanations for its slower growth compared to some other economies are reviewed.

During the 1980s the increased penetration of imports, particularly in such prominent industries as automobiles and electrical products, and the deterioration in the US trade balance provoked a wide-ranging academic and political debate over US competitiveness, particularly productivity. In fact the record on productivity since 1945 falls into two distinct periods. In the first phase, from 1945 to 1969, US productivity increased very substantially and those years ranked as highly successful in historical terms. However, productivity growth slowed in the late 1960s and the fall became more precipitate during the 1970s. This poses the question of why there was a decline. In part the answer is simply that productivity growth slowed in all industrial economies after 1970. However a comparative perspective poses a different question. While the United States held a substantial productivity lead, aggregate indicators placed US productivity growth below the rates achieved in Japan, Germany or in the developing economies of Southeast Asia since 1950. All countries experienced lower productivity growth after 1969, but again the US performance was below the rates achieved in some other economies. The question of productivity performance can then be addressed both in terms of why US growth rates declined after 1970, but also as why were US growth rates generally low by international standards. The difference between these two questions can lead to a contrasting search for discontinuities which depressed productivity after 1970, or efforts to identify long-term factors responsible for 'slow' post-war growth. Since the US record was one of retardation rather than absolute decline, there were no complete obstacles to development and the uncertain nature of productivity data compound the problem of finding clear-cut explanations.

The numerous analyses of the post-war exeperience may be divided into three broad, often overlapping, categories. First optimistic interpretations, such as that of Lawrence, highlighted continuing strengths in the US economy as harbingers of future achievements.[1] The persistence of a US lead in absolute levels of productivity across many industries, despite relatively slow growth, indicated competitive advantages. The post-1970 slowdown and later problems are presented as the product of short-run conditions in the early 1980s, namely recession and the rising value of the dollar which drew in imported goods, but readjustment and recovery are to be expected rather than decline. A second view, exemplified by Abramovitz, adopted a long-run perspective on international trends and viewed postwar events as a process of technological convergence among industrial economies.[2] In this context the post-1970 fall in productivity growth was seen as a common feature due to a mix of specific adverse conditions, but the focus is on long-term technological influences and on the effective policies pursued by other nations as much as on US failings. Third, a set of more jaundiced interpretations have argued that the United States has been losing its competitive edge to other economies. This line encompassed very different explanations of the extent and sources of relative decline, ranging from low levels of saving and investment to institutional weaknesses such as flaws in production or poor education.[3] The resulting public policy prescriptions have included deregulation, new state industrial policies, incentives for increased saving and capital investment, and more or different educational provision. A comparative approach can be used, but there are problems, given the small number of cases and the risks of exaggerating differences between the United States and other economies, or often of setting US experience against a composite version of the attributes of several countries, none of which correspond to the ideal. In many respects the discussion resembled the continuing and inconclusive debate over Britain's economic performance since 1870.

Productivity performance, 1945–69

The period from 1945 to 1969 fits with ideas of convergence. Levels of productivity in the United States were the international exemplar, and the economy's earlier advantages from its natural resources and mass-production industries were augmented by high levels of expenditure on research and development and increases in average levels of education. New investment and rates of productivity growth returned to their long-term trend, regaining ground lost in the 1930s and contributing to post-war economic growth. Given the starting point of wartime growth which compensated for the below-trend performance during the 1930s, US productivity growth in the 1950s and 1960s was impressive. These advantages were retained throughout the 1950s and 1960s, although other economies' cheaper labour offset part of the gap in production costs.

At the same time US growth rates in investment, output and productivity were generally below those in other industrial economies and the

Table 11.1 *Ratio of world gross fixed non-residential investment to Gross Domestic Product at current price, 1901–87 (%)*

Years	France	Germany	Japan	UK	USA
1901–10	10.4	n.a.	11.0	7.4	15.7
1911–20	n.a.	n.a.	14.9	6.2	12.5
1921–30	12.1	11.9	13.9	6.4	12.7
1931–40	11.1	10.1	14.7	6.5	9.7
1941–50	9.1	8.4	14.3	6.3	9.9
1951–60	13.8	16.6	20.1	12.4	12.6
1961–73	17.0	17.6	26.6	14.7	13.5
1974–87	14.9	14.6	23.9	14.1	13.6

Source: Angus Maddison, *Dynamic Forces in Capitalist Development: A Long-Run Comparative View* (Oxford, 1991), p. 41, table 2.3.&

international average. More critical interpretations of the US productivity record argued that the economy had the potential for faster growth. Rates of savings and fixed capital formation in the US were low compared to other nations, though precise comparisons are difficult. A similar situation was apparent in the narrower measure of fixed non-residential investment which indicated expenditure on plant and equipment (Table 11.1). A lower level of investment in new plant and equipment would delay the introduction of more efficient methods and, thus, affect productivity or lead to the workforce increasing faster than the supply of equipment. Such tendencies restricted productivity growth while other economies gained from higher levels of investment.

Inevitably a good deal of the explanation lay overseas. Other economies began from a more depressed point in the late 1940s and had more scope to transfer resources from low-productivity agriculture. With educational advances and a commitment to modernisation, they were able to generate rapid growth by upgrading their plant and equipment and adopting US technology and practices more extensively.[4] Moreover US corporations contributed directly to this process, selling technologies and expertise to foreign firms and investing directly in production and even research and development abroad throughout the post-war years. It was harder for the United States to achieve spectacular growth rates from its position of leadership. [5] In this light the US performance was in some sense in line with its potential rather than a case of retardation. Indeed the US productivity lead remained intact in most sectors to 1970 and as technological and productivity differences narrowed growth rates elsewhere could be expected to slow. Nonetheless there were signs of a loss of leadership to Germany and Japan in sectors such as steel, textiles and automobiles with import penetration by the 1960s reflecting technological advances overseas, not simply lower labour costs.

A rather different interpretation emphasised the role of the defence sector which absorbed a larger share of total research expenditure than was the case in most other economies. Critics, such as Seymour Melman, argued that the defence sector diverted resources into unproductive activities, effectively 'crowding out' more productive forms of investment: while Germany and Japan concentrated on investments and research directly related to industrial productivity, the defence sector failed to generate comparable results.[6] For Paul Kennedy the extension of US commitments overseas after 1945 resulted in 'overstretch' beyond the nation's resources, though this does not necessarily make defence spending the cause of retardation.[7] The case for misallocation of resources hinges on the extent of 'spin-offs' from defence investment and an assumption that in its absence similar resources would have been transferred into more productive fields. Certainly defence dominated federal support for research and development and it is reasonable to assume their specialist character limited the extent of 'spin-offs', but there is no neat fit with the trend in productivity.[8] Defence spending accounted for its largest share of national income and research funding during the 1945 to 1965 period and was associated with innovations, notably in aerospace, electronics and computing which filtered into civilian use, and the aerospace industry retained international competitiveness. The possible draining effects of defence expenditure are problematic, since productivity growth slowed alongside a decline in defence spending as a share of national income in the decade after 1966, and when military expenditure then rose dramatically after 1975, there was no obvious impact on productivity.

Why slower productivity growth in the 1970s and 1980s?

Various explanations for the pronounced slackening of productivity growth since 1970 have been advanced, but it remains difficult to establish clear causal relationships. Indeed Denison's exhaustive analysis concluded that the sources of slower productivity growth in the 1970s are a 'mystery'.[9] Maddison's growth-accounting model identified only 39 per cent of the deceleration in US GDP growth after 1973.[10] It appeared that new investment in plant and equipment failed to keep pace with higher total employment and that the economy benefited less from the virtuous cycle of investment, technical change and productivity growth. Yet non-residential investment rose as a proportion of national income (Table 11.1) even though government borrowing drove down overall rates of saving in the 1980s. The growth accounting models offered the rise in the proportion of the workforce who were young or less experienced, in spite of the simultaneous improvements in average levels of education, and the acceleration of the shift to service employment as further contributory factors in the slower productivity growth. Both Denison and Maddison concluded that the largest part of the decline in productivity occurred in the residual, the catch-all category which Denison labelled as 'advances in knowledge plus factors not included elsewhere'.

A different approach is to treat post-1970 growth rates less as a case of retardation and more as the resumption of long-term trends. The lower rates of productivity growth were in line with the economy's long-run performance whereas both the depressed 1930s and booming economy between 1945 and 1970 represented distinct deviations, though the existence of such pronounced deviations over the last sixty years casts doubt on the relevance of average growth rates.[11] Conceivably the 1970s and 1980s constituted one of the periodic downswings in the Kondratieff cycle, an exhaustion of the impact of key technologies which exerts a general drag on economic activity. Such an interpretation supplies an explanation for the persistence of slower growth, but carries the risk of a circular argument in which the sources of retardation are assumed rather than specified. A less grand version of events would be that since all economies experienced slower growth in the 1970s and 1980s this is indicative of convergence in economic structures and performance, with the very high growth rates becoming hard to maintain after the completion of a phase of 'catching-up' development after 1945. Assuming that more nations possess comparable resources and that there are economies of scale, technological leadership is likely to be diffused with no one economy dominating. The longer-run implications, however, are uncertain since the dynamic and destabilising aspects of technological change could mean that the cumulative effects of a small initial lead or the impact of a major breakthrough would result in wide differences in national growth rates.

The notion of convergence suggested a blurring of national differences. However, given similar technologies, cultural or institutional differences exerted a profound influence on ways in which technologies are used and on efficiency. Porter, for instance, argued that broad cultural factors, such as education and state policies, produced very different national forms of competitive advantage.[12] Covergence theories, for instance, often operated on the assumption that higher incomes altered patterns of consumption and work effort by permitting consumers to satisfy preferences for more leisure, and such forces might be expected to operate in the United States. By implication, the roots of slower growth lay in similar broad influences, but if cultural factors were central then the prospects of easy solutions, and even the notion of convergence, were in doubt. Nonetheless there has been no shortage of analyses which proclaimed deficiencies in US education, management, industrial relations and consumerism or propose either more or less government intervention in industrial and social policy.[13] The success of the Japanese economy has been variously ascribed to state intervention, innovative production systems, education and a culture based on trust and service, but often pundits emphasised only one element and downplayed others. As Rosenberg argued, the complex economic and social relationships which contributed to technological change made it difficult to transfer or imitate other nations' technologies.[14] Imitation was particularly difficult since Japan's competitive advantage lay in incremental innovations and efficiencies in co-ordinating activities rather than in a specific piece of machinery.[15]

The United States experienced slower growth throughout the post-war period compared to many economies and this tendency persisted through recessions and recoveries, so it seems reasonable to look for continuities. There was some contribution from the changing composition of employment, which involved a transfer of resources from industrial activities for which there are conventional measures of productivity to the far more diverse service sector, where both inputs, output and quality are even less easy to define. Certainly productivity growth was slower in the expanding service industries, though this was also true of other economies and the US record was good by international standards. Recent slower productivity growth may be the cumulative result of the relatively low levels of savings and new investment since 1945, but the pronounced fall in productivity growth began in the late 1960s whilst the most dramatic decline in the rate of saving occurred in the 1980s. In any case rates of fixed capital formation, a more direct influence on productivity, improved slightly (Table 11.1).

Key decisions about investment and technological change lay with individual firms and their role has been the subject of debate. Despite the evidence on aggregate savings, it was not clear that US firms were short of capital, especially given excellent profits to 1969. For some critics there was a long-run tendency for US managers to focus on short-term financial objectives rather than being committed to sustaining investments in research and development and productivity. Such attitudes were fostered by a financial system which lacked the links between large industrial and financial institutions apparent in Japan and rather focused on corporate takeovers, thereby highlighting short-term dividends and share prices.

Business historians and management theorists identified aspects of the pre-1970 corporate culture as harbingers of disaster. Chandler, whose portrayal of US business to the early 1960s was predicated on its technical and organisational superiority, asserted that excessive diversification created companies lacking economies of scope and beyond the capacity of managers to control.[16] It is not clear that the criticism can be applied throughout industry since the chapter on US business highlighted the diversity of business forms. However, this critique carries considerable weight in certain key sectors where US business lost ground, particularly heavy industries such as cars and steel. The dominance of a few major corporations in those industries made their business decisions particularly critical. Chandler and other writers have argued that US management changed its character during the 1950s and 1960s in ways which departed from the sources of its pre-war efficiency. Hayes and Abernathy concluded that American senior executives became detached from operational matters in terms of their personal expertise and through their reliance on financial measures of performance.[17] In the same vein H. Thomas Johnson suggested that from the 1950s firms were increasingly 'managed by numbers' in that executives relied on financial indicators, and an increase in the proportion of chief executives with backgrounds in accountancy or other financial careers indicated this tendency. Halberstam detected such influences in the automobile industry in the form of an over-emphasis on financial measures plus a conformist culture which restrained innovation.[18] Lazonick suggested that as top managers increasingly possessed stock options, their decision-making shifted toward raising short-term share values.[19] Chandler placed more emphasis on mergers and acquisitions as distracting managements from longer-term interest and investments in production methods and research.[20] Mowery suggested that US industrial research changed in character after 1945 as firms responded to anti-trust policies by emphasising basic research aimed at developing major new technologies through their in-house laboratories.[21] According to Mowery, this was a departure from the pre-war focus on incremental research that was more closely linked to immediate production problems, though it presumably reflected the pace of scientific changes and the greater availability of trained personnel. Like Chandler, Mowery considered conglomerates as less likely to promote research and development and less well-equipped to exploit the full potential of any innovation. Whatever the precise mechanism, such interpretations take changing managerial priorities as the source of investment decisions based on short-term financial concerns rather than commitments to long-term programmes such as research and development or close attention to manufacturing efficiency.

The precise form of these financial influences remains a matter of debate. Recently Roe has argued that American financial institutions were relatively weak due to a regulatory framework which reflected pre-war political decisions designed to constrain the growth of powerful banks.[22] Although the shareholdings of insurance companies and other institutional investors increased after 1945, Roe's analysis suggests that the relationships were more limited and less likely to supply long-term finance to corporations than was the case in Japan or Germany. Rather, the financial sector promoted speculative deal-making. The comparative perspective requires care since it is consistent with efficient and flush capital markets, a contrast to the conditions under which Japanese corporations, for instance, developed. In the United States short- and medium-term bank loans were used to finance corporate investments and at times involved continuing relationships between banks and industry. Conversely, to the extent that corporate executives enjoyed a degree of autonomy from bank oversight, this formulation places greater emphasis on the responsibility of corporate managements for the emphasis on short-term returns and dividends. Share-ownership by such institutional investors as pension funds and insurance companies increased rapidly from the 1960s, and the conglomerate movement and the financing of mergers and de-mergers in the 1980s testified to a combination of remarkable capacities to mobilise capital for acquisitions in search of immediate gains. Yet far from being evidence of managerial control or autonomy, the 1980s suggested that both corporate and financial institutions were locked into a similar short-run perspective, which begs the question of whether different bank structures would have altered policy fundamentally.

Any emphasis on continuity risked blurring the impact of new conditions as a source of slower productivity growth. Maddison concluded that the destabilising effects of new conditions in the 1970s 'eroded' the basis of post-war prosperity. Mansfield detected fragmentary signs of a loss of support for, and rates of, innovation during the 1970s.[23] There was a fall in the share of national income devoted to research and development, slower growth in employment of technical personnel and a decline in corporate support for high-risk and basic research projects. The retrenchment was consistent with US firms acting cautiously in the face of unpredictable economic conditions as well as limiting new investment as profit margins declined. Such reactions would constrain productivity growth. Federal support for research and development may also become less influential. The aerospace industries' international success indicated the potential advantages from military research and development, but from the early 1970s there may have been fewer general benefits, especially for the troubled mass-production industries, from specialised military products and production processes.[24]

The combination of supply shocks plus the impact of recessions on demand created profound uncertainties for producers and consumers and forced major adjustments. The low price of oil was brought to an end as OPEC's policies drove up oil prices sharply, triggering a general rise in energy costs.[25] The resulting shift in the terms of trade between primary producers and manufactures transferred resources both within the US economy and to other economies. Public policy in the United States had previously deliberately kept energy prices low and the economy, traditionally a heavy user of resources, consumed vast quantities of energy. The framework of institutions and technology was then particularly vulnerable to the dramatic rise in energy costs. Energy consumption per unit of GNP fell by 23 per cent between 1973 and 1985, but the adjustments away from resource- and energy-intensive manufacturing was reflected in industrial contraction, and the challenge from overseas competitors which demonstrated a greater capacity to adjust did so because their prior choices of technology were more directed to saving on energy costs.[26]

As inflation rates accelerated, employers and workers endeavoured to keep pace, adding to price and wage increases. The volatility of interest rates in the 1970s and their high real level in the 1980s plus pronounced swings in stock prices from the mid-1980s were added uncertainties for lenders, business and consumers. The precise mechanisms linking price swings to productivity are unclear. Inflation gathered momentum during the 1960s and tensions between industrialists and workers over profits and wages became more intense as a result, but these conflicts appear more an effect than a cause of lower productivity. Indeed since inflation fell in the 1980s and union influence declined, the outcome might have been expected to stimulate productivity. There was an improvement in manufacturing productivity, but neither the fall in energy prices, lower inflation or changed industrial relations produced a strong rebound in US productivity overall.[27] The main drag came from the service sector, where productivity growth remained sluggish.

One possible area where shifting conditions had an impact was on technological change. Under the changing conditions of the 1970s existing technologies were not always appropriate for the changing patterns of demand and costs while new investments were fraught with greater uncertainty than usual. American managers were unprepared for more challenging times.[28] Aaronson argued that US business schools, an increasing source of executives since the 1950s via MBA programmes, provided little or no training or encouragement to entrepreneurship. [29] Instead they trained managers to fit particular careers or disciplines. Other commentators argued for a more general decline in the value of earlier corporate strategies; Piore and Sabel suggested that conglomerate growth offered less support as demand slackened across many sectors. The conglomerate philosophy often appeared as a flexible rationalisation of opportunistic or *ad-hoc* deal-making. Such evidence is consistent with a study of mergers in manufacturing between 1950 and 1976 which concluded that financial performance was poor.[30] Many accounts see the 1970s as a watershed between different systems of production, with US mass-production arrangements being too inflexible compared to new manufacturing methods used by Japanese companies.[31] This perspective directed attention to the deployment of investment rather than its aggregate level and to the ways in which institutions, such as firms, systems of production and distribution and social values operate. A good deal of the analysis focuses on industries, particularly automobiles, where import penetration has been most influential. This approach had the advantage of trying to identify concrete sources of productivity problems, and emphasised the interrelationship between developments in the US and overseas. Nonetheless the polarity between forms of production, highlighted by Piore and Sabel, mixed short-term responses to recession and longer-term changes. It also tended to underplay the earlier diversity of US corporate forms, the variety of different scales of production and understated the continuing relevance of mass-production methods.

The debates surrounding productivity and competitiveness remain, therefore, confused and yet have had considerable impact on public policy. From 1945 to the late 1960s, the most persuasive explanations for slower US productivity growth are a combination of readjustment from an exaggerated lead in 1945 plus a process of 'catching up' by Europe and Japan. With other economies emerging as more potent rivals in particular sectors, the US economy was less pre-eminent. The destabilising impact of recessions and inflation placed US business on the defensive during the 1970s. In manufacturing the technical shortcomings and short-term emphasis of US firms and financial markets ensured a retrenchment of new investment during the 1970s which diminished the capacity of the US economy to sustain its position of dominance. Such tendencies mattered more as overseas multinationals turned ever more determinedly to the US market via exports and direct investment. The continuing shift of employment to services exerted a drag on productivity which office automation and computing plus the impact of recession on, say, financial employment have not countered. The future prospects for the US economy hinge upon its capacity to sustain recent improvements in industrial productivity growth and innovation rather than relying on forms of protectionism or relocating to Mexico in search of cheaper labour.

Notes

1 Robert Z. Lawrence, *Can America Compete?* (Washington, DC, 1984).
2 Moses Abramovitz, 'Catching Up, Forging Ahead, and Falling Behind', *Journal of Economic History*, 46(2), 1986, pp. 385–406.
3 Michael Dertouzos *et al.*, *Made in America: Regaining the Productive Edge* (Cambridge, MA, 1989); William Lazonick, *Competitive Advantage on the Shop-Floor* (Cambridge, MA, 1990).
4 Abramovitz, 'Catching Up, Forging Ahead, and Falling Behind'.
5 Edward Denison, *Why Growth Rates Differ: Postwar Experience in Nine Western Countries* (Washington, DC, 1967), pp. 330–1.
6 Seymour Melman, *Pentagon Capitalism: The Political Economy of War* (New York, 1990).
7 Paul Kennedy, *The Rise and Fall of the Great Powers: Economic Change and Military Conflict from 1500 to 2000* (London, 1988), pp. 442–6, 514–25, 531–5.
8 Richard R. Nelson and Gavin Wright, 'The Rise and Fall of American Technological Leadership', *Journal of Economic Literature*, 30(4), 1992, pp. 1931–64.
9 Edward Denison, *Accounting For Slower Economic Growth: The United States in the 1970s* (Washington, DC, 1979), p. 4.
10 Maddison, *Dynamic Forces in Capitalist Development*, chapter 5.
11 William J. Baumol, 'Productivity Growth, Convergence and Welfare: What The Long Run Data Show', *American Economic Review*, 76, 1986, pp. 1072–85.
12 Michael E. Porter, *The Competitive Advantage of Nations* (London, 1990).
13 Lazonick, *Competitive Advantage on the Shop-Floor*.

14 Nathan Rosenberg, *Exploring the Black Box: Technology, Economics and History* (Cambridge, 1982), esp. chapter 1.
15 *Ibid.*, pp. 125–6.
16 Alfred D. Chandler, *Scale and Scope: The Dynamics of Industrial Capitalism* (Cambridge, MA, 1990), pp. 621–6.
17 Robert H. Hayes and William J. Abernathy, 'Managing Our Way To Economic Decline', *Harvard Business Review*, July-August 1980, pp. 67–77.
18 David Halberstam, *The Reckoning* (New York, 1986); Lee Iacocca with William Novak, *Iacocca: An Autobiography* (New York, 1986).
19 William Lazonick, 'Organizational Capabilities in American Industry: The Rise and Decline of Managerial Capitalism', *Business and Economic History*, 19, 1990, pp. 51–3. Also see Carliss Y. Baldwin and Kim B. Clark, 'Capital-Budgeting Systems and Capabilities Investments in US Companies after the Second World War', *Business History Review*, 68, 1994, pp. 73–109.
20 Chandler, *Scale and Scope*, pp. 621–6.
21 David C. Mowery, 'The Boundaries of the US Firm in R & D' in Naomi Lamoreaux and Daniel Raff (eds), *Coordination and Information: Historical Perspectives on the Organization of Enterprise* (Chicago, 1995), pp. 147–76.
22 Mark J. Roe, *Strong Managers, Weak Owners: The Political Roots of American Corporate Finance* (Princeton, NJ, 1994).
23 Edwin Mansfield, 'Technology and Productivity in the United States' in Martin Feldstein (ed.), *The American Economy in Transition* (Chicago, 1980), pp. 563–96.
24 Nelson and Wright, 'The Rise and Fall of American Technological Leadership'. On the specialist character of products and specialised manufacturing processes in defence industries see Ann Markusen and Joel Yudken, *Dismantling the Cold War Economy* (New York, 1992).
25 Robert J. Gordon, 'Postwar Macroeconomics: The Evolution of Events and Ideas' in Feldstein (ed.), *The American Economy in Transition*, pp. 156–7.
26 Rosenberg, *Exploring the Black Box*, pp. 172–8.
27 Maddison, *Dynamic Forces in Capitalist Development*, p. 177; Alice M. Rivlin, *Reviving the American Dream: The Economy, the States and the Federal Government* (Washington, DC, 1992).
28 Harold C. Livesay, 'Entrepreneurial Dominance in Business Large and Small, Past and Present', *Business History Review*, 63, 1989, pp. 1–21.
29 Susan Ariel Aaronson, 'Serving America's Business? Graduate Business Schools and American Business, 1945–60', *Business History*, 34(1), 1992, pp. 160–82.
30 David J. Ravenscraft and F. M. Scherer, *Mergers, Sell-offs and Economic Efficiency* (Washington, DC, 1987) cited in F. M. Scherer and David Ross, *Industrial Market Structure and Economic Performance* (3rd edn, Boston, MA, 1990), pp. 172–3.
31 Michael J. Piore and Charles Sabel, *The Second Industrial Divide: Possibilities For Prosperity* (New York, 1984); Stephen Cohen and John Zysman, *Manufacturing Matters* (New York, 1986); Dertouzos *et al.*, *Made in America*; James Womack *et al.*, *The Machine That Changed The World* (Cambridge, MA, 1991).

Bibliography

Aaron, Henry J., *Politics and the Professors: The Great Society in Perspective* (Washington, DC, 1978).

Aaronson, Susan Ariel, 'Serving America's Business? Graduate Business Schools and American Business, 1945–60', *Business History*, 34(1), 1992, pp. 160–82.

Abbott, Carl, *The New Urban America: Growth and Politics in Sunbelt Cities* (Chapel Hill, NC, 1981).

Abo Tetsuo, (ed.), *Hybrid Factory: The Japanese Production System in the United States* (New York, 1994).

Abraham, Katharine G. and McKersie, Robert B. (eds), *New Developments in the Labor Market: Toward a New Institutional Paradigm* (Cambridge, MA, 1990).

Abramovitz, Moses, 'Catching Up, Forging Ahead, and Falling Behind', *Journal of Economic History*, 46(2), 1986, pp. 385–406.

Adams, Judith A., *The American Amusement Park Industry* (Boston, MA, 1991).

Alston, L. J. and Ferrie, J. P., 'Resisting the Welfare State: Southern Opposition to the Farm Security Administration', *Research in Economic History*, supplement 4, 1985, pp. 83–120.

Anderson, Alan B. and Pickering, George W., *Confronting the Color Line: The Broken Promise of the Civil Rights Movement in Chicago* (Athens, GA, 1986).

Anderson, Gregory (ed.), *The White-Blouse Revolution: Female Office Workers since 1870* (Manchester, 1988).

Armstrong, Philip *et al.*, *Capitalism Since 1945* (Oxford, 1994 edn).

Arsenault, Raymond, 'The End of the Long Hot Summer: The Air Conditioner and Southern Culture', *Journal of Southern History*, 50(4), 1984, pp. 597–628.

Asher, Robert and Edsforth, Ronald (eds), *Autowork*, (Albany, NY, 1995).

Auletta, Ken, *The Underclass* (New York, 1982).

Averitt, Robert T., *The Dual Economy* (New York, 1968).

Baldassare, Mark, *Residential Overcrowding in Urban America* (Berkeley, CA, 1979).

Baldwin, Carliss Y. and Clark, Kim B., 'Capital-Budgeting Systems and Capabilities Investments in US Companies after the Second World War', *Business History Review*, 68, 1994, pp. 73–109.

Barbash, Jack, 'Trade Unionism From Roosevelt To Reagan', *The Annals of The American Academy of Political and Social Science*, 473, 1984, pp. 11–22.

Baumol, William J., 'Productivity Growth, Convergence and Welfare: What The Long Run Data Show', *American Economic Review*, 76, 1986, pp. 1072–85.

Belden, Joseph N., *et al.*, *Dirt Rich, Dirt Poor: America's Food and Farm Crisis* (New York, 1986).

Bell, Daniel, *The Cultural Contradictions of Capitalism* (London, 1976).

Berger, Bennett M., *Working-Class Suburb: A Study of Auto Workers in Suburbia* (Berkeley, CA, 1960).

Berkowitz, Edward and McQuaid, Kim, *Creating the Welfare State: The Political Economy of Twentieth Century Reform* (2nd edn, New York, 1988).

Bernard, Richard M. (ed.), *Snowbelt Cities: Metropolitan Politics in the Northeast and Midwest since World War II* (Bloomington, IN, 1990).

Bernard, Richard M. and Rice, Bradley R. (eds), *Sunbelt Cities: Politics and Growth since World War II* (Austin, TX, 1983).

Bernstein, Michael A. and Adler, David E. (eds), *Understanding American Economic Decline* (Cambridge, 1994).

Bianchi, Suzanne M. and Spain, Daphne, *American Women in Transition* (New York, 1986).

Bingham, Richard D. and Eberts, Randall W. (eds), *Economic Restructuring of the American Midwest: Proceedings of the Midwest Economic Restructuring Conference of the Federal Reserve Bank of Cleveland* (Boston, MA, 1990).

Blackford, Mansel G., *A History of Small Business in America* (New York, 1991).

Blackford, Mansel G., *The Lost Dream: Businessmen and City Planning on the Pacific Coast, 1890–1920* (Columbus, OH, 1993).

Bloom, Jack M., *Class, Race and the Civil Rights Movement* (Bloomington, IN, 1987).

Bluestone, Barry and Harrison, Bennett, *The Deindustrialization of America: Plant Closings, Community Abandonment, and the Dismantling of Basic Industry* (New York, 1982).

Bolton, Roger E., *Defense Purchases and Regional Growth* (Washington, DC, 1966)

Bowden, Sue and Offer, Avner, 'Household appliances and the use of time: the United States and Britain since the 1920s', *Economic History Review*, 62(4), 1994, pp. 735–48.

Bradshaw, Michael, *Regions and Regionalism in the United States* (London, 1988).

Braeman, John *et al.* (eds), *The New Deal: The National Level*, volume 1 (Columbus, OH, 1975).

Brauer, Carl M., 'Kennedy, Johnson and the War on Poverty', *Journal of American History*, 69, 1982, pp. 98–119.

Bremner, Robert H. and Reichard, Gary W. (eds), *Reshaping America: Society and Institutions, 1945–1960* (Columbus, OH, 1982).

Bremner, Robert H., Reichard, Gary W. and Hopkins, Richard J. (eds), *American Choices: Social Dilemmas and Public Policy since 1960* (Columbus, OH, 1986).

Brody, David, *In Labor's Cause: Main Themes on the History of the American Worker* (New York, 1993).

Brownell, Blaine A. and Goldfield, David R. (eds), *The City in Southern History: The Growth of Urban Civilisation in the South* (London, 1977).

Bruchey, Stuart (ed.), *Small Business in American Life* (New York, 1980).

Buenger, Walter L. and Pratt, Joseph A., *But Also Good Business: Texas Commerce Banks and the Financing of Houston and Texas, 1886–1986* (College Station, TX, 1986).

Bugos, Glenn E., 'Programming the American Aerospace Industry, 1954–1964: The Business Structure of Technical Transactions', *Business and Economic History*, 22(1), 1993, pp. 210–22.

Bullard, Robert D. (ed.), *In Search of the New South: The Black Urban Experience in the 1970s and 1980s* (Tuscaloosa, AL, 1989).

Campbell, John L. *et al.* (eds), *Governance and the American Economy* (Cambridge, 1991).

Caplovitz, David, *The Poor Pay More: Consumer Practices of Low Income Families* (London, 1963).

Cell, John W., *The Highest Stage of White Supremacy: The Origins of Segregation in South Africa and the American South* (Cambridge, 1982).

Chafe, W. H., *The American Woman: Her Changing Social, Economic and Political Roles, 1920–1970* (Oxford, 1972).

Chafe, William H., *Civilities and Civil Rights: Greensboro, North Carolina, and the Black Struggle for Freedom* (Oxford, 1980).

Chafe, William H., *The Unfinished Journey: America since World War II* (2nd edn, Oxford, 1991).

Chandler, Alfred D., *Strategy and Structure* (Cambridge, MA, 1962).

Chandler, Alfred D., *The Visible Hand: The Managerial Revolution in American Business* (Cambridge., MA, 1977)

Chandler, Alfred D., *Scale and Scope: The Dynamics of Industrial Capitalism* (Cambridge, MA, 1990).

Chandler, Alfred D., 'The Competitive Performance of US Industrial Enterprises since the Second World War', *Business History Review*, 68, 1994, pp. 1–72.

Cherlin, Andrew J., *Marriage Divorce Remarriage* (Cambridge, MA, 1981).

Clark, Gordon L., *Unions and Communities under Siege: American Communities and the Crisis of Organized Labor* (Cambridge, 1989).

Clarke, Sally, 'Innovation in U.S. Agriculture: A Role for New Deal Regulation', *Business and Economic History*, 21, 1992, pp. 46–55.

Clayton, James L., 'The Impact of the Cold War on the Economies of California and Utah', *Pacific Historical Review*, 36, 1967, pp. 449–73.

Clayton, James L. (ed.), *The Economic Impact of the Cold War: Sources and Readings* (New York, 1970).

Cleveland, Harold van B. and Huertas, Thomas F., *Citibank, 1812–1970* (London, 1985).

Cobb, James C., *The Selling of the South: The Southern Crusade for Industrial Development, 1936–1980* (Baton Rouge, LA, 1982).

Cobb, James C., *Industrialization and Southern Society, 1877–1984* (Lexington, KY, 1984).

Cobb, James C., 'Beyond Planters and Industrialists: A New Perspective on the New South', *Journal of Southern History*, 54(1), 1988, pp. 45–68.

Cobb, James C, '"Somebody Done Nailed Us On The Cross": Federal Farm Policy and Welfare Policies and the Civil Rights Movement in the Mississippi Delta', *Journal of American History*, 77(3), 1990, pp. 912–36.

Cobble, Dorothy Sue, *Dishing it Out: Waitresses and their Unions in the Twentieth Century* (Urbana, IL, 1991).

Cochran, Thomas C., *American Business in the Twentieth Century* (Cambridge, MA, 1972).

Cochrane, Willard W., *The Development of American Agriculture: A Historical Analysis* (Minneapolis, MN, 1979), p. 127

Cochrane, Willard W. and Ryan, Mary E., *American Farm Policy, 1948–1973* (Minneapolis, MN, 1976).

Cohen, Stephen and Zysman, John, *Manufacturing Matters* (New York, 1986).

Colburn, David R., *Racial Change and Community Crisis: St Augustine, Florida, 1877–1980* (New York, 1985).

Collins, Robert M., *The Business Response to Keynes, 1929–1964* (New York, 1981).

Cowan, Ruth Schwartz, *More Work For Mother: The Ironies of Household Technology from the Open Hearth to the Microwave* (New York, 1983).

Cramer, M. Richard, 'School Desegregation and New Industry: The Southern Community Leaders' Viewpoint', *Social Forces*, May 1963, pp. 384–9.

Cuff, R. D., 'An Organisational Perspective on the Military–Industrial–Complex', *Business History Review*, 52, 1978, pp. 250–67.

Cumbler, John T., *A Social History of Economic Decline: Business, Politics, and Work in Trenton* (New Brunswick, NJ, 1989).

Curme, Michael A., Hirsch, Barry T. and Macpherson, David A., 'Union Membership and Contract Coverage in the United States, 1983–1988', *Industrial and Labor Relations Review*, 44(1), 1990, pp. 5–33.

Dallek, Robert, *Lone Star Rising: Lyndon Johnson and his times, 1908–1960* (New York, 1991).

Daniel, Pete, *Breaking The Land: The Transformation of Cotton, Tobacco, and Rice Cultures since 1880* (Chicago, 1985).

Daniel, Pete, 'Going Among Strangers: Southern Reactions to World War II', *Journal of American History*, 77(3), 1990, pp. 886–911.

Daniels, Roger, *Coming To America: A History of Immigration and Ethnicity in American Life* (New York, 1990).

Davies, Gareth, 'War on Dependency: Liberal Individualism and the Economic Opportunity Act of 1964', *Journal of American Studies*, 26(2), 1992, pp. 205–31.

Davis, Gerald F. *et al.*, 'The Decline and Fall of the Conglomerate Firm in the 1980s: The Deinstitutionalization of an Organizational Form', *American Sociological Review*, 59, 1994, pp. 547–70.

Davis, Lance *et al.*, *American Economic Growth: An Economist's History of the United States* (New York, 1972).

Davis, Mike, *City of Quartz: Excavating the Future in Los Angeles* (London, 1990).

Day, Richard H., 'The Economics of Technological Change and the Demise of the Share-cropper', *American Economic Review*, 57(3), 1967, pp. 427–49.

DeLamarter, Richard Thomas, *Big Blue: IBM's Use and Abuse of Power* (New York, 1986).

Denison, Edward, *Why Growth Rates Differ: Postwar Experience in Nine Western Countries* (Washington, DC, 1967).

Denison, Edward, *Accounting For Slower Economic Growth: The United States in the 1970s* (Washington, DC, 1979).

Derthick, Martha, *Policymaking for Social Security* (Washington, DC, 1979).

Dertouzos, Michael *et al.*, *Made in America: Regaining the Productive Edge* (Cambridge, MA, 1989).

Deslippe, Denis, '"We Had An Awful Time With Our Women": Iowa's United Packinghouse Workers of America', *Journal of Women's History*, 5(1), 1993, pp. 10–32.

Dicke, Thomas S., *Franchising in America: The Development of a Business Method, 1840–1980* (Chapel Hill, NC, 1992).

Didricksen, Jon, 'The Development of Diversified and Conglomerate Firms in the US, 1920–1970', *Business History Review*, 46(2), 1972, pp. 202–19.

Donaldson, Scott, *The Suburban Myth* (New York, 1969).

Dorfman, Nancy S., 'Route 128: The Development of a Regional High Technology Economy', *Research Policy*, 12 (1983), pp. 299–318.

Doti, Lynne Pierson and Schweikart, Larry, *Banking in the American West: From the Gold Rush to Deregulation* (Norman, OK, 1991).

DuBoff, Richard B., *Accumulation and Power: An Economic History of the United States* (New York, 1989).

Dunning, John H., 'Explaining Patterns of International Production: In Defence of the Eclectic Theory', *Oxford Bulletin of Economics and Statistics*, 41(4), 1979, pp. 269–96.

Dunning, John H., *Multinational Enterprises and the Global Economy* (Wokingham, 1993).

Dyer, Davis, 'Necessity as the Mother of Convention: Developing the ICBM, 1954–1958', *Business and Economic History*, 22(1), 1993, pp. 194–209.

Eagles, Charles W. and Lewis, David L. (eds), *The Civil Rights Movement in America* (Jackson, MS, 1986).

Easterlin, Richard A., *Birth and Fortune: The Impact of Numbers on Personal Welfare* (New York, 1980).

Economic Report of the President (Various issues, Washington, DC).

Egerton, John, *The Americanization of Dixie: The Southernization of America* (New York, 1974).

Ehrlich, Paul, *The Population Bomb* (New York, 1968).

Eisner, Marc Allan, *The State in the American Political Economy: Public Policy and the Evolution of State-Economy Relations* (Englewood Cliffs, NJ, 1995).

Ellwood, David T. and Crane, Jonathan, 'Family Change Among Black Americans: What Do We Know?', *Journal of Economic Perspectives*, 4(4), 1990, pp. 65–84.

Encyclopedia of American Social History, volume II (New York, 1993).

Estall, Robert, *New England: A Study in Industrial Adjustment* (London, 1966).

Estall, Robert, *A Modern Geography of the United States* (London, 1978).

Ewen, Stuart, *Captains of Consciousness: Advertising and the Social Roots of the Consumer Culture* (New York, 1976).

Ewen, Stuart, *All Consuming Images: The Politics of Style in Contemporary Culture* (New York, 1988).

Fairclough, Adam, 'Historians and the Civil Rights Movement', *Journal of American Studies*, 24(3), 1990, pp. 387–98.

Fairclough, Adam, *To Redeem The Soul of America: The Southern Christian Leadership Conference and Martin Luther King, Jr.* (Athens, GA, 1987).

Falk, William W. and Lyson, Thomas A., *High Tech, Low Tech, No Tech: Recent Industrial and Occupational Change in the South* (Albany, NY, 1988).

Farley, Reynolds, 'Family Types and Family Headship: A Comparison of Trends Among Blacks and Whites', *Journal of Human Resources*, 6, 1971, pp. 275–96.

Farley, Reynolds and Allen, Walter R., *The Color Line and the Quality of Life in America* (New York, 1987).

Fearon, Peter, *War, Prosperity and Depression: The US Economy, 1917–1945* (Oxford, 1987).

Feldstein, Martin (ed.), *The American Economy in Transition* (Chicago, 1980), p. 238.

Finkle, Lee, 'The Conservative Aims of Black Militant Rhetoric: Black Protest during World War II', *Journal of American History*, 60, 1973, pp. 692–713.

Fisher, Franklin M., McKie, James W. and Mancke, Richard B., *IBM and the US Data Processing Industry: An Economic History* (New York, 1983).

Fisher, Robert, *Let The People Decide: Neighbourhood Organizing in America* (Boston, MA, 1984).

Fite, Gilbert C., *American Farmers: The New Minority* (Bloomington, IN, 1981).

Fite, Gilbert C., *Cotton Fields No More: Southern Agriculture, 1865–1980* (Lexington, KY, 1984).

Fligstein, Neil, *The Transformation of Corporate Control* (Cambridge, MA, 1990).

Flowerdew, Robin, 'Spatial Patterns of Residential Segregation in a Southern City', *Journal of American Studies*, 13(1), 1979, pp. 93–107.

Fones-Wolf, Elizabeth A., *Selling Free Enterprise: The Business Assault on Labor and Liberalism, 1945–60* (Chicago, 1994).

Foster, Mark S., *Henry J Kaiser: Builder in the Modern American West* (Austin, TX, 1989).

Fraser, Steve and Gerstle, Gary (eds), *The Rise and Fall of the New Deal Order, 1930–1980* (Princeton, NJ, 1989).

Frazier, E. Franklin, *Black Bourgeoisie* (Glencoe, IL, 1957).

French, Michael J., *The US Tire Industry: A History* (Boston, MA, 1990).

Furner, Mary O. and Supple, Barry (eds), *The State and Economic Knowledge: The American and British Experiences* (Cambridge, 1990).

Galambos, Louis, 'Technology, Political Economy and Professionalisation: Central Themes of the Organisational Synthesis', *Business History Review*, 57(4), 1983, pp. 471–93.

Galambos, Louis (ed.), *The New American State: Bureaucracies and Policies since World War II* (Baltimore, MD, 1987).

Galbraith, J. K., *The Affluent Society* (London, 1957).

Galbraith, John Kenneth, *The New Industrial State* (New York, 1967).

Galston, William A., *A Tough Row To Hoe: The 1985 Farm Bill and Beyond* (Lanham, NY, 1985).

Gans, Herbert J., *The Urban Villagers: Group and Class in the Life of Italian-Americans* (New York, 1962).

Gans, Herbert J., *The Levittowners: Ways of Life and Politics in a New Suburban Community* (London, 1967).

Garreau, Joel, *The Nine Nations of North America* (New York, 1981).

Gatlin, Rochelle, *American Women since 1945* (London, 1987).

Giglio, James N., 'New Frontier Agricultural Policy: The Commodity Side, 1961–1963', *Agricultural History*, 61(3), 1987, pp. 53–70.

Glasgow, Douglas, *The Black Underclass: Poverty, Unemployment and Entrapment of Ghetto Youth* (New York, 1981).

Goldfield, David R., *Cotton Fields and Skyscrapers: Southern City and Region, 1607–1980* (Baton Rouge, LA, 1982).

Goldfield, David R., *Promised Land: The South Since 1945* (Arlington Heights, IL, 1987).

Goldfield, David R., *Black, White and Southern: Race Relations and Southern Culture 1940 to the Present* (Baton Rouge, LA, 1990).

Goldfield, Michael, *The Decline of Organized Labor in the United States* (Chicago, 1987).

Goldin, Claudia, *Understanding the Gender Gap* (New York, 1990).

Goldsmith, Raymond W., *The National Wealth of the United States in the Postwar Period* (Princeton, NJ, 1962).

Gordon, David M., Edwards, Richard and Reich, Michael, *Segmented Work, Divided Workers: The Historical Transformation of Labor in the United States* (Cambridge, 1982).

Gordon, Robert A., *Economic Instability and Growth: The American Record* (New York, 1974).

Gray, Maureen Boyle, 'Consumer Spending on Durables and Services in the 1980s', *Monthly Labor Review*, 115(5), 1992, pp. 18–26.

Greenberg, Stanley B., *Race and State in Capitalist Development: Comparative Perspectives* (New Haven, CT, 1980).

Griffith, Robert, 'Dwight D. Eisenhower and the Corporate Commonwealth', *American Historical Review*, 77, 1982, pp. 87–122.

Grim, Valerie, 'The Impact of Mechanized Farming on Black Farm Families in the Rural South: A Study of Farm Life in the Brooks Farm Community, 1940–1970', *Agricultural History*, 68(2), 1994, pp. 169–84.

Gronemann, Carol and Norton, Mary Beth (eds), *'To Toil The Livelong Day': America's Women At Work, 1780–1980* (Ithaca, NY, 1987).

Gutman, Herbert G., *The Black Family in Slavery and Freedom, 1750–1925* (Oxford, 1976).

Halberstam, David, *The Reckoning* (New York, 1986).

Hall, Peter and Markusen, Ann (eds), *Silicon Landscapes* (Boston, MA, 1984).

Hallam, Arne (ed.), *Size, Structure, and the Changing Face of American Agriculture* (Boulder, CO, 1993).

Halle, David, *America's Working Man: Work, Home and Politics among Blue-Collar Property Owners* (Chicago, 1984).

Harl, Neil E., *The Farm Debt Crisis of the 1980s* (Ames, IA, 1990).

Harrington, Michael, *The Other America: Poverty in the United States* (New York, 1962).

Harris, Howell John, *The Right To Manage: Industrial Relations Policies of American Business in the 1940s* (Madison, WI, 1982).

Harris, Howell John and Lichtenstein, Nelson (eds), *Industrial Democracy in America: The Ambiguous Promise* (Cambridge, 1993).

Harris, Seymour E., *The Economics of New England: Case Study of an Older Area* (Cambridge, MA, 1982).

Harrison, Bennett, *Lean and Mean: The Changing Landscape of Corporate Power in the Age of Flexibility* (New York, 1994).

Hartmann, Susan M., *American Women in the 1940s: The Home Front and Beyond* (Boston, MA, 1982).

Harvey, James C., *Black Civil Rights during the Johnson Administration* (Jackson, MS, 1973).

Haveman, Robert H. (ed.), *A Decade of Federal Antipoverty Programs: Achievements, Failures and Lessons* (New York, 1977).

Hawley, Ellis W., *The New Deal and the Problem of Monopoly: A Study in Economic Ambivalence* (Princeton, NJ, 1966).

Hayes, Robert H. and Abernathy, William J., 'Managing Our Way To Economic Decline', *Harvard Business Review*, July–August 1980, pp. 67–77.

Hays, Samuel P., *Beauty, Health and Permanence: Environmental Politics in the United States, 1955–1985* (Cambridge, 1987).

Hekman, John S. and Strong, John S., 'The Evolution of New England Industry', *New England Economic Review*, March/April 1981, pp. 35–67.

Henry, D. K. and Oliver, R. P., 'The Defense Build-Up, 1977–85: Effects on Production and Employment', *Monthly Labor Review*, 110(8), 1987, pp. 3–11.

Higbee, Edward, *Farms and Farmers in an Urban Age* (New York, 1963).

Higgs, Robert, *Crisis and Leviathan: Critical Episodes in the Growth of American Government* (Oxford, 1987).

Higgs, Robert, 'The Cold War Economy: Opportunity Cost, Ideology and the Politics of Crisis', *Explorations in Economic History*, 31(3) 1994, pp. 283–312.

Hill, Herbert, 'Racial Equality in Employment: Patterns of Discrimination', *The Annals of the American Academy of Political and Social Science*, 357, 1965, pp. 30–47.

Hirsch, Arnold, *Making the Second Ghetto:Race and Housing in Chicago* (Cambridge, 1983).

Hofstadter, Richard, *The Age of Reform: From Bryan to FDR* (New York, 1955).

Holman, Mary A., *The Political Economy of the Space Program* (Palo Alto, CA, 1974).

Hooks, Gregory, 'The Rise of the Pentagon and US State Building: The Defense Program as Industrial Policy', *American Journal of Sociology*, 96(2), 1990, pp. 358–404.

Hughes, Jonathan R. T., *The Governmental Habit Redux: Economic Controls From Colonial Times to the Present* (Princeton, NJ, 1991).

Hunter, Guy (ed.), *Industrialisation and Race Relations: A Symposium* (London, 1965).

Iacocca, Lee with Novak, William, *Iacocca: An Autobiography* (New York, 1986).

Ingham, John N., *Making Iron and Steel: Independent Mills in Pittsburgh, 1820–1920* (Columbus, OH, 1991).

Iowa State University Center for Agricultural and Economic Development, *Food Goals, Future Structural Changes, and Agricultural Policy: A National Basebook* (Ames, IA, 1969).

Jackson, Kenneth T., *Crabgrass Frontier: The Suburbanization of the United States* (New York, 1985).

Jacoby, Sanford, *Employing Bureaucracy: Managers, Unions, and the Transformation of Work in American Industry, 1900–1945* (New York, 1985).

Jacoway, Elizabeth and Colburn, David R. (eds), *Southern Businessmen and Desegregation* (Baton Rouge, LA, 1982).

Jaynes, Gerald D., 'The Labor Market Status of Black Americans: 1939–1985', *Journal of Economic Perspectives*, 4(4) 1990, pp. 9–24.

Jones, Charles O. (ed.), *The Reagan Legacy: Promise and Performance* (Chatham, NJ, 1988).

Juster, F. Thomas (ed.), *The Distribution of Economic Well-Being* (Cambridge, MA, 1977).

Kaplan, Marshall and Cuciti, Peggy L. (eds), *The Great Society and its Legacy: Twenty Years of US Social Policy* (Durham, NC, 1986).

Katz, Michael B., *The Undeserving Poor: From the War on Poverty to the War on Welfare* (New York, 1989).

Katz, Michael B. (ed.), *The Underclass Debate: Views from History* (Princeton, NJ, 1993).

Kaufman, Allen and Englander, Ernest J., 'Kohlberg Kravis Roberts & Co. and the Challenge to Managerial Capitalism', *Business and Economic History*, 21, 1992, pp. 97–108.

Kearns, Doris, *Lyndon Johnson and the American Dream* (New York, 1976).

Kennedy, Paul, *The Rise and Fall of the Great Powers: Economic Change and Military Conflict from 1500 to 2000* (London, 1988).

Kenney, Martin and Florida, Richard, *Beyond Mass Production: The Japanese System and its Transfer to the United States* (New York, 1993).

Kerr, Norwood Allen, 'Drafted into the War on Poverty: USDA Food and Nutrition Programmes, 1961–1969', *Agricultural History*, 64(2), 1990, pp. 154–66.

Kessler-Harris, Alice, *Out To Work: A History of Wage-Earning Women in the United States* (Oxford, 1982).

King, Mary, 'Occupational Segregation by Race and Sex, 1940–1988', *Monthly Labor Review*, 115(4), 1992, pp. 30–7.

Kirby, Jack Temple, *Rural Worlds Lost: The American South, 1920–1960* (Baton Rouge, LA, 1987).

Koistinen, Paul A. C., *The Military–Industrial Complex: A Historical Perspective* (New York, 1980).

Kolko, Gabriel, *Wealth and Power in America: An Analysis of Social Class and Income Distribution* (London, 1962).

Kolko, Gabriel, *Triumph of Conservatism: A Reinterpretation of American History, 1900–1916* (New York, 1973).

Korstad, Robert and Lichtenstein, Nelson, 'Opportunities Lost and Found: Labour, Radicals and the Early Civil Rights Movement', *Journal of American History*, 75, 1988, pp. 786–811.

Kramer, John (ed.), *North American Suburbs: Politics, Diversity, and Change* (Berkeley, CA, 1972).

Kravis, Irving B., *The Structure of Income: Some Quantitative Essays* (Philadelphia, PA, 1962).

Krueger, Anne O., *Economic Policies at Cross-Purposes: The United States and Developing Countries* (Washington, DC, 1993).

Krugman, Paul A., *The Age of Diminished Expectations: US Economic Policy in the 1990s* (Cambridge, MA, 1990).

Kusmer, Kenneth L., 'African Americans in the City since World War II: From the Industrial to the Post-Industrial Era', *Journal of Urban History*, 21(4), 1995, pp. 458–504.

Kutscher, Ronald E., 'Historical Trends, 1950–92, and Current Uncertainties', *Monthly Labor Review*, 116(11), 1993, pp. 3–10.

Kuznets, Simon, *Shares of Upper-Income Groups in Income and Savings* (New York, 1953).

Kyrk, Hazel, 'Who Works and Why', *The Annals of the American Academy of Political and Social Science*, 251, 1947, pp. 44–52.

Lamoreaux, Naomi, *The Great Merger Movement in American Business, 1895–1904* (Cambridge, 1985).

Lamoreaux, Naomi and Raff, Daniel M. G. (eds), *Coordination and Information: Historical Perspectives on the Organization of Enterprise* (Chicago, 1995).

Langlois, Richard N., 'Creating External Capabilities: Innovation and Vertical Disintegration in the Microcomputer Industry', *Business and Economic History*, 19, 1990, pp. 93–102.

Langlois, Richard N., 'External Economies and Economic Progress: The Case of the Microcomputer Industry', *Business History Review*, 1992, pp. 1–52.

Lash, Scott and Urry, John *The End of Organized Capitalism* (Madison, WI, 1987).

Lawrence, Robert Z., *Can America Compete?* (Washington, DC, 1984).

Lawson, Steven F., *Black Ballots: Voting Rights in the South, 1944–1969* (New York, 1976).

Lazonick, William, *Competitive Advantage on the Shop-Floor*, (Cambridge, MA, 1990).

Lazonick, William, 'Organizational Capabilities in American Industry: The Rise and Decline of Managerial Capitalism', *Business and Economic History*, 19, 1990, pp. 51–3.

Leary, William M (ed.), *Encyclopedia of American History and Biography: The Airline Industry* (New York, 1992).

Lebergott, Stanley, *Pursuing Happiness: American Consumers in the Twentieth Century* (Princeton, NJ, 1993).

Leiter, Jeffrey *et al.* (eds), *Hanging By A Thread: Social Change in Southern Textiles* (Ithaca, NY, 1991).

Lemann, Nicholas, *The Promised Land: The Great Black Migration and How it Changed America* (London, 1991).

Leslie, Stuart W., *The Cold War and American Science: The Military–Industrial–Academic Complex at MIT and Stanford* (New York, 1993).

Levenstein, Harvey, *Paradox of Plenty: A Social History of Eating in Modern America* (Oxford, 1993).

Levitan, Sar A. and Shapiro, Isaac, *Working But Poor: America's Contradiction* (Baltimore, MD, 1987).

Levy, Frank, *Dollars and Dreams: The Changing American Income Distribution* (New York, 1987).

Lichtenstein, Nelson, *Labor's War At Home: The CIO in World War II* (Cambridge, 1982).

Lichtenstein, Nelson and Mayer, Stephen (eds), *On The Line: Essays in the History of Auto Work* (Urbana, IL, 1989).

Lipset, Seymour Martin (ed.), *Unions In Transition: Entering the Second Century* (San Francisco, CA, 1986).

Lipsky, David B. and Donn, Clifford B. (eds), *Collective Bargaining in American Industry: Contemporary Perspectives and Future Directions* (Lexington, KY, 1987).

Little, Jane Sneddon, 'The Dollar, Structural Change, and the New England Miracle', *New England Economic Review*, September/October 1989, pp. 47–57.

Livesay, Harold C., 'Entrepreneurial Dominance in Business Large and Small, Past and Present', *Business History Review*, 63, 1989, pp. 1–21.

Logan, Rayford W. (ed.), *What The Negro Wants* (Chapel Hill, NC, 1944).

Long, Larry, *Migration and Residential Mobility in the United States* (New York, 1988).

Lotchin, Roger W., *Fortress California, 1910–1961: From Warfare to Welfare* (New York, 1992).

Lotchin, Roger W., 'World War II and Urban California: City Planning and the Transformation Hypothesis', *Pacific Historical Review*, 62, 1993, pp. 143–71.

Lyson, Thomas A., *Two Sides To The Sunbelt: The Growing Divergence Between the Rural and Urban South* (New York, 1989).

Lyson, Thomas A. and Falk, William W. (eds), *Forgotten Places: Uneven Development in Rural America* (Lawrence, KS, 1993).

McAdam, Doug, *Political Process and the Development of Black Insurgency, 1930–1970* (Chicago, 1982).

McColloch, Mark, *White Collar Workers in Transition: The Boom Years, 1940–1970* (Westport, CN, 1983).

McComb, David G., *Houston: A History* (Austin, TX, 1981).

McCraw, Thomas K., *America Versus Japan* (Boston, MA, 1986).

McDougall, Walter A., ... *The Heavens and the Earth: A Political History of the Space Age* (New York, 1985).

McMillen, Neil R., *The Citizen's Council: Organised Resistance to the Second Reconstruction* (Urbana, IL, 1971).

McMillen, Neil R., 'Black Enfranchisement in Mississippi: Federal Enforcement and Black Protest in the 1960s', *Journal of Southern History*, 43(3), 1977, pp. 364–6.

McQuaid, Kim, *Big Business and Presidential Power: From FDR to Reagan* (New York, 1982).

Maddison, Angus, *Dynamic Forces in Capitalist Development: A Long-Run Comparative View* (Oxford, 1991).

Mandell, Lewis, *The Credit Card Industry: A History* (Boston, MA, 1990).

Marable, Manning, *Race, Reform and Rebellion: The Second Reconstruction in Black America, 1945–1982* (London, 1984).

Markusen, Ann, *Regions: The Economics and Politics of Territory* (Totowa, NJ, 1987).

Markusen, Ann, *et al.*, *The Rise of the Gunbelt: The Military Remapping of Industrial America* (New York, 1991).

Markusen, Ann and Yudken, Joel, *Dismantling the Cold War Economy* (New York, 1992).

Markusen, Ann Roell, *Profit Cycles, Oligopoly and Regional Development* (Cambridge, MA, 1987).

Massey, Douglas S. and Denton, Nancy A., *American Apartheid: Segregation and the Making of the Underclass* (Cambridge, MA, 1993).

Matthaei, Julie A., *An Economic History of Women in America: Women's Work, the Sexual Division of Labor, and the Development of Capitalism* (New York, 1982).

Matusow, Allen J., *The Unravelling of America: American Liberalism in the 1960s* (New York, 1984).

May, Elaine Tyler, *Homeward Bound: American Families in the Cold War Era* (New York, 1988).

Mead, Lawrence, *Beyond Entitlement: The Social Obligations of Citizenship* (New York, 1986).

Meier, August and Bracey, John H., 'The NAACP as a Reform Movement, 1909–1965: To Reach the Conscience of America', *Journal of Southern History*, 59(1), 1993, pp. 3–30.

Meier, August and Rudwick, Elliot, *From Plantation to Ghetto* (London, 1970).

Meier, August and Rudwick, Elliot, *Black Detroit and the Rise of the UAW* (New York, 1979).

Melman, Seymour, *Pentagon Capitalism: The Political Economy of War* (New York, 1990).

Meyer, Robert N., *The Consumer Movement: Guardians of the Marketplace* (Boston, MA, 1989).

Milkman, Ruth, *Gender At Work: The Dynamics of Job Segregation by Sex during World War II* (Chicago, 1987).

Mills, C. Wright, *The Power Elite* (Oxford, 1956).

Milner, Clyde A. *et al.* (eds), *The Oxford History of the American West* (New York, 1994).

Min, Pyong Gap, 'From White-Collar Occupations to Small Business: Korean Immigrants' Occupational Adjustment', *Sociological Quarterly*, 25, 1984, pp. 333–52.

Mitchell, Jeremy and Maidment, Richard (eds), *The United States in the Twentieth Century: Culture* (Milton Keynes, 1994).

Mohl, Raymond A., 'Making the Second Ghetto in Metropolitan Miami, 1940–1960', *Journal of Urban History*, 21(3), 1995, pp. 395–427.

Moody, Kim, *An Injury to All: the Decline of American Unionism* (London, 1988).

Moorhouse, Herbert F., *Driving Ambitions: An Analysis of the American Hot Rod Enthusiasm* (Manchester, 1990).

Morgan, David, 'Terminal Flight: The Air Traffic Controllers' Strike of 1981', *Journal of American Studies*, 18(2), 1984, pp. 165–83.

Morgan, Iwan W., *Eisenhower Versus 'The Spenders': The Eisenhower Administration, the Democrats and the Budget, 1953–1960* (London, 1990).

Morgan, Iwan W., *Beyond the Liberal Consensus: A Political History of the United States since 1965* (London, 1994).

Morgan, Iwan W., *Deficit Government: Taxing and Spending in Modern America* (Chicago, 1995).

Morgan, S. Philip *et al.*, 'Racial Differences in Household and Family Structure at the Turn of the Century', *American Journal of Sociology*, 98(2), 1993, pp. 799–828.

Morris, Aldon D., *The Origins of the Civil Rights Movement: Black Communities Organizing* (New York, 1984).

Morse, H. Wayne and Josling, Timothy E., *Agricultural Policy Reform: Politics and Process in the EC and the USA* (New York, 1990).

Moynihan, Daniel P., *The Negro Family: The Case for National Action* (Washington, DC, 1967).

Mrozek, Donald J., 'The Truman Administration and the Enlistment of the Aviation Industry in Post-war Defense', *Business History Review*, 48(1), 1974, pp. 73–94.

Murray, Charles, *Losing Ground: American Social Policy, 1950–1980* (New York, 1984).

Nash, Gerald D., *The American West Transformed: The Impact of the Second World War* (Bloomington, IN, 1985).

Nash, Gerald D. and Etulain, Richard W. (eds), *The Twentieth Century West: Historical Interpretations*, (Albuquerque, NM, 1989).

Nelson, Daniel, *Farm and Factory: Workers in the Midwest, 1880–1990* (Bloomington, IN, 1995).

Nelson, Richard R. and Wright, Gavin, 'The Rise and Fall of American Technological Leadership', *Journal of Economic Literature*, 30(4), 1992, pp. 1931–64.

Newman, Katherine S., *Falling From Grace: The Experience of Downward Mobility in the American Middle-Class* (New York, 1988).

Newman, Robert J., *Growth in the American South: Changing Regional Employment and Wage Patterns in the 1960s and 1970s* (New York, 1984).

Norrell, Robert J., 'Caste in Steel: Jim Crow Careers in Birmingham, Alabama', *Journal of American History*, 73, 1986–87, pp. 669–94.

OECD, *OECD Economic Surveys: United States, 1993* (Paris, 1993).

Olney, Martha L., *Buy Now, Pay Later: Advertising, Credit, and Consumer Durables in the 1920s* (Chapel Hill, NC, 1991).

Olson, Mancur, *The Rise and Decline of Nations* (New Haven, CT, 1982).

Olson, Mancur, 'The South Will Fall Again', *Southern Economic Journal*, 49, 1982–83, pp. 917–32.

Omi, Michael and Winant, Howard, *Racial Formation in the United States: From the 1960s to the 1980s* (New York, 1986).

Packard, Vance, *The Hidden Persuaders* (London, 1957).

Parsons, Donald O., 'The Decline in Male Labor Force Participation', *Journal of Political Economy*, 88(1), 1980, pp. 117–34.

Parsons, Talcott and Clark, Kenneth (eds), *The Negro American* (Boston, MA, 1965)

Patterson, James T., *America's Struggle Against Poverty, 1900–1985* (London, 1986).

Patterson, James T., *The Welfare State in America,1930–1980* (Durham, NC, 1981).

Patterson, James T., *Grand Expectations: The United States, 1945–1974* (Oxford, 1996).

Perloff, Harvey S., *Regions, Resources, and Economic Growth* (Baltimore, MD, 1960).

Perry, David C. and Watkins, Alfred J. (eds), *The Rise of the Sunbelt Cities*, Urban Affairs Annual Reviews, 14, 1977.

Peterson, Trudy Huskamp, *Agricultural Exports, Farm Income, and the Eisenhower Administration* (Lincoln, NB, 1979).

Pinkney, Alphonso, *The Myth of Black Progress* (Cambridge, 1984).

Piore, Michael J. and Sabel, Charles, *The Second Industrial Divide: Possibilities for Prosperity* (New York, 1984).

Piven, Frances and Cloward, Richard, *Regulating the Poor: The Functions of Public Welfare* (revised edn, New York, 1993).

Piven, Frances Fox and Cloward, Richard A., *Poor People's Movements: Why They Succeed, How They Fail* (New York, 1977).

Porter, Michael, *Competitive Strategy: Techniques for Analysing Industries and Competitors* (New York, 1980).

Porter, Michael, *Competitive Advantage: Creating and Sustaining Superior Performance* (New York, 1985).

Porter, Michael E., *The Competitive Advantage of Nations* (London, 1990).

Portes, Alejandro and Rumbaut, Ruben G., *Immigrant America: A Portrait* (Berkeley, CA, 1990).

Pratt, Joseph A., *The Growth of a Refining Region* (Greenwich, CT, 1980).

Rae, John B., *The American Automobile Industry: A History* (Boston, MA, 1984).

Rainwater, Lee and Yancey, William L., *The Moynihan Report and the Politics of Controversy* (Cambridge, 1967).

Rasmussen, Wayne D., 'A Postscript; Twenty-five Years of Change in Farm Productivity', *Agricultural History*, 49(1), 1975, pp. 84–6.

Raup, Philip M., 'Corporate Farming in the United States', *Journal of Economic History*, 33(1), 1973, pp. 274–90.

Ravitch, Diane, *The Troubled Crusade: American Education, 1945–1980* (New York, 1983).

Rawlings, Steve W., *Household and Family Characteristics: March 1992*, US Bureau of the Census, Current Population Reports, P20–467 (Washington, DC, 1993).

Reimers, David M., *Still a Golden Door: The Third World Comes to America* (New York, 1985).

Reskin, Barbara F. and Hartmann, Heidi I. (eds), *Women's Work, Men's Work: Sex Segregation on the Job* (Washington, DC, 1986).

Rivlin, Alice M., *Reviving the American Dream: The Economy, the States and the Federal Government* (Washington, DC, 1992).

Rockoff, Hugh, *Drastic Measures: A History of Wage and Price Controls in the United States* (Cambridge, 1984).

Rodwin, Lloyd and Sazanami, Hidehiko (eds), *Deindustrialisation and Regional Economic Transformation: The Experience of the United States* (Boston, MA, 1989).

Roe, Mark J., *Strong Managers, Weak Owners: The Political Roots of American Corporate Finance* (Princeton, NJ, 1994).

Romer, Christine, 'Is the Stabilization of the Post-War Economy a Figment of the Data?', *American Economic Review*, 76(3), 1986, pp. 314–34.

Rose, Mark H., *Interstate: Express Highway Politics, 1941–1956* (Lawrence, KS, 1979).

Rosenberg, Nathan, *Technology and American Economic Growth* (New York, 1972).

Rosenberg, Nathan, *Inside the Black Box: Technology and Economics* (Cambridge, 1982).

Rosenberg, Nathan, *Exploring the Black Box: Technology, Economics and History* (Cambridge, 1994).

Rostow, W. W., *Stages of Economic Growth: A Non-communist Manifesto* (Cambridge, 1960).

Rubinstein, James M., *The Changing US Auto Industry: A Geographical Analysis* (New York, 1992).

Ruggles, Steven, 'The Origins of African-American Family Structure', *American Sociological Review*, 59, 1994, pp. 136–51.

Sandholtz, Wayne *et al.* (eds), *The Highest Stakes: The Economic Foundations of the Next Security System* (New York, 1992).

Sawers, Larry and Tabb, William K. (eds), *Sunbelt/Snowbelt: Urban Development and Regional Restructuring* (New York, 1984).

Saxenian, AnnaLee, *Regional Advantage: Culture and Competition in Silicon Valley and Route 128* (Cambridge, MA, 1994).

Sayre, Charles R., 'Cotton Mechanization since World War II', *Agricultural History*, 53(1), 1979, pp. 105–24.

Scanzoni, John H., *The Black Family in Modern Society* (Boston, MA, 1971).

Schapsmeier, Edward L. and Schapsmeier, Frederick H., 'Eisenhower and Ezra Taft Benson: Farm Policy in the 1950s', *Agricultural History*, 44(4), 1970, pp. 369–78.

Schatz, Ronald W., *The Electrical Workers: A History of Labor at General Electric and Westinghouse, 1923–60* (Chicago, 1993).

Scherer, F. M. and Ross, David, *Industrial Market Structure and Economic Performance* (3rd edn, Boston, MA, 1990).

Schoolman, Morton and Majid, Alvin (eds), *Reindustrializing New York State: Strategies, Implications and Challenges* (Albany, NY, 1986).

Schulman, Bruce J., *From Cotton Belt to Sunbelt: Federal Policy, Economic Development and the Transformation of the South, 1938–1980* (New York, 1991).

Schwarz, John E., *America's Hidden Success: A Reassessment of Public Policy from Kennedy to Reagan* (London, 1983).

Schweninger, Loren, 'A Vanishing Breed: Black Farm Owners in the South, 1651–1982', *Agricultural History*, 63(3), 1989, pp. 41–60.

Scott, Allen J., *Metropolis: From The Division of Labor to Urban Form* (Berkeley, CA, 1988).

Servan-Schreiber, J. J., *The American Challenge* (New York, 1968).

Shover, John L., *First Majority-Last Minority: The Transforming of Rural Life in America* (De Kalb, IL, 1976), pp. 167–8.

Simon, Julian L., *The Economic Consequences of Immigration* (Oxford, 1989).

Sitkoff, Harvard, *The Struggle For Black Equality, 1954–1980* (New York, 1981).

Sloan, John W., *Eisenhower and the Management of Prosperity* (Lawrence, KS, 1991).

Smith, Michael Peter and Feagin, Joe R. (eds), *The Capitalist City: Global Restructuring and Community Politics* (Oxford, 1987).

Sobel, Robert, *The Age of Giant Corporations: A Microeconomic History of American Business, 1914–1984* (2nd edn, Westport, CT, 1984).

Sobel, Robert, *The Rise and Fall of the Conglomerate Kings* (New York, 1984).

Spulber, Nicolas, *Managing the American Economy From Roosevelt to Reagan* (Bloomington, IN, 1989).

Starr, Kevin, *Inventing the Dream: California through the Progressive Era* (New York, 1985).

Starr, Kevin, *Material Dreams: Southern California through the 1920s* (New York, 1990).

Starr, Paul, *The Social Transformation of American Medicine* (New York, 1982).

Stein, Herbert, *Presidential Economics: The Making of Economic Policy from Roosevelt to Reagan and Beyond* (New York, 1984).

Stein, Herbert, *The Fiscal Revolution in America* (Washington, DC, 1990).

Stockman, David A., *The Triumph of Politics: How the Reagan Revolution Failed* (New York, 1986).

Stokes, Melvyn and Halpern, Rick (eds), *Race and Class in the American South since 1890* (Oxford, 1994).

Storper, M. and Christopher, S. 'Flexible Specialization and Regional Agglomerations: The Case of the U.S. Motion Picture Industry', *Annals of the Association of American Geography*, 77, 1987, pp. 104–17.

Street, James H., *The New Revolution in the Cotton Economy: Mechanization and Its Consequences* (Chapel Hill, NC, 1957)

Sundquist, James L., *Politics and Policy: The Eisenhower, Kennedy and Johnson Years* (Washington, DC, 1968).

Taeuber, Karl E. and Taeuber, Alma F., *Negroes in Cities: Residential Segregation and Neighbourhood Change* (Chicago, 1965).

Teaford, Jon C., *Cities of the Heartland: The Rise and Fall of the Industrial Midwest* (Bloomington, IN, 1993).

Teaford, Jon C., *The Twentieth Century American City* (2nd edn, Baltimore, MD, 1993).

Tedlow, Richard, *New and Improved: The Story of Mass Marketing in America* (Oxford, 1990).

Thernstrom, Stephan, *The Other Bostonians: Poverty and Progress in the American Metropolis, 1880–1970* (Cambridge, MA, 1973).

Thompson, Grahame (ed.), *Markets*, (Milton Keynes, 1994).

Tolliday, Steven and Zeitlin, Jonathan (eds), *Shop Floor Bargaining and the State* (Cambridge, 1985).

Tucker, Barbara, 'Agricultural Workers in World War II: The Reserve Army of Children, Black Americans and Jamaicans', *Agricultural History*, 68(1), 1994, pp. 54–73.

Ulrich, Hugh, *Losing Ground: Agricultural Policy and the Decline of the American Farm* (Chicago, 1989).

US Bureau of the Census, Current Population Reports, series P-23, 26, *Recent Trends in the Social and Economic Condition of Negroes in the United States* (Washington, DC, 1968).

US Bureau of the Census, Current Population Reports, P23–180, *Marriage, Divorce and Remarriage in the 1990s* (Washington, DC, 1989).

US Bureau of the Census, Current Population Reports, series P-25, No. 1023, *US Population Estimates and Components of Change: 1970 to 1987* (Washington, DC, 1988).

US Bureau of the Census, *Historical Statistics of the United States, Colonial Times to 1970, Bicentennial Edition* (Washington, DC, 1975).

US Bureau of the Census, *Statistical Abstract of the United States* (various years, Washington, DC).

US Bureau of the Census, jointly with the Department of Agriculture, Current Population Reports, series P-27, No. 59, *Farm Population of the United States: 1984* (Washington, DC, 1988).

US Bureau of the Census, jointly with the Department of Agriculture, Current Population Reports, series P-27, No. 61, *Rural and Rural Farm Population: 1987* (Washington, DC, 1988).

Valdes, Dennis Nodin, 'Machine Politics in California Agriculture, 1945–1990s', *Pacific Historical Review*, 63(2), 1994, pp. 203–24.

Vance, Rupert B. and Demerath, Nicholas J. (eds), *The Urban South* (Chapel Hill, NC, 1954).

Vatter, Harold G., *The US Economy in the 1950s: An Economic History* (Chicago, 1963).

Vernon, R., 'International Investment and International Trade in the Product Cycle', *Quarterly Journal of Economics*, 80, 1966, pp. 190–207.

Vernon, R., 'The Product Cycle Hypothesis in a New International Environment', *Oxford Bulletin of Economics and Statistics*, 41, 1979, pp. 255–67.

Vernon, Raymond, *Sovereignty at Bay: The Multinational Spread of US Enterprises* (New York, 1971).

Vietor, Richard H. K., *Contrived Competition: Regulation and Deregulation in America* (Cambridge, MA, 1994).

Vietor, Richard H. K., 'Contrived Competition: Economic Regulation and Deregulation, 1920s-1980s', *Business History*, 36(4), 1994, pp. 1–32.

Viorst, Milton, *Fire in the Streets: America in the 1960s* (New York, 1979).

Vogel, David, *Fluctuating Fortunes: The Political Power of Business in America* (New York, 1989).

Wacquant, Loic J. D. and Wilson, William Julius, 'The Cost of Racial and Class

Exclusion in the Inner City', *The Annals of the American Academy of Political and Social Science*, 501, 1989, pp. 8–25.

Weaver, Robert, *The Negro Ghetto* (New York, 1948).

Weinstein, Bernard L. and Firestine, Robert E., *Regional Growth and Decline in the United States: The Rise of the Sunbelt and the Decline of the Northeast* (New York, 1978).

Weir, Margaret *et al.* (eds), *The Politics of Social Policy in the United States* (Princeton, NJ, 1988).

Weitzman, Leonore J., *The Divorce Revolution: The Unexpected Social and Economic Consequences for Women and Children in America* (New York, 1985).

West, Peter J., *Foreign Investment and Technology Transfer: The Tire Industry in Latin America* (Greenwich, CT, 1984).

Westcolt, Diane Nilsen, 'Blacks in the 1970s: Did They Scale the Job Ladder?', *Monthly Labor Review*, 105(2), 1982, pp. 29–38.

Wetzel, James R., 'American Families: 75 Years of Change', *Monthly Labor Review*, 113(3), 1990, pp. 4–13.

White, Richard, *It's Your Misfortune and None of My Own: A History of the American West* (Norman, OK, 1991).

Whyte, William H., *The Organisation Man* (London, 1957).

Wiggins, Sarah Woolfolk(comp.), *From Civil War to Civil Rights: Alabama, 1860–1960* (Tuscaloosa, AL, 1987).

Wiley, Peter and Gottlieb, Robert, *Empires in the Sun: The Rise of the New American West* (Tucson, AZ, 1982)

Wilkins, Mira, *The Maturing of Multinational Enterprise: American Business Abroad from 1914 to 1970* (Cambridge, MA, 1974).

Wilkins, Mira, 'Japanese Multinationals in the United States: Continuity and Change, 1879–1990', *Business History Review*, 64(4), 1990, pp. 585–629.

Williams, Donald R., 'Women's Part-Time Employment: A Gross Flow Analysis', *Monthly Labor Review*, April 1995, pp. 36–44.

Wilson, David A. (ed.), 'Universities and the Military', *The Annals of the American Academy of Political and Social Science*, 502, 1989, pp. 9–154.

Wilson, John Donald, *The Chase: The Chase Manhattan Bank, N.A., 1945–1985* (Boston, MA, 1986).

Wilson, William Julius, *The Declining Significance of Race: Blacks and Changing American Institutions* (Chicago, 1978).

Wilson, William Julius, *The Truly Disadvantaged: The Inner City, the Underclass, and Public Policy* (Chicago, 1987).

Wolfe, Alan (ed.), *America at Century's End* (Berkeley, CA, 1992).

Womack, James *et al.*, *The Machine that Changed the World* (Cambridge, MA, 1991).

Woodruff, Nan Elizabeth, 'Pick or Fight: The Emergency Farm Labor Program in the Arkansas and Mississippi Deltas During World War II', *Agricultural History*, 64(2), 1990, pp. 74–86.

Woodward, C. Vann, *The Strange Career of Jim Crow* (Oxford, 1966).

Wright, Gavin, *Old South, New South: Revolutions in the Southern Economy Since the Civil War* (New York, 1986).

Wynn, Neil A., *The Afro-American and the Second World War* (London, 1976).

Yans-McLaughlin, Virginia (ed.), *Immigration Reconsidered: History, Sociology and Politics* (Oxford, 1990).

Youngson, A. J., *Possibilities of Economic Progress* (Cambridge, 1959).

Zieger, Robert H. (ed.), *Organized Labor in the Twentieth Century South* (Knoxville, TN, 1991).

Index